BLADE RUNNER 2029

TITAN COMICS

ALCON ENTERTAINMENT

BLADE RUNNER 2029 – VOL 3: REDEMPTION

EDITED BY David Leach

TITAN COMICS

GROUP EDITOR | Jake Devine
SENIOR CREATIVE EDITOR | David Leach
EDITOR | Phoebe Hedges
EDITORIAL ASSISTANT | Calum Collins
PRODUCTION CONTROLLERS | Caterina Falqui | Kelly Fenlon
PRODUCTION MANAGER | Jackie Flook
ART DIRECTOR | Oz Browne
SALES & CIRCULATION MANAGER | Steve Tothill

MARKETING COORDINATOR | Lauren Noding
PUBLICIST | Phoebe Trillo
DIGITAL AND MARKETING MANAGER | Jo Teather
HEAD OF RIGHTS | Jenny Boyce
ACQUISITIONS EDITOR | Duncan Baizley
PUBLISHING DIRECTORS | Ricky Claydon | John Dziewiatkowsk
OPERATIONS DIRECTOR | Leigh Baulch
PUBLISHERS | Vivian Cheung | Nick Landau

ALCON PUBLISHING

EDITOR | Jeff Conner
ASSOCIATE EDITOR | Al Cuenca
COO/CEO | Scott Parish
LEGAL/BUSINESS AFFAIRS | Jeannette Hill
PUBLISHERS | Andrew Kosove & Broderick Johnson

BLADE RUNNER 2029: REDEMPTION
APRIL 2022. Published by Titan Comics, a division of Titan Publishing Group, Ltd. 144 Southwark Street, London SE1 0UP. Titan Comics is a registered trademark of Titan Publishing Group, Ltd. All rights reserved. © 2022 – Blade Runner 2029 and all related marks and characters are trademarks and copyrights of Alcon Publishing ®. All rights reserved. Licensed by Alcon Publishing ®. All rights reserved.

Published by Titan Comics, a division of Titan Publishing Group, Ltd. Titan Comics is a registered trademark of Titan Publishing Group, Ltd.
144 Southwark Street, London SE1 0UP

STANDARD EDITION ISBN 9781787737372

A CIP catalogue for this title is available from the British Library.

First Edition: April 2022

10 9 8 7 6 5 4 3 2 1

Printed in Spain.

www.titan-comics.com
Follow us on twitter@ComicsTitan | Visit us at facebook.com/comicstitan
For rights information contact: jenny.boyce@titanemail.com

BLADE RUNNER 2029

2029

REDEMPTION

WRITTEN BY

MIKE JOHNSON

CREATIVE CONSULTANTS

MELLOW BROWN
MICHAEL GREEN
K. PERKINS

ART BY

ANDRES GUINALDO

COLORS BY

MARCO LESKO

LETTERING BY

JIM CAMPBELL

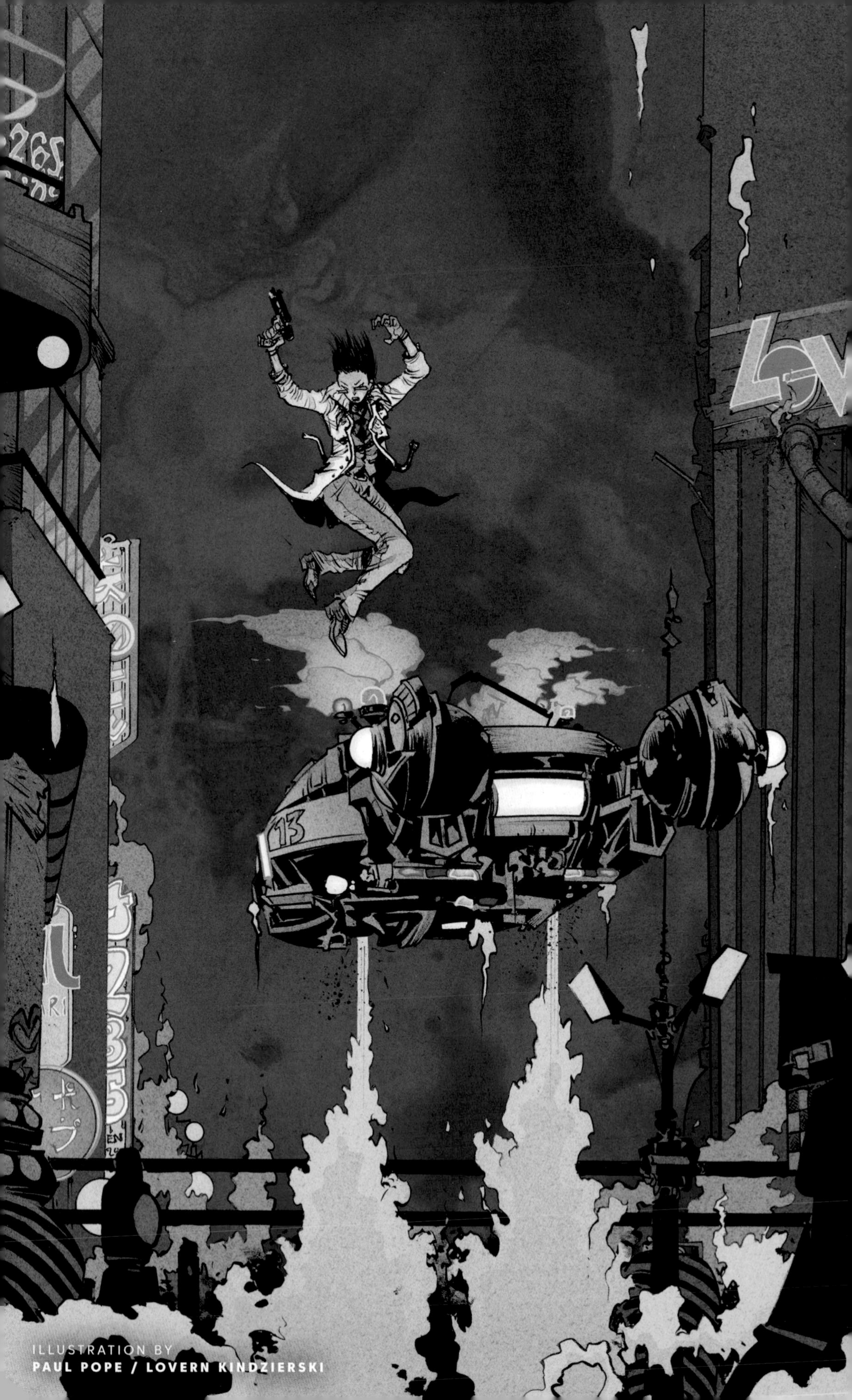
13

ILLUSTRATION BY
PAUL POPE / LOVERN KINDZIERSKI

Early in the 21st Century, **THE TYRELL CORPORATION** advanced Robot evolution into the **NEXUS** phase – a being virtually identical to a human – known as a **REPLICANT**.

Replicants were used Off-world as slave labor. Those who escaped to Earth were hunted by **BLADE RUNNER UNITS** ordered to kill any trespassing Replicant upon detection.

In 2022, a Replicant attack on the Tyrell Corporation forced the company into bankruptcy and erased all records of existing Replicants. The surviving Nexus 8 models disappeared with the help of the **REPLICANT UNDERGROUND.** Many Replicants remained in servitude.

In 2027, **AAHNA "ASH" ASHINA**, a former Blade Runner, rejoined the department to hunt down fugitive Replicants. Her superiors are unaware that her loyalties are divided. Her lover, **FREYSA**, is a leader in the Replicant Underground.

While investigating a report of a rogue Replicant, Ash discovered that a Nexus 6 Replicant, **YOTUN**, whom she had failed to retire 12 years previously, had somehow outlived his expiration date and become the leader of a Replicant guerrilla army.

Yotun captured Ash and ordered his army to launch an all-out attack upon Los Angeles, and called on all Replicants in the city to revolt against their masters. Then he destroyed the Seawall and took over the **LAPD** Tower, before rigging it for demolition.

Rescued from Yotun's clutches by members of the Replicant Underground, Ash raced back to the city to save her lover, whom Yotun mistakenly believed had joined his cause. Instead, she sabotaged his plan and in retaliation he blinded her in one eye and left her to die in the burning **LAPD** Tower.

Faced with killing Yotun or rescuing Freysa, Ash chose her wounded lover, leaving Yotun to escape...

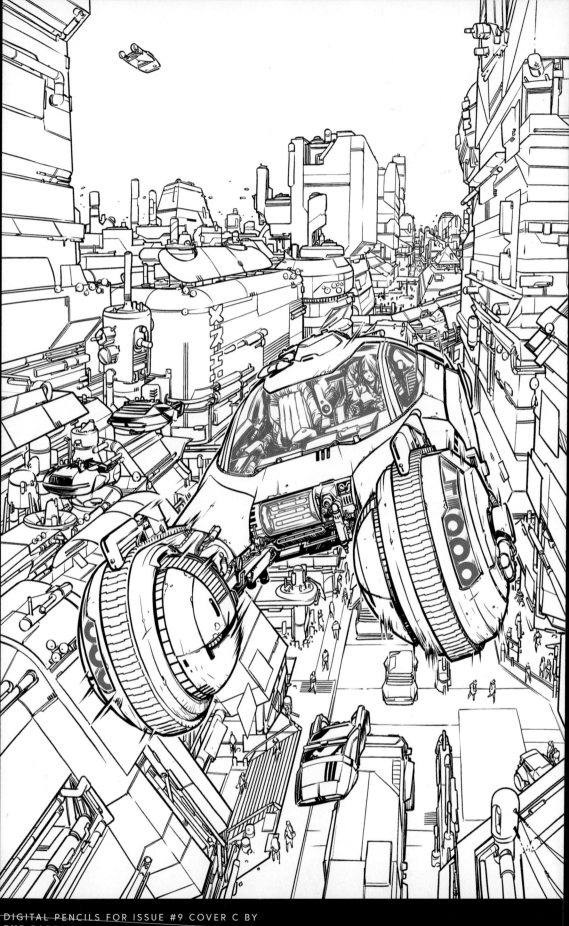

DIGITAL PENCILS FOR ISSUE #9 COVER C BY
PYE PARR

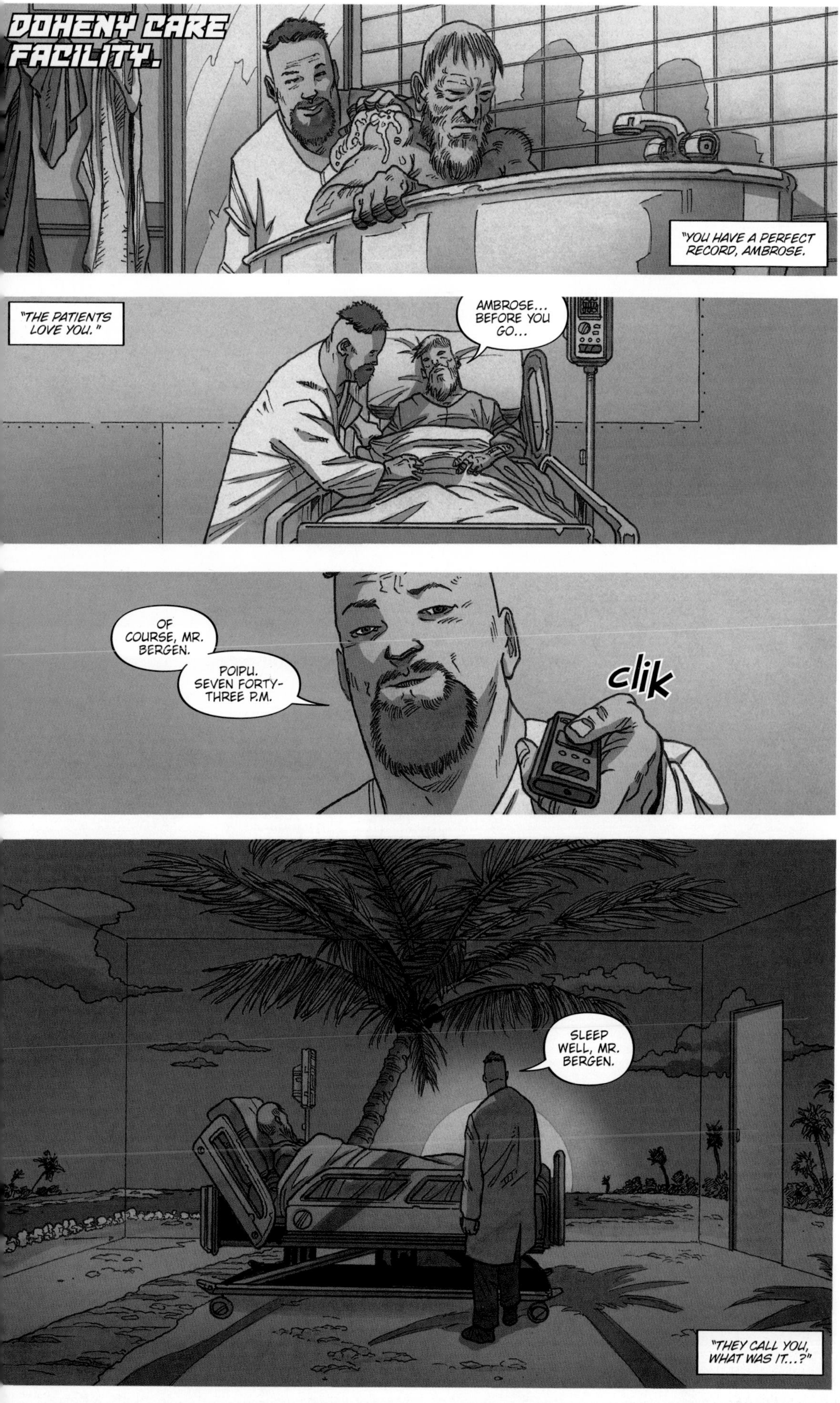
DOHENY CARE FACILITY.
"YOU HAVE A PERFECT RECORD, AMBROSE.
"THE PATIENTS LOVE YOU."
AMBROSE... BEFORE YOU GO...
OF COURSE, MR. BERGEN.
POIPU. SEVEN FORTY-THREE P.M.
clik
SLEEP WELL, MR. BERGEN.
"THEY CALL YOU, WHAT WAS IT...?"

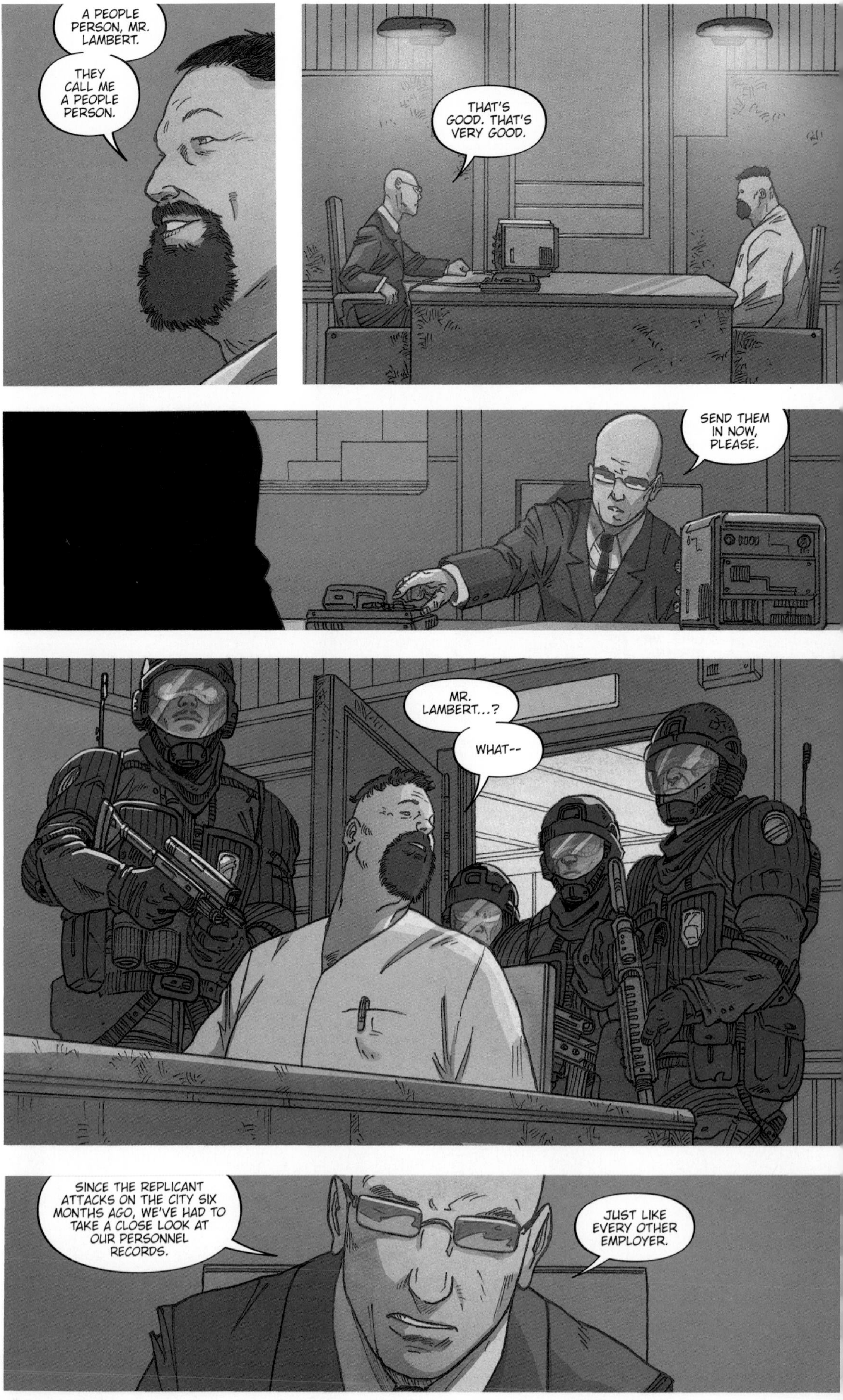
A PEOPLE PERSON, MR. LAMBERT.
THEY CALL ME A PEOPLE PERSON.
THAT'S GOOD. THAT'S VERY GOOD.
SEND THEM IN NOW, PLEASE.
MR. LAMBERT...?
WHAT--
SINCE THE REPLICANT ATTACKS ON THE CITY SIX MONTHS AGO, WE'VE HAD TO TAKE A CLOSE LOOK AT OUR PERSONNEL RECORDS.
JUST LIKE EVERY OTHER EMPLOYER.

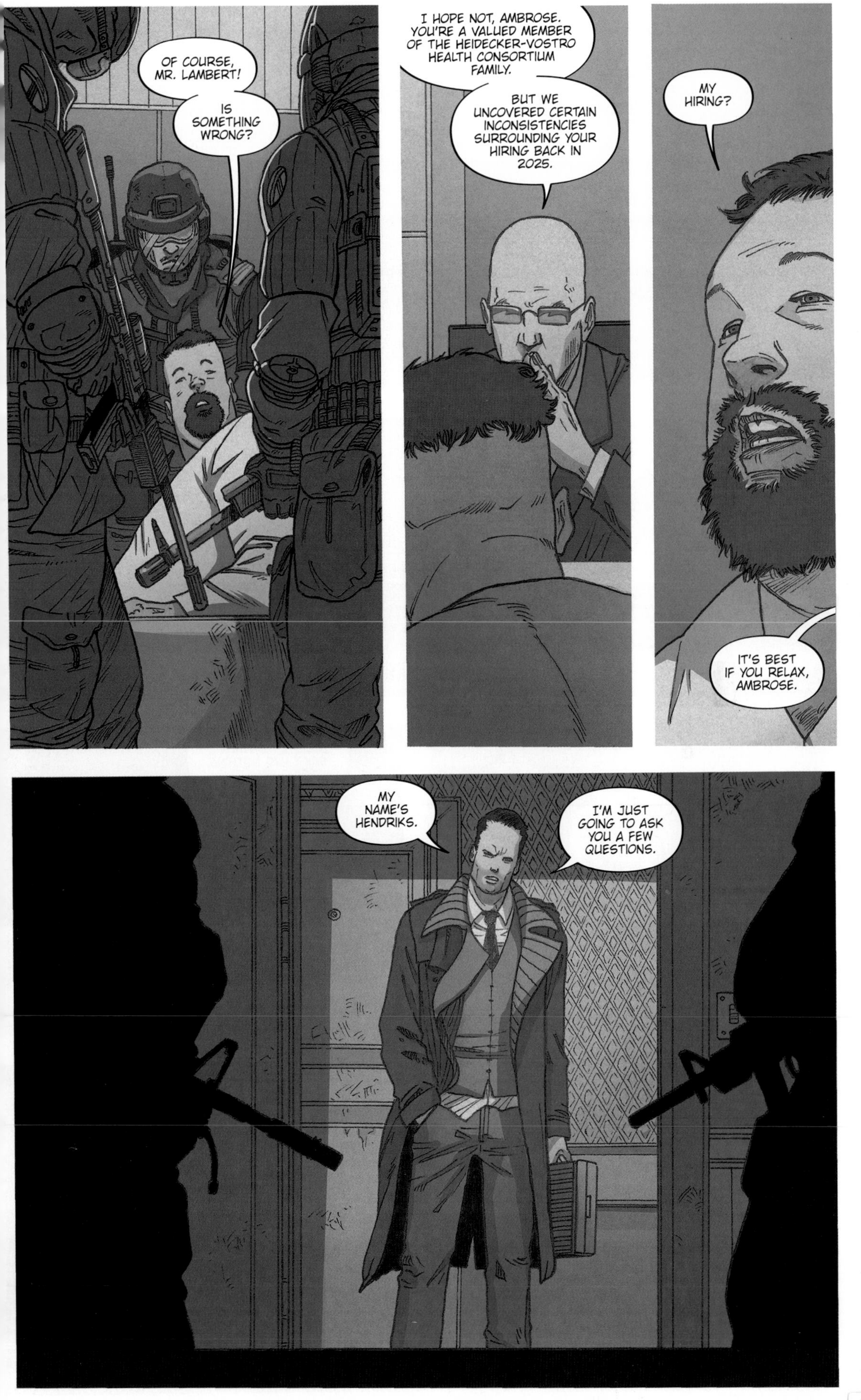
OF COURSE, MR. LAMBERT!
IS SOMETHING WRONG?
I HOPE NOT, AMBROSE. YOU'RE A VALUED MEMBER OF THE HEIDECKER-VOSTRO HEALTH CONSORTIUM FAMILY.
BUT WE UNCOVERED CERTAIN INCONSISTENCIES SURROUNDING YOUR HIRING BACK IN 2025.
MY HIRING?
IT'S BEST IF YOU RELAX, AMBROSE.
MY NAME'S HENDRIKS.
I'M JUST GOING TO ASK YOU A FEW QUESTIONS.

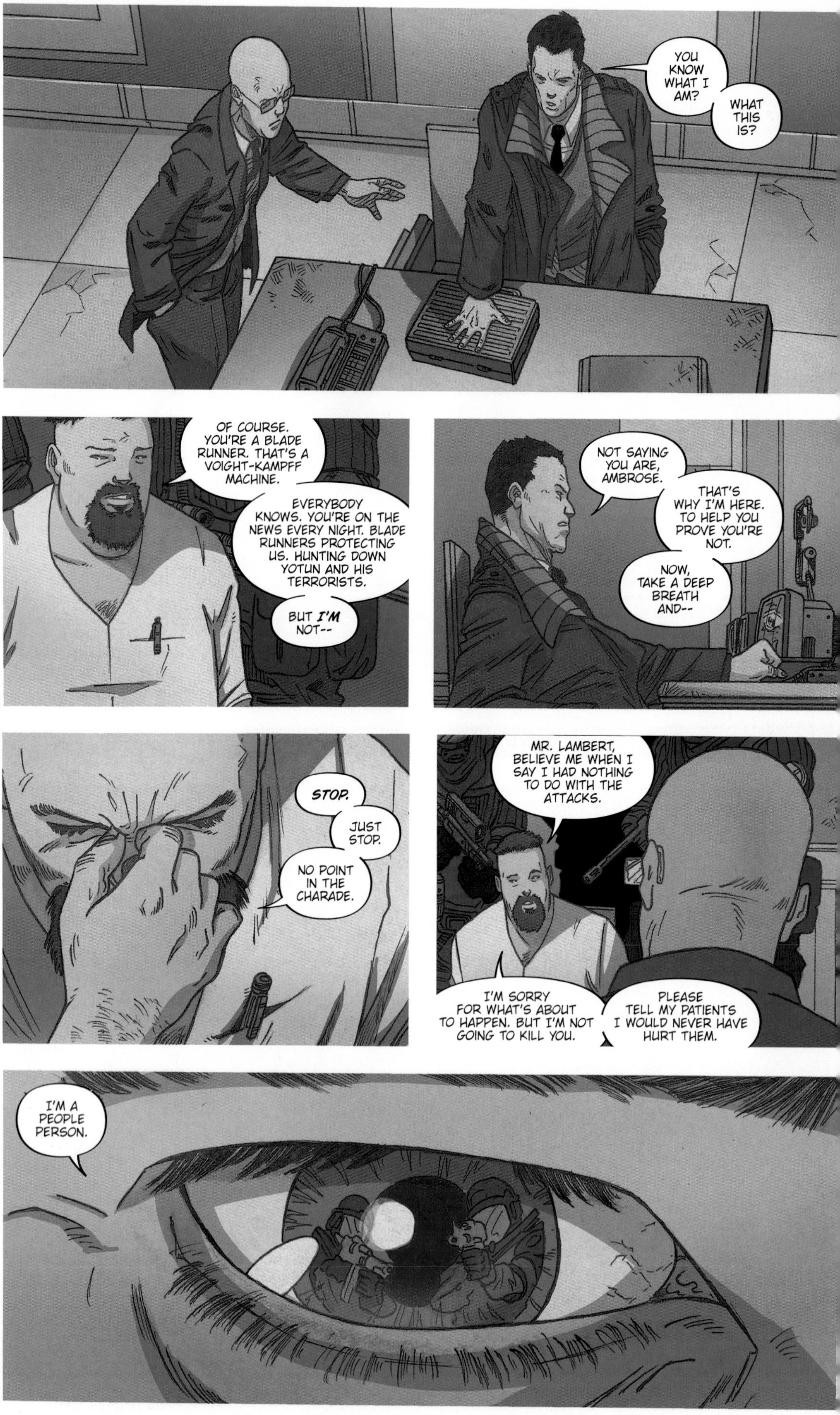
YOU KNOW WHAT I AM?
WHAT THIS IS?
OF COURSE. YOU'RE A BLADE RUNNER. THAT'S A VOIGHT-KAMPFF MACHINE.
EVERYBODY KNOWS. YOU'RE ON THE NEWS EVERY NIGHT. BLADE RUNNERS PROTECTING US. HUNTING DOWN YOTUN AND HIS TERRORISTS.
BUT *I'M* NOT--
NOT SAYING YOU ARE, AMBROSE.
THAT'S WHY I'M HERE. TO HELP YOU PROVE YOU'RE NOT.
NOW, TAKE A DEEP BREATH AND--
STOP.
JUST STOP.
NO POINT IN THE CHARADE.
MR. LAMBERT, BELIEVE ME WHEN I SAY I HAD NOTHING TO DO WITH THE ATTACKS.
PLEASE TELL MY PATIENTS I WOULD NEVER HAVE HURT THEM.
I'M SORRY FOR WHAT'S ABOUT TO HAPPEN. BUT I'M NOT GOING TO KILL YOU.
I'M A PEOPLE PERSON.

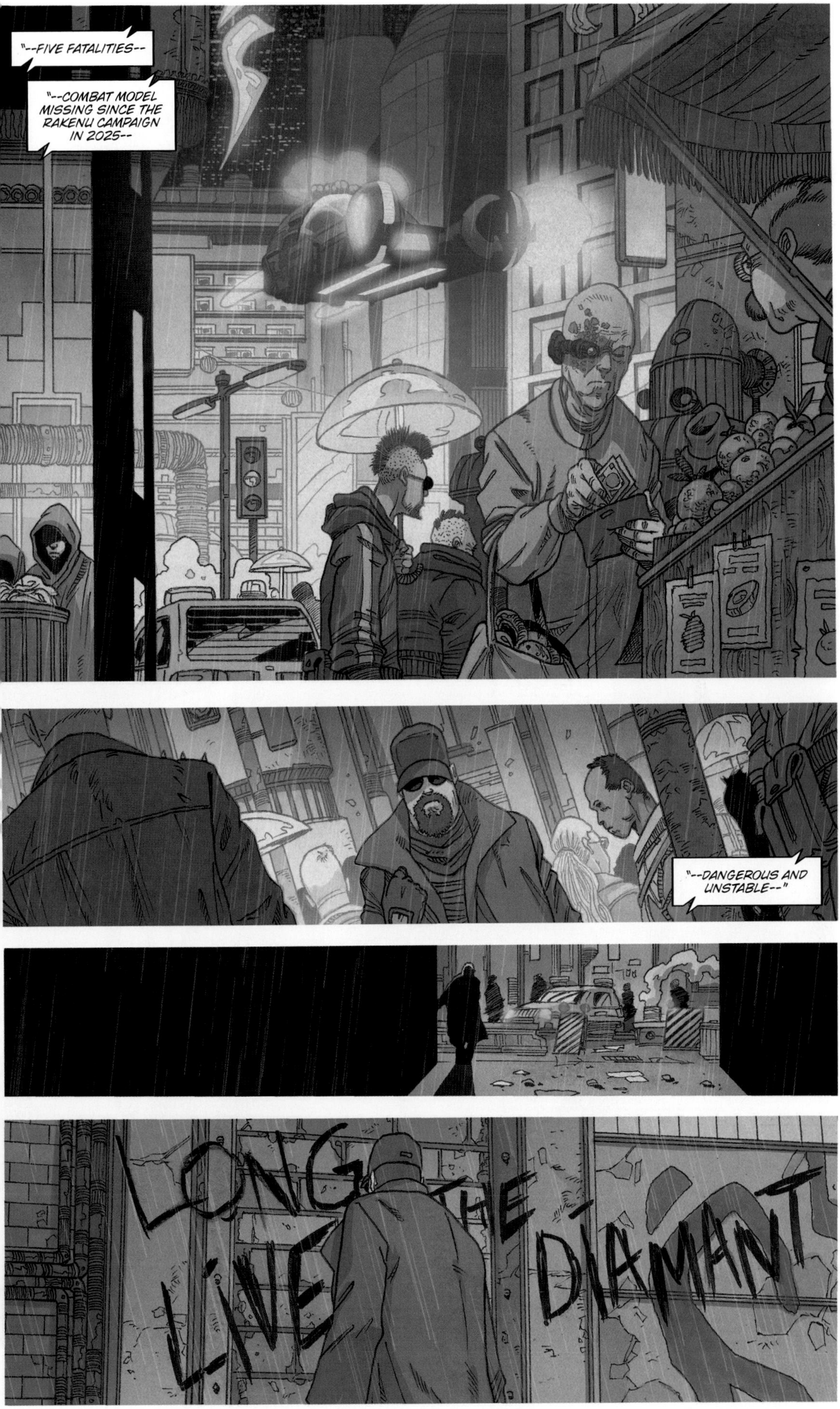
"--FIVE FATALITIES--
"--COMBAT MODEL MISSING SINCE THE RAKENU CAMPAIGN IN 2025--
"--DANGEROUS AND UNSTABLE--"
LONG LIVE THE DIAMANT

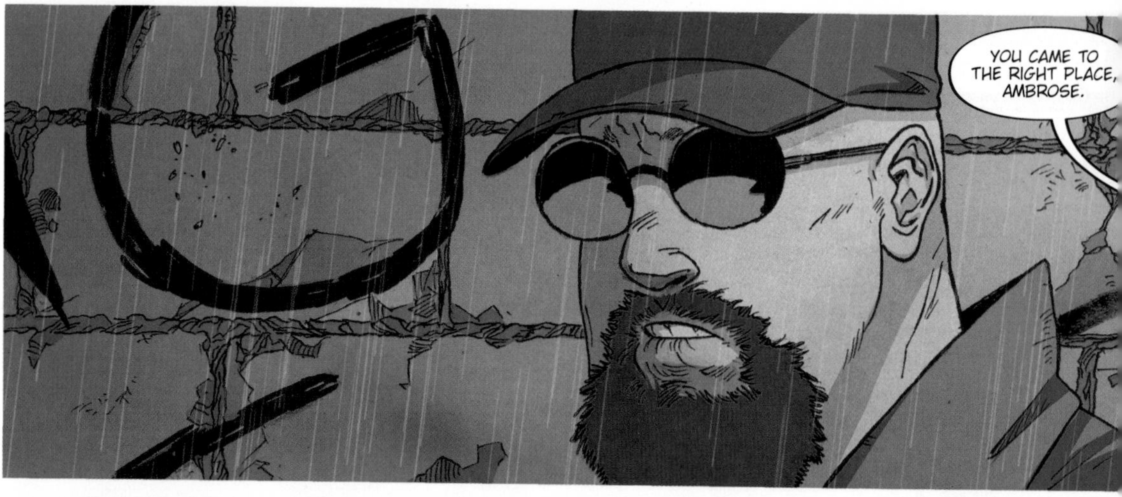
YOU CAME TO THE RIGHT PLACE, AMBROSE.

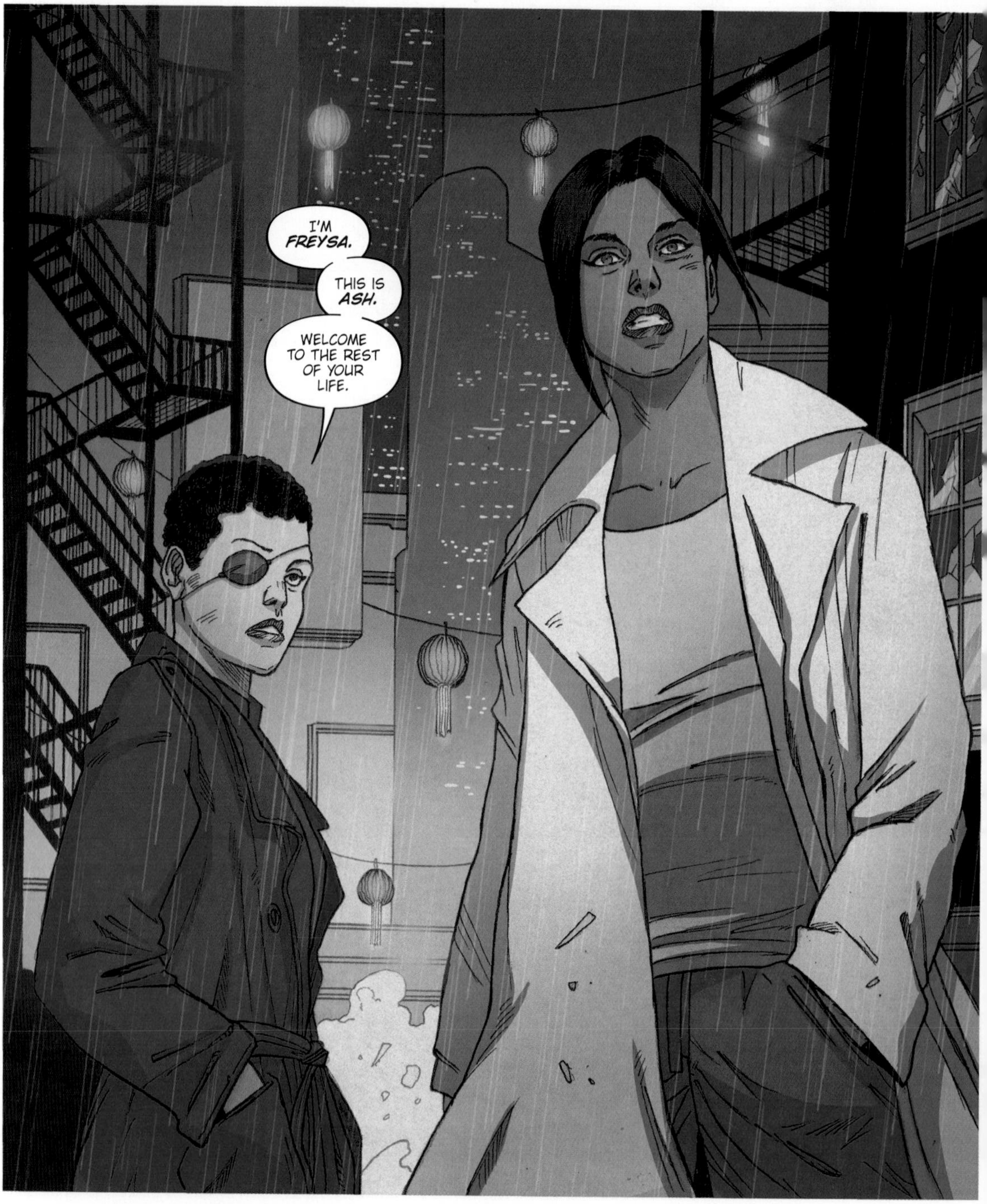
I'M FREYSA.
THIS IS ASH.
WELCOME TO THE REST OF YOUR LIFE.

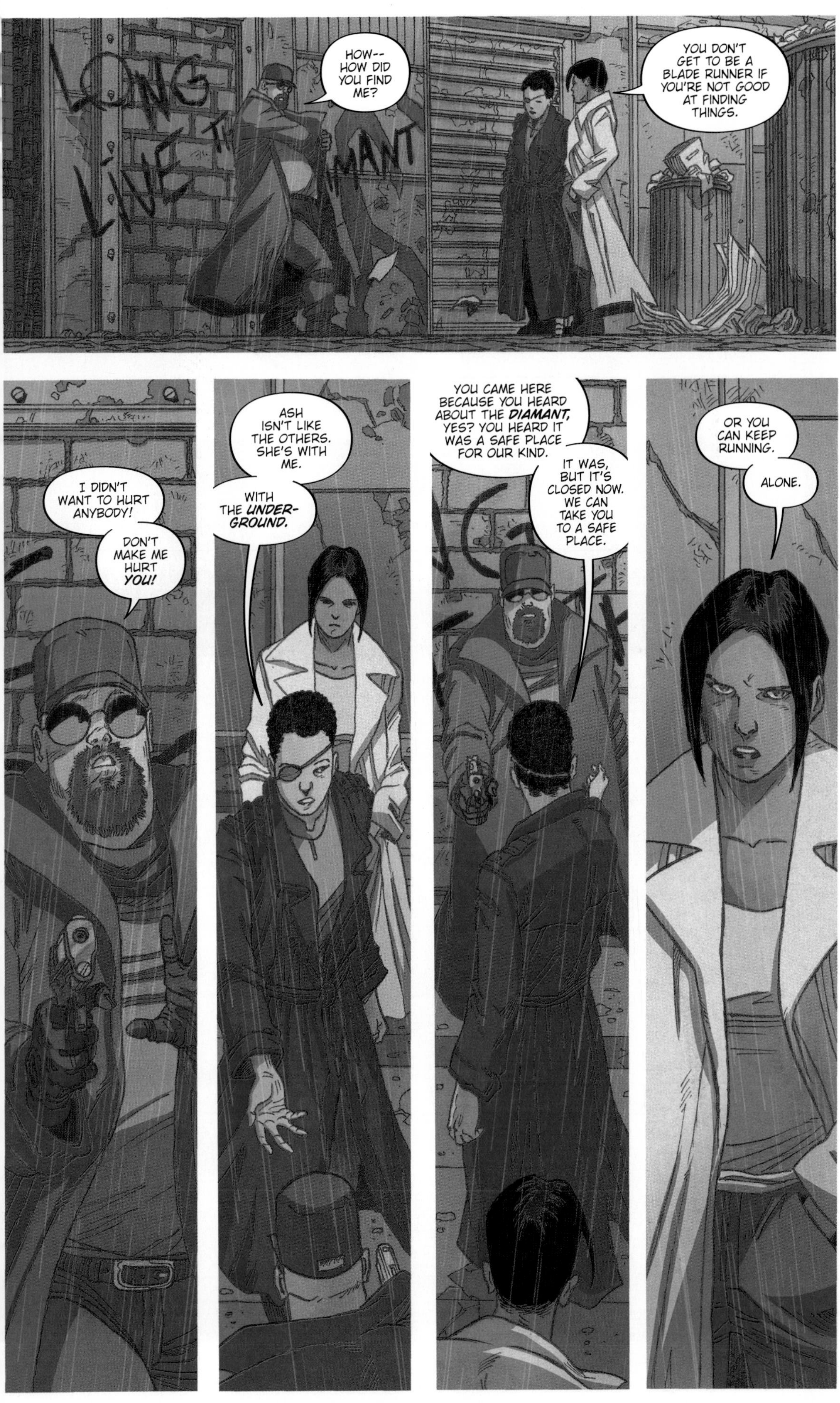
LONG LIVE TH... DIAMANT
HOW-- HOW DID YOU FIND ME?
YOU DON'T GET TO BE A BLADE RUNNER IF YOU'RE NOT GOOD AT FINDING THINGS.
I DIDN'T WANT TO HURT ANYBODY!
DON'T MAKE ME HURT *YOU!*
ASH ISN'T LIKE THE OTHERS. SHE'S WITH ME.
WITH THE ***UNDER-GROUND.***
YOU CAME HERE BECAUSE YOU HEARD ABOUT THE ***DIAMANT,*** YES? YOU HEARD IT WAS A SAFE PLACE FOR OUR KIND.
IT WAS, BUT IT'S CLOSED NOW. WE CAN TAKE YOU TO A SAFE PLACE.
OR YOU CAN KEEP RUNNING.
ALONE.

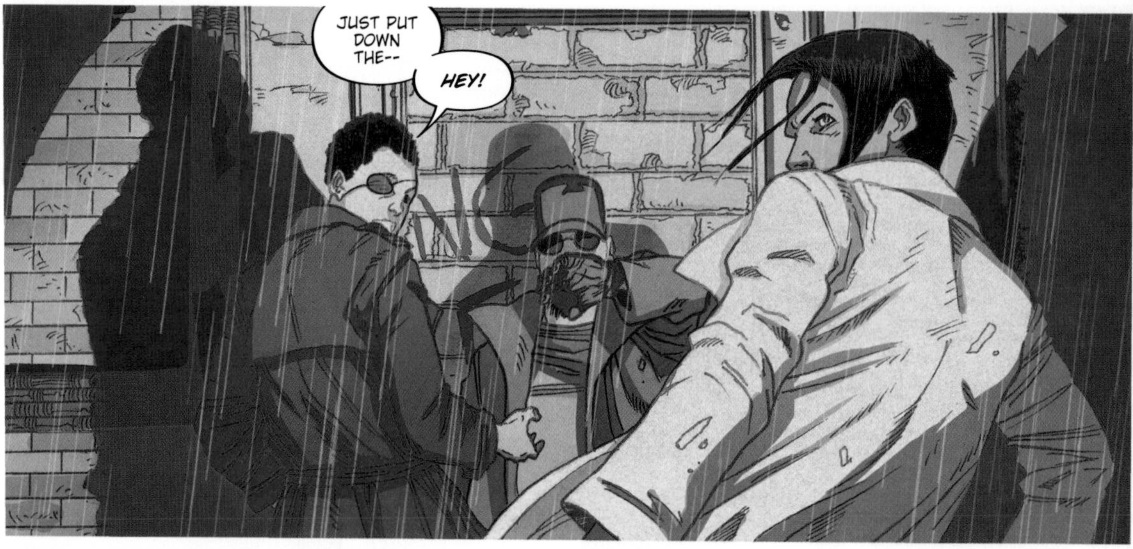
JUST PUT DOWN THE--
HEY!

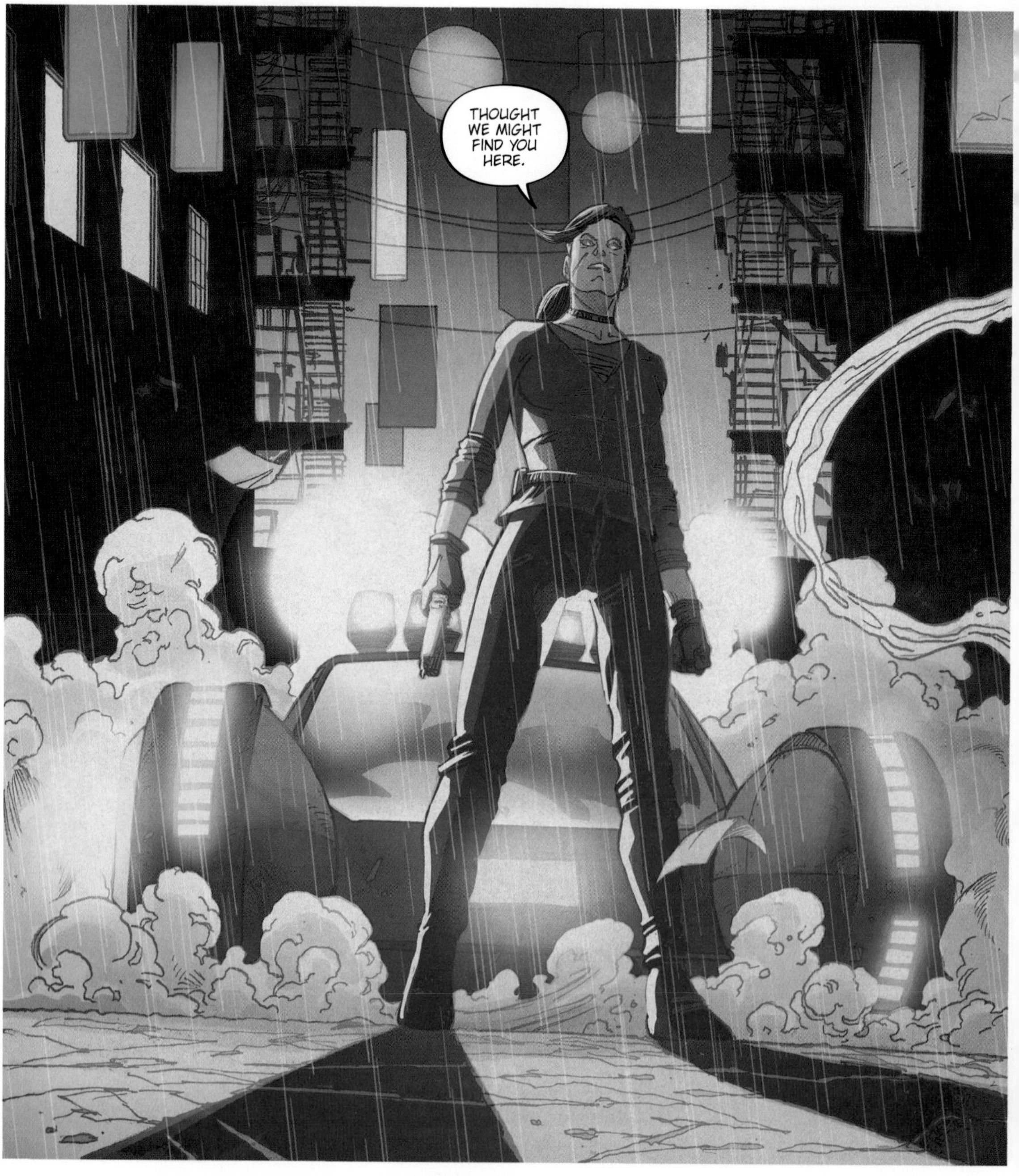
THOUGHT WE MIGHT FIND YOU HERE.

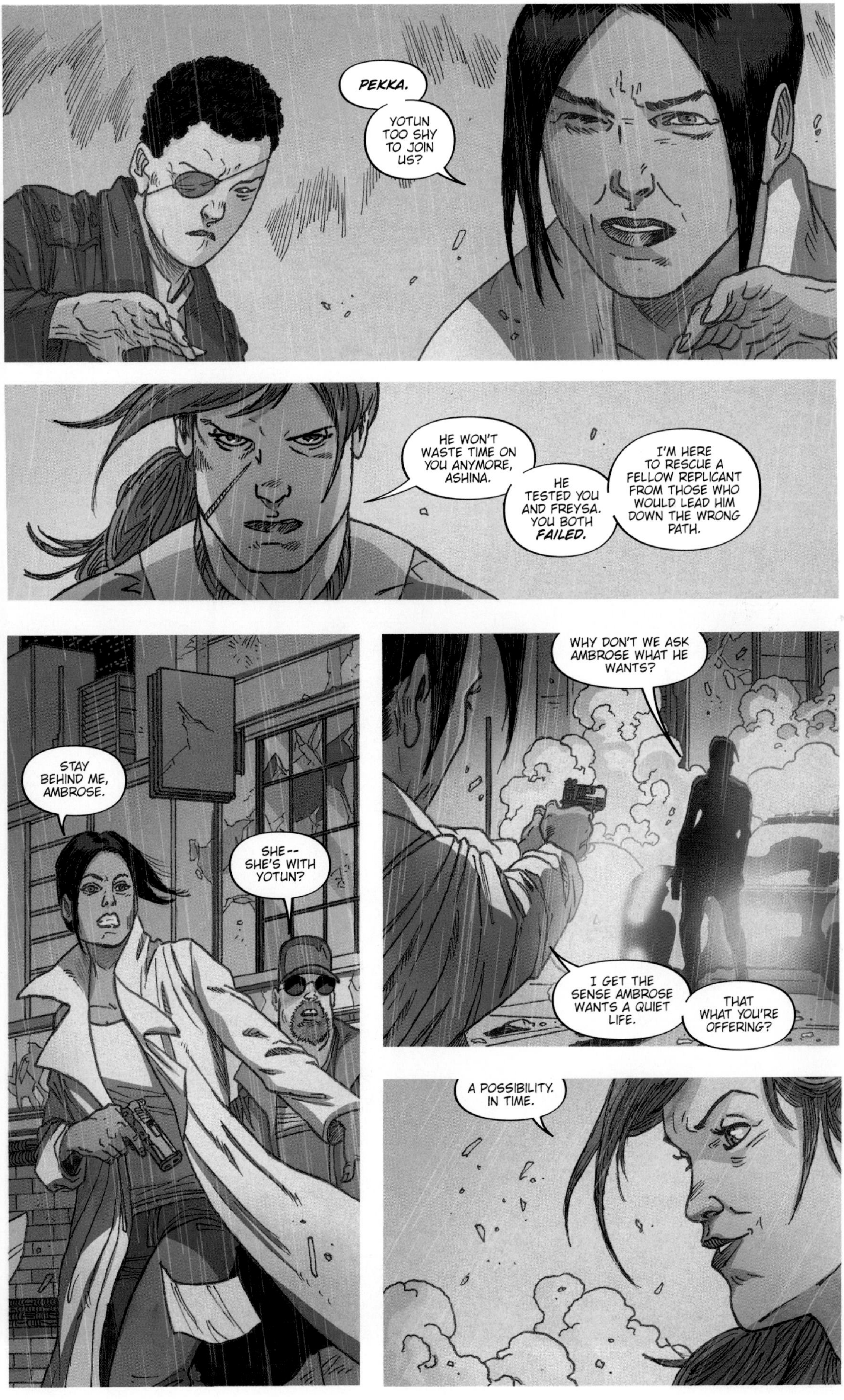
PEKKA.
YOTUN TOO SHY TO JOIN US?
HE WON'T WASTE TIME ON YOU ANYMORE, ASHINA.
HE TESTED YOU AND FREYSA. YOU BOTH FAILED.
I'M HERE TO RESCUE A FELLOW REPLICANT FROM THOSE WHO WOULD LEAD HIM DOWN THE WRONG PATH.
STAY BEHIND ME, AMBROSE.
SHE-- SHE'S WITH YOTUN?
WHY DON'T WE ASK AMBROSE WHAT HE WANTS?
I GET THE SENSE AMBROSE WANTS A QUIET LIFE.
THAT WHAT YOU'RE OFFERING?
A POSSIBILITY. IN TIME.

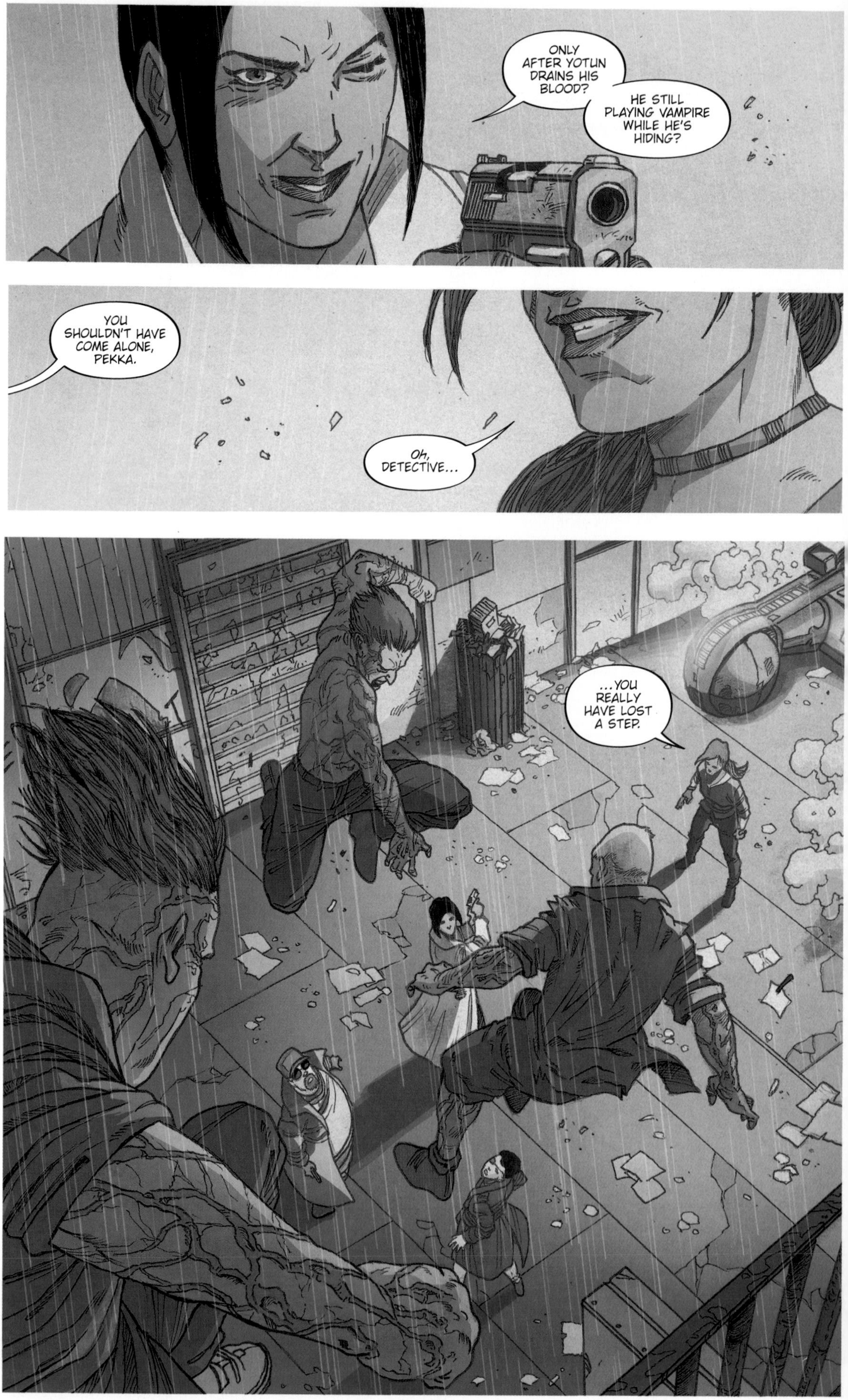
ONLY AFTER YOTUN DRAINS HIS BLOOD?
HE STILL PLAYING VAMPIRE WHILE HE'S HIDING?
YOU SHOULDN'T HAVE COME ALONE, PEKKA.
Oh, DETECTIVE...
...YOU REALLY HAVE LOST A STEP.

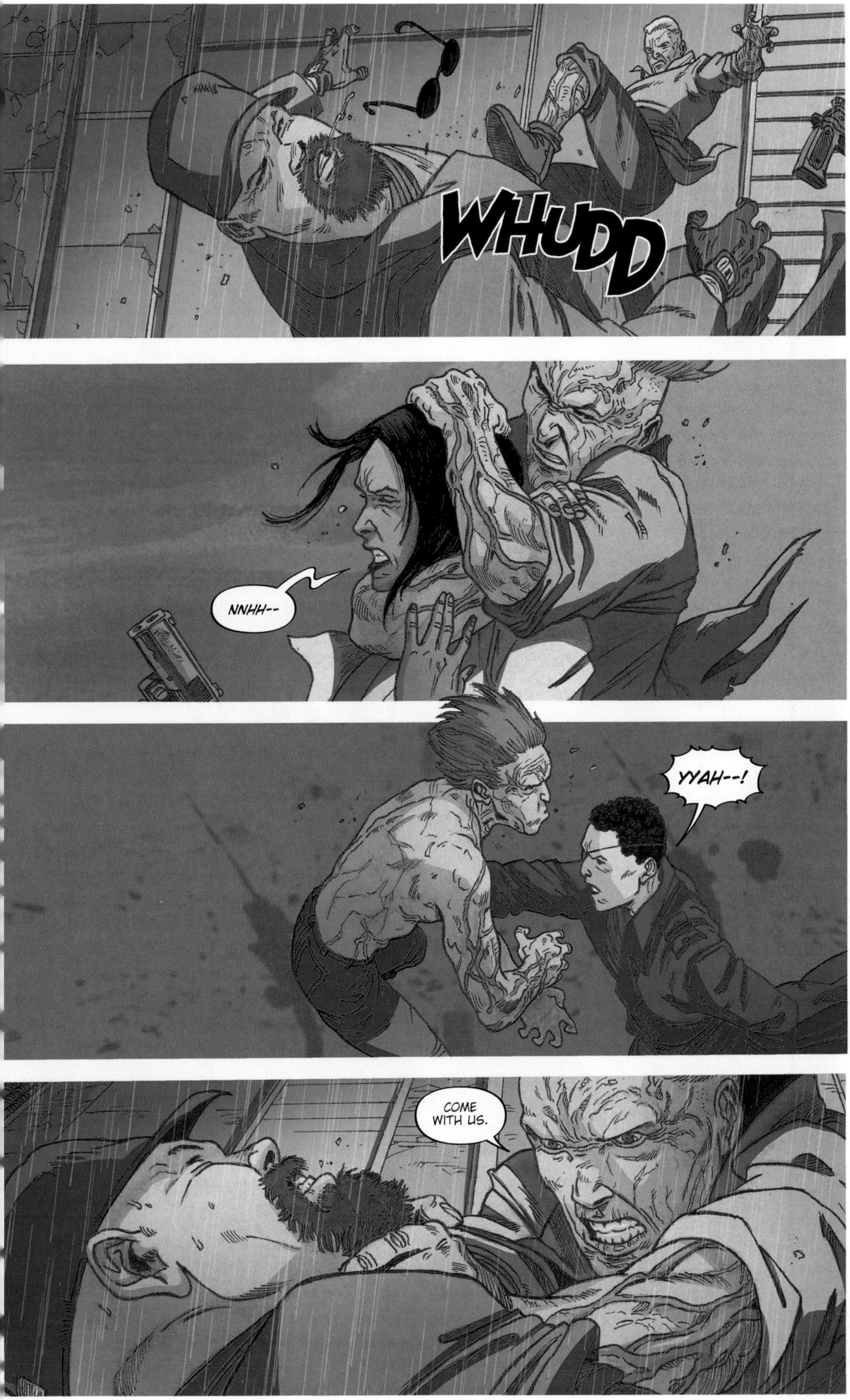
WHUDD
NNHH--
YYAH--!
COME WITH US.

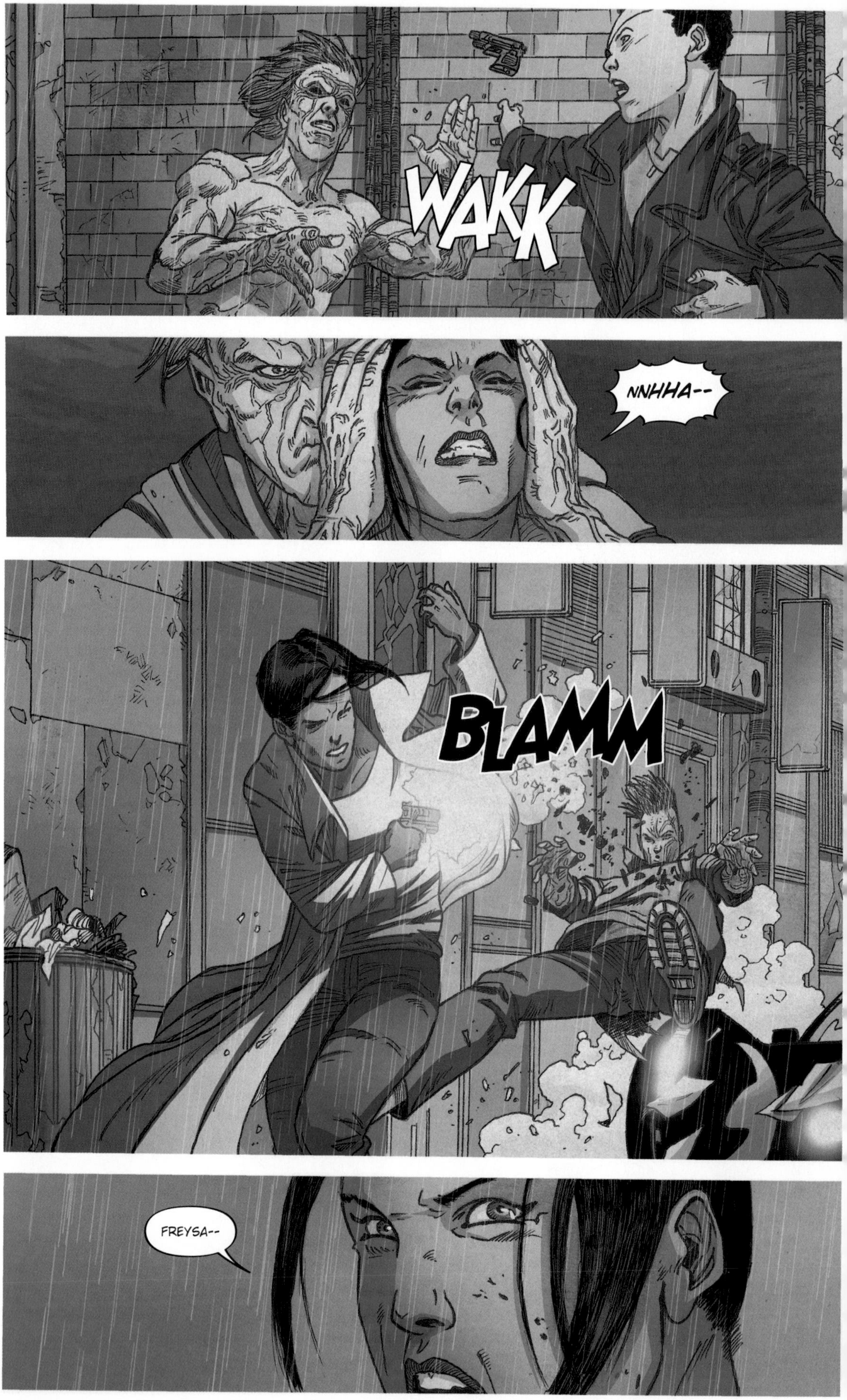
WAKK
NNHHA--
BLAMM
FREYSA--

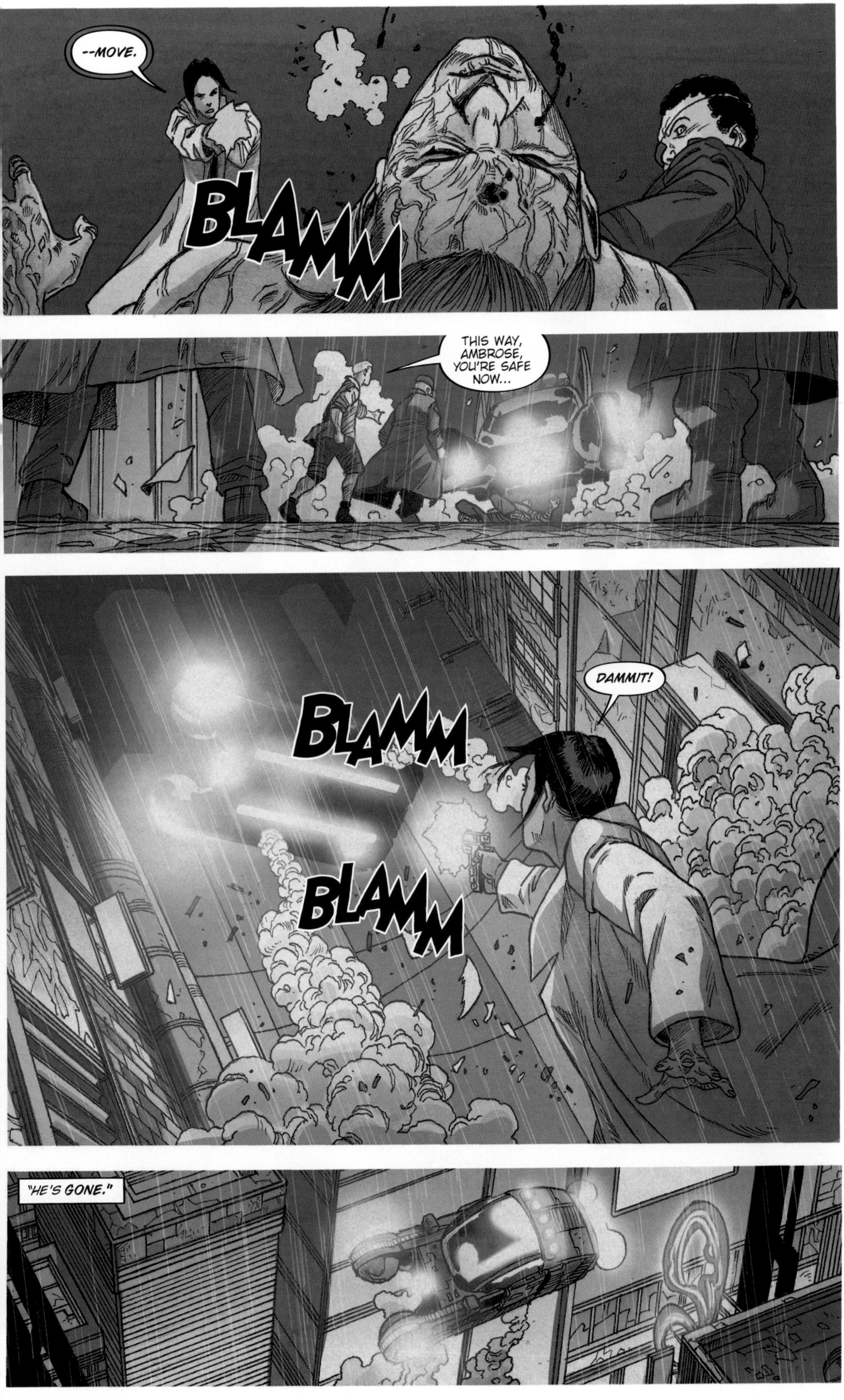
--MOVE.
BLAMM
THIS WAY, AMBROSE, YOU'RE SAFE NOW...
DAMMIT!
BLAMM
BLAMM
"HE'S GONE."

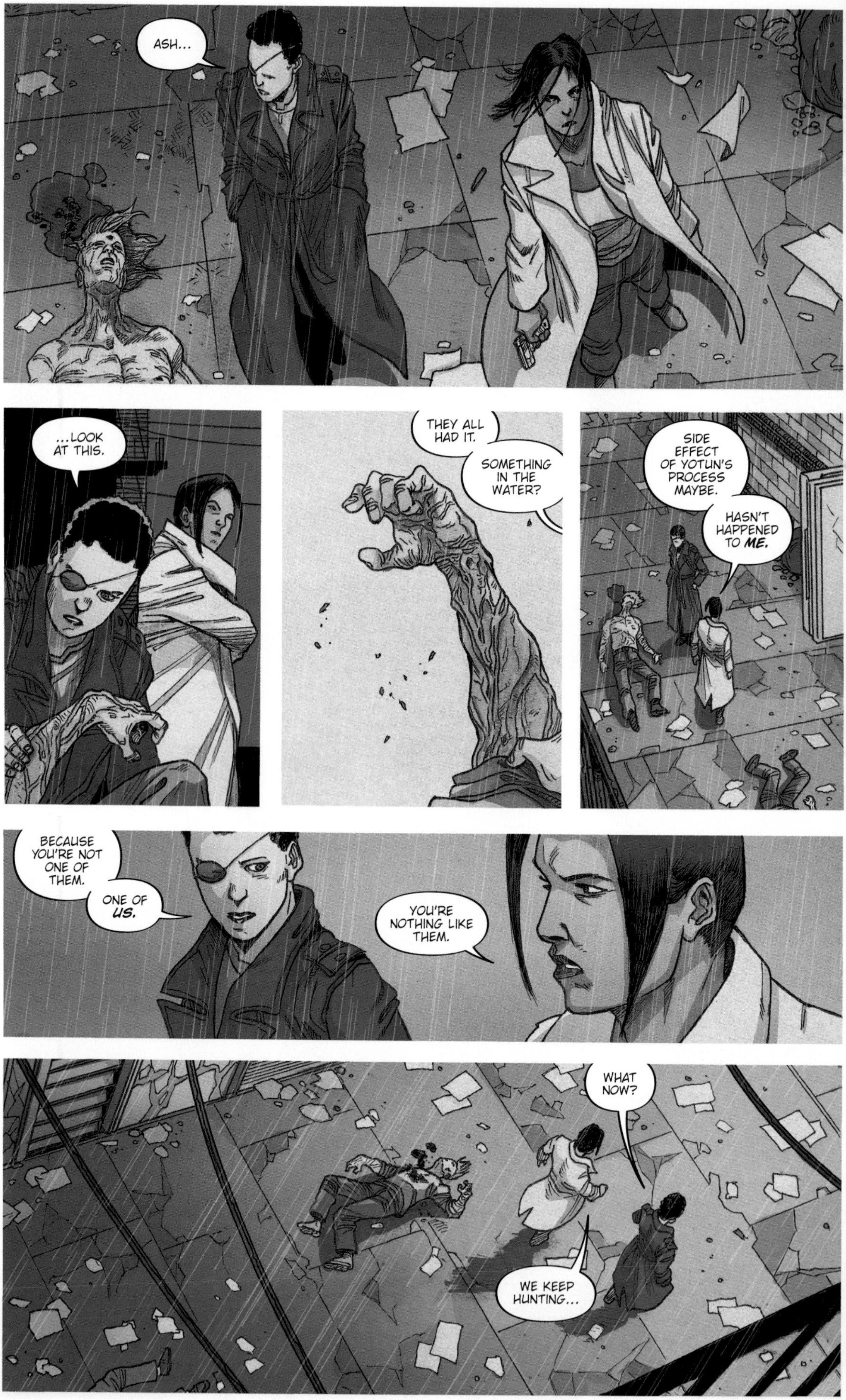
ASH...
...LOOK AT THIS.
THEY ALL HAD IT.
SOMETHING IN THE WATER?
SIDE EFFECT OF YOTUN'S PROCESS MAYBE.
HASN'T HAPPENED TO *ME.*
BECAUSE YOU'RE NOT ONE OF THEM.
ONE OF *US.*
YOU'RE NOTHING LIKE THEM.
WHAT NOW?
WE KEEP HUNTING...

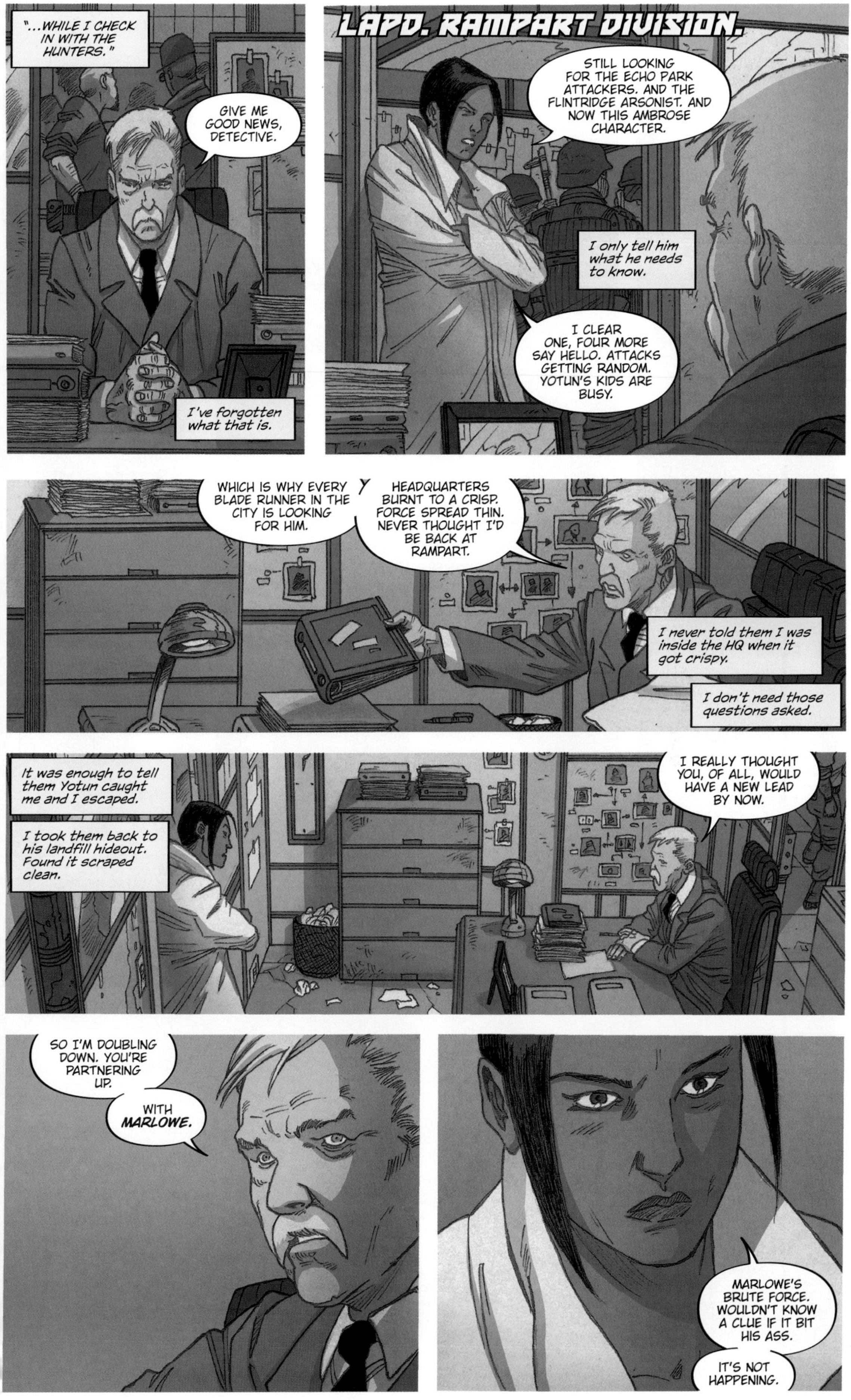
"...WHILE I CHECK IN WITH THE HUNTERS."
GIVE ME GOOD NEWS, DETECTIVE.
I've forgotten what that is.
LAPD. RAMPART DIVISION.
STILL LOOKING FOR THE ECHO PARK ATTACKERS. AND THE FLINTRIDGE ARSONIST. AND NOW THIS AMBROSE CHARACTER.
I only tell him what he needs to know.
I CLEAR ONE, FOUR MORE SAY HELLO. ATTACKS GETTING RANDOM. YOTUN'S KIDS ARE BUSY.
WHICH IS WHY EVERY BLADE RUNNER IN THE CITY IS LOOKING FOR HIM.
HEADQUARTERS BURNT TO A CRISP. FORCE SPREAD THIN. NEVER THOUGHT I'D BE BACK AT RAMPART.
I never told them I was inside the HQ when it got crispy.
I don't need those questions asked.
It was enough to tell them Yotun caught me and I escaped.
I took them back to his landfill hideout. Found it scraped clean.
I REALLY THOUGHT YOU, OF ALL, WOULD HAVE A NEW LEAD BY NOW.
SO I'M DOUBLING DOWN. YOU'RE PARTNERING UP.
WITH MARLOWE.
MARLOWE'S BRUTE FORCE. WOULDN'T KNOW A CLUE IF IT BIT HIS ASS.
IT'S NOT HAPPENING.

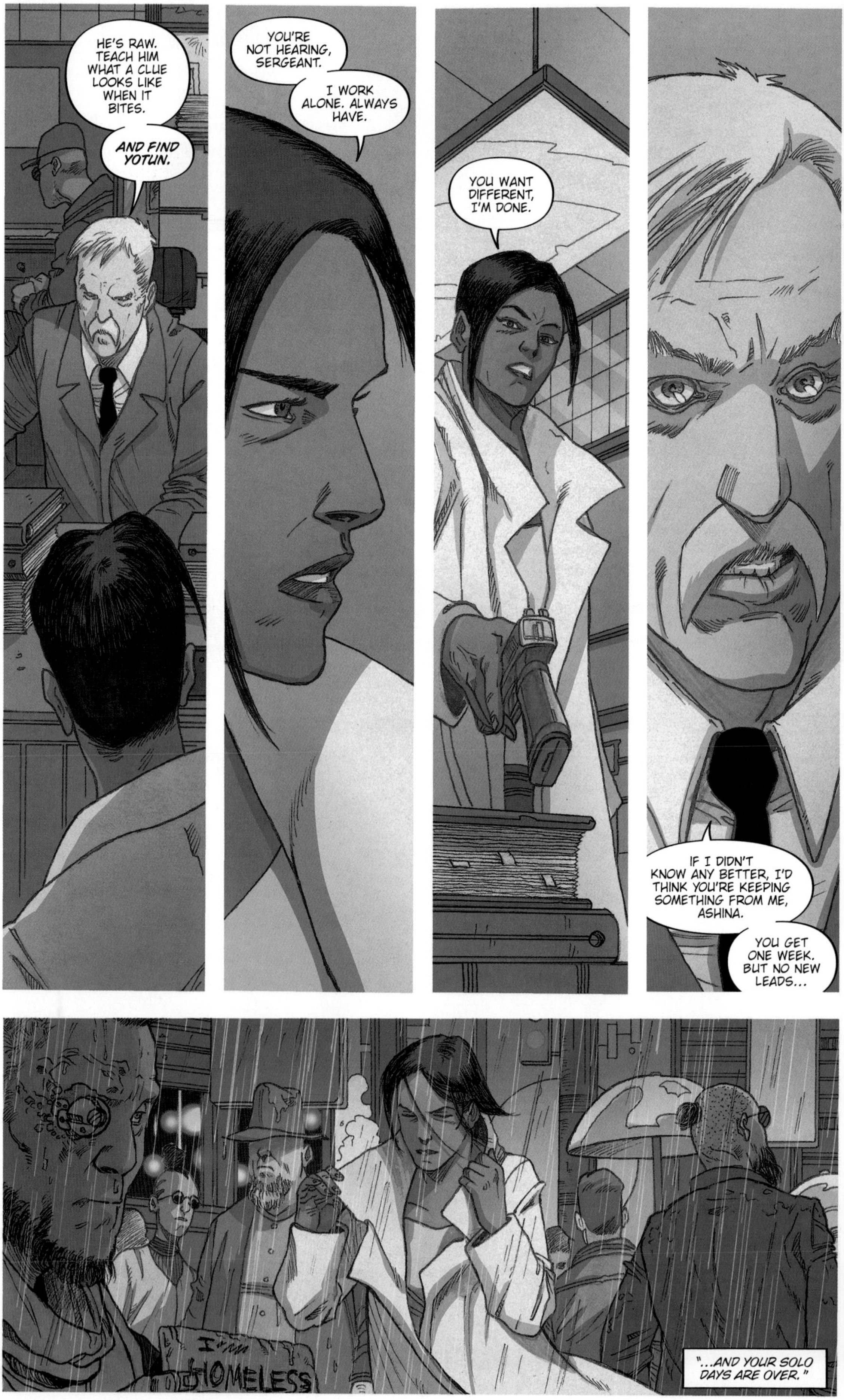
HE'S RAW. TEACH HIM WHAT A CLUE LOOKS LIKE WHEN IT BITES.
AND FIND YOTUN.
YOU'RE NOT HEARING, SERGEANT.
I WORK ALONE. ALWAYS HAVE.
YOU WANT DIFFERENT, I'M DONE.
IF I DIDN'T KNOW ANY BETTER, I'D THINK YOU'RE KEEPING SOMETHING FROM ME, ASHINA.
YOU GET ONE WEEK. BUT NO NEW LEADS...
"...AND YOUR SOLO DAYS ARE OVER."

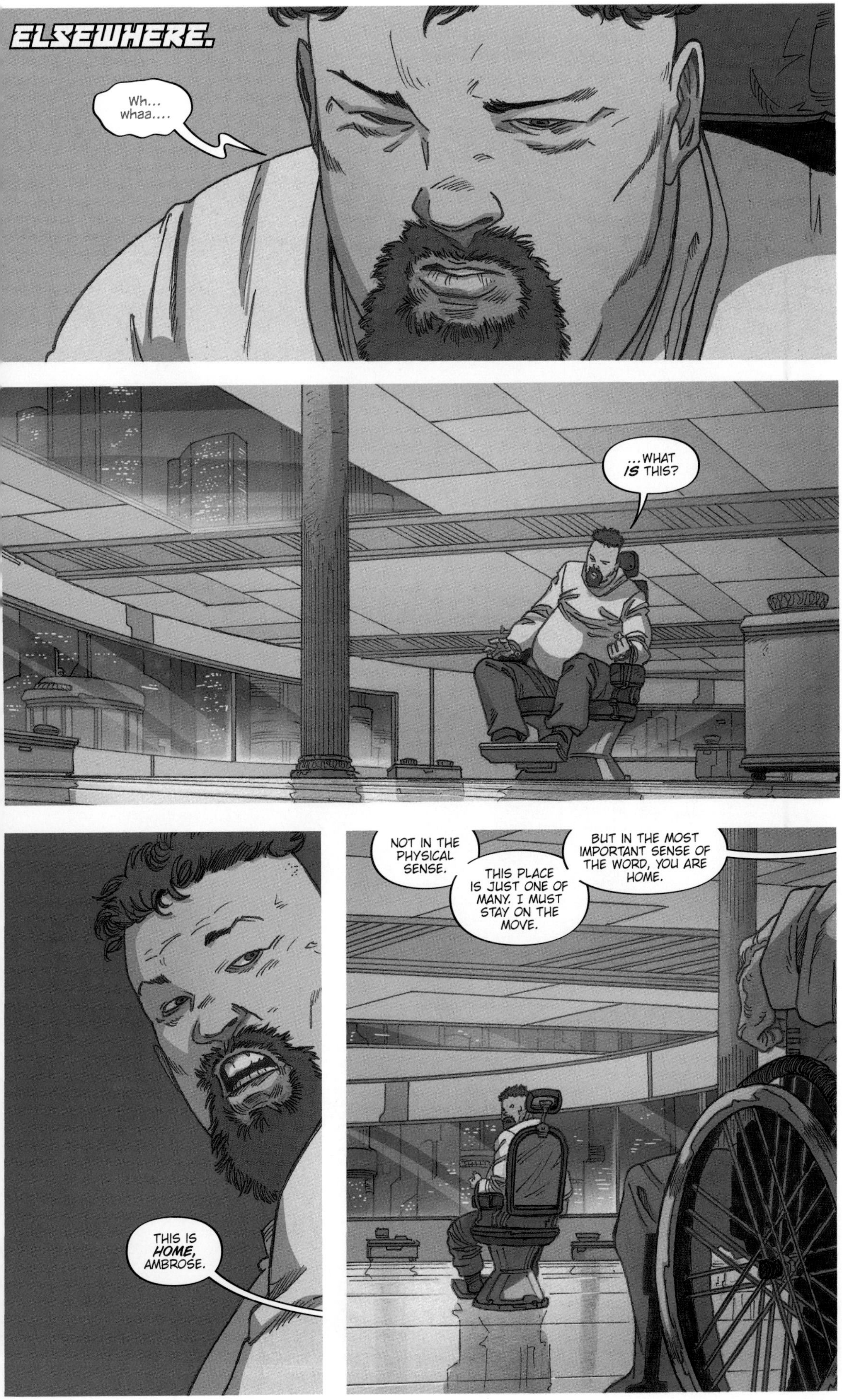
ELSEWHERE.
Wh... whaa....
...WHAT IS THIS?
THIS IS HOME, AMBROSE.
NOT IN THE PHYSICAL SENSE.
THIS PLACE IS JUST ONE OF MANY. I MUST STAY ON THE MOVE.
BUT IN THE MOST IMPORTANT SENSE OF THE WORD, YOU ARE HOME.

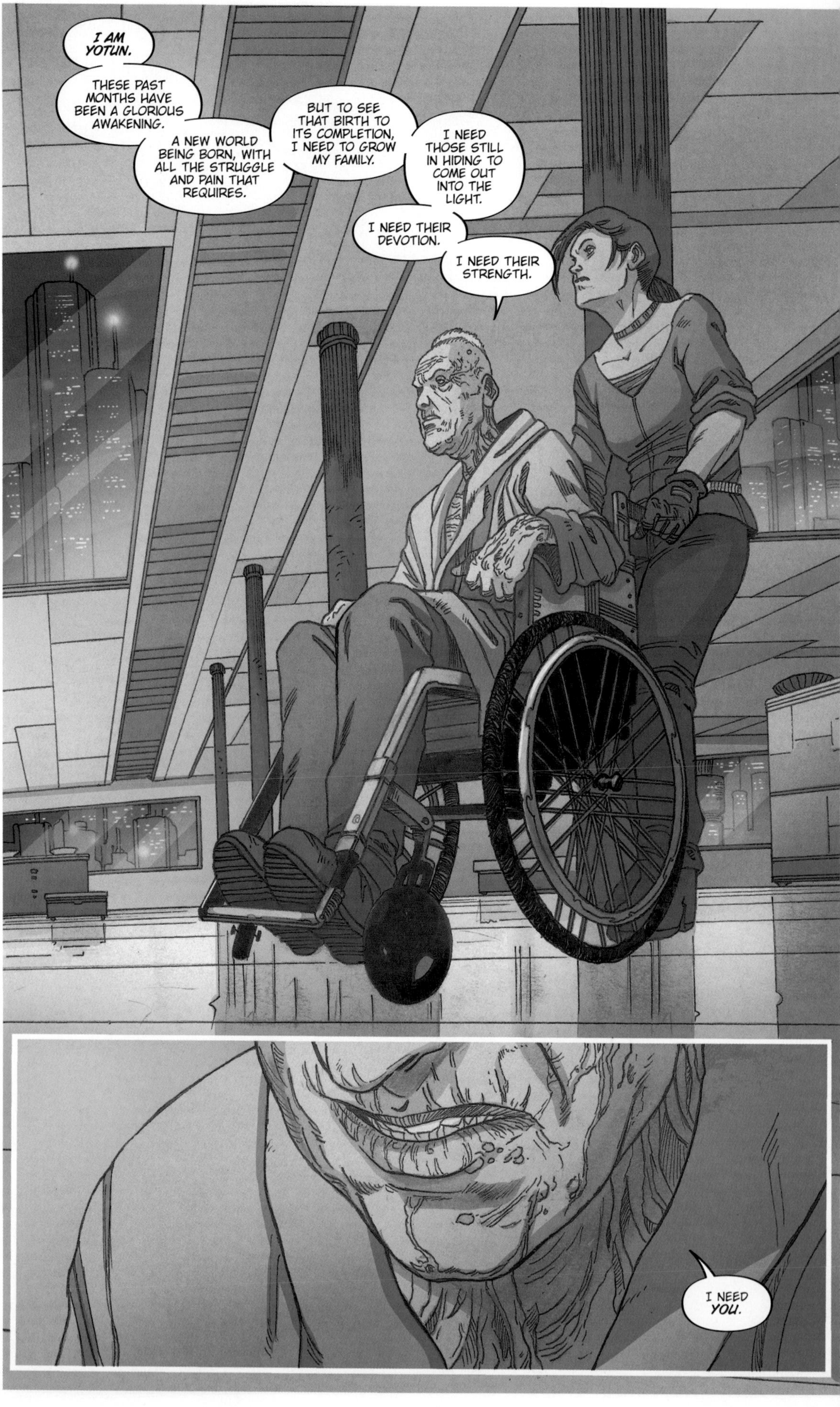
I AM YOTUN.
THESE PAST MONTHS HAVE BEEN A GLORIOUS AWAKENING.
A NEW WORLD BEING BORN, WITH ALL THE STRUGGLE AND PAIN THAT REQUIRES.
BUT TO SEE THAT BIRTH TO ITS COMPLETION, I NEED TO GROW MY FAMILY.
I NEED THOSE STILL IN HIDING TO COME OUT INTO THE LIGHT.
I NEED THEIR DEVOTION.
I NEED THEIR STRENGTH.
I NEED YOU.

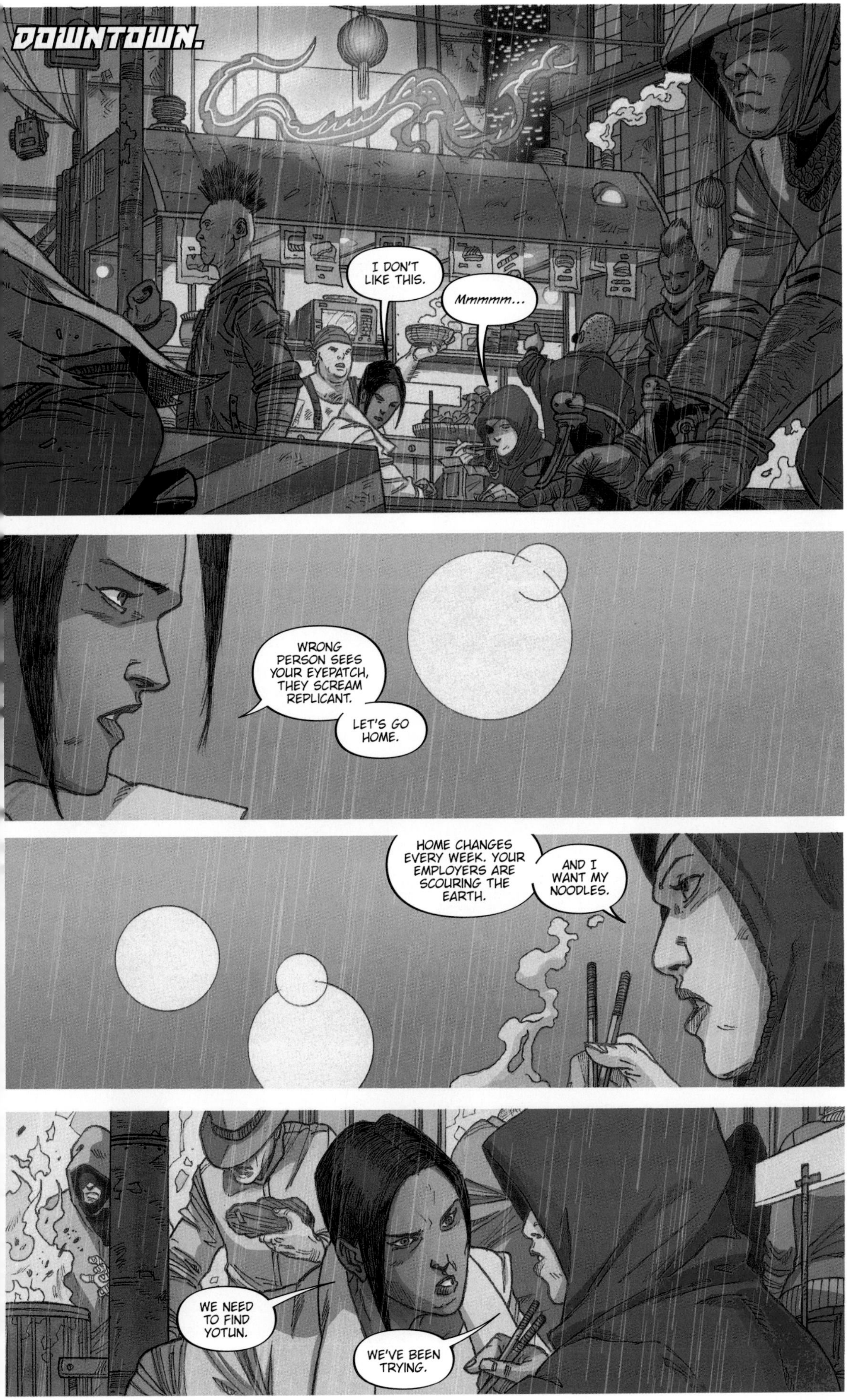
DOWNTOWN.
I DON'T LIKE THIS.
Mmmmm...
WRONG PERSON SEES YOUR EYEPATCH, THEY SCREAM REPLICANT.
LET'S GO HOME.
HOME CHANGES EVERY WEEK. YOUR EMPLOYERS ARE SCOURING THE EARTH.
AND I WANT MY NOODLES.
WE NEED TO FIND YOTUN.
WE'VE BEEN TRYING.

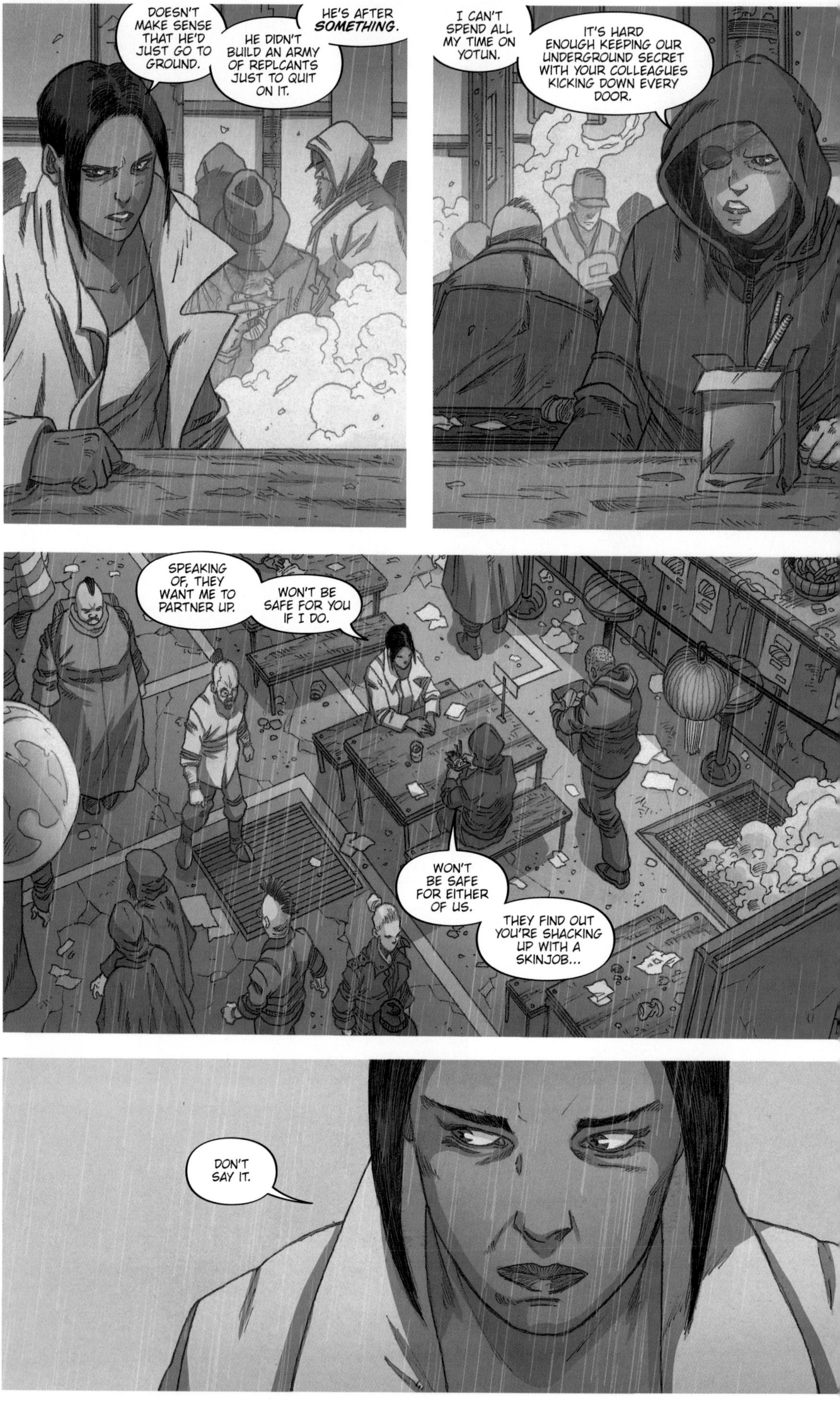
DOESN'T MAKE SENSE THAT HE'D JUST GO TO GROUND.
HE DIDN'T BUILD AN ARMY OF REPLCANTS JUST TO QUIT ON IT.
HE'S AFTER *SOMETHING*.
I CAN'T SPEND ALL MY TIME ON YOTUN.
IT'S HARD ENOUGH KEEPING OUR UNDERGROUND SECRET WITH YOUR COLLEAGUES KICKING DOWN EVERY DOOR.
SPEAKING OF, THEY WANT ME TO PARTNER UP.
WON'T BE SAFE FOR YOU IF I DO.
WON'T BE SAFE FOR EITHER OF US.
THEY FIND OUT YOU'RE SHACKING UP WITH A SKINJOB...
DON'T SAY IT.

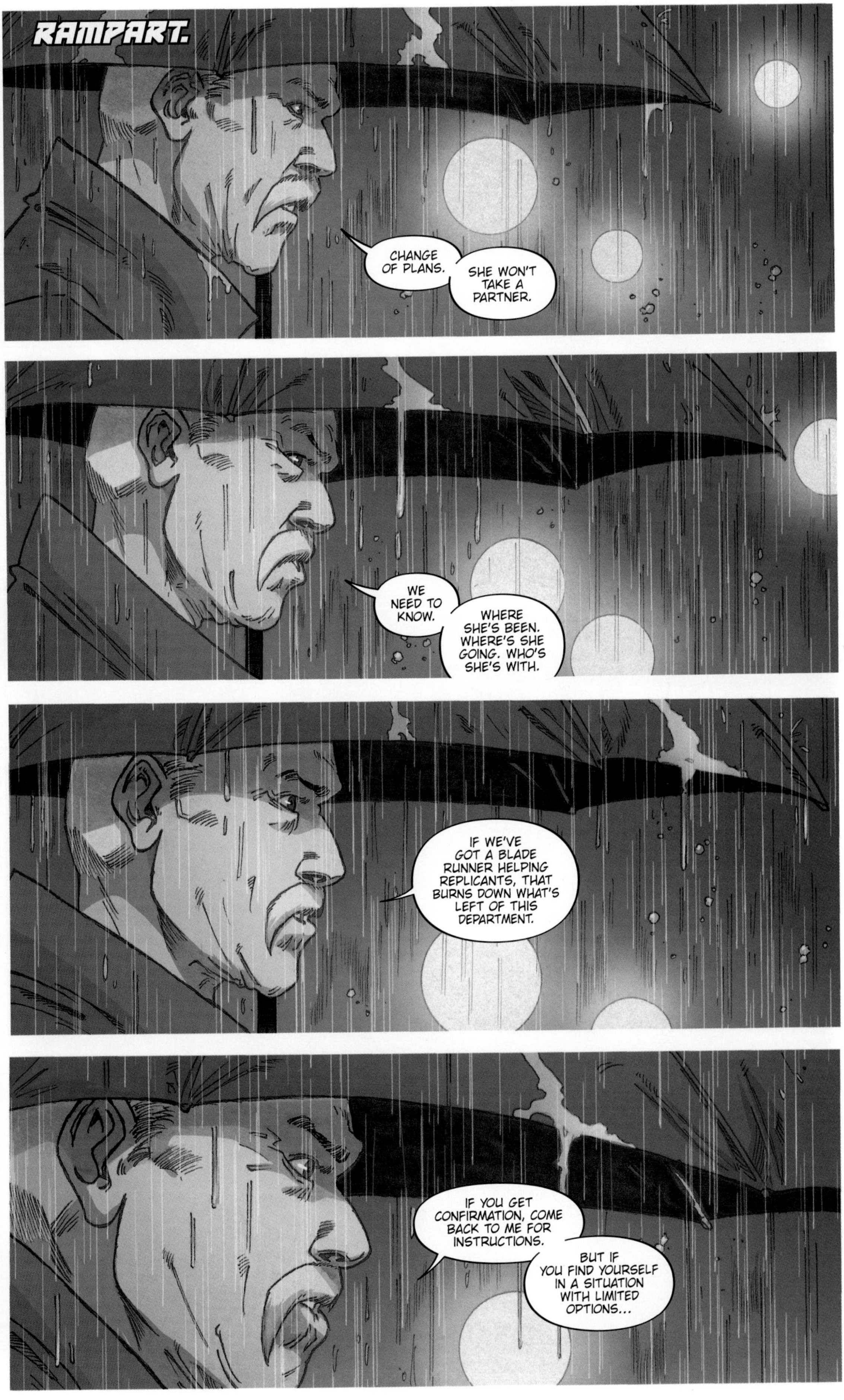
RAMPART.
CHANGE OF PLANS.
SHE WON'T TAKE A PARTNER.
WE NEED TO KNOW.
WHERE SHE'S BEEN. WHERE'S SHE GOING. WHO'S SHE'S WITH.
IF WE'VE GOT A BLADE RUNNER HELPING REPLICANTS, THAT BURNS DOWN WHAT'S LEFT OF THIS DEPARTMENT.
IF YOU GET CONFIRMATION, COME BACK TO ME FOR INSTRUCTIONS.
BUT IF YOU FIND YOURSELF IN A SITUATION WITH LIMITED OPTIONS...

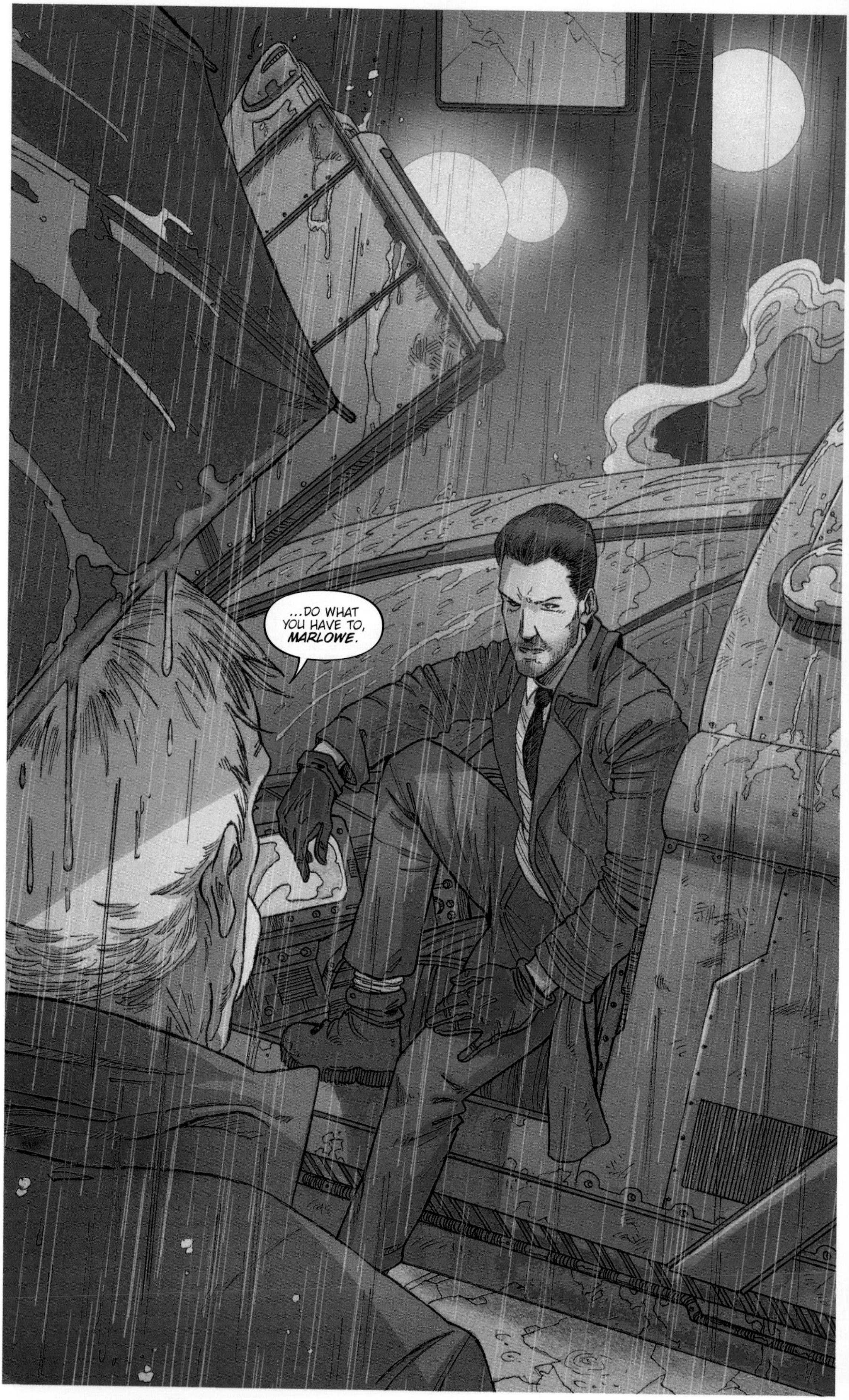
...DO WHAT YOU HAVE TO, MARLOWE.

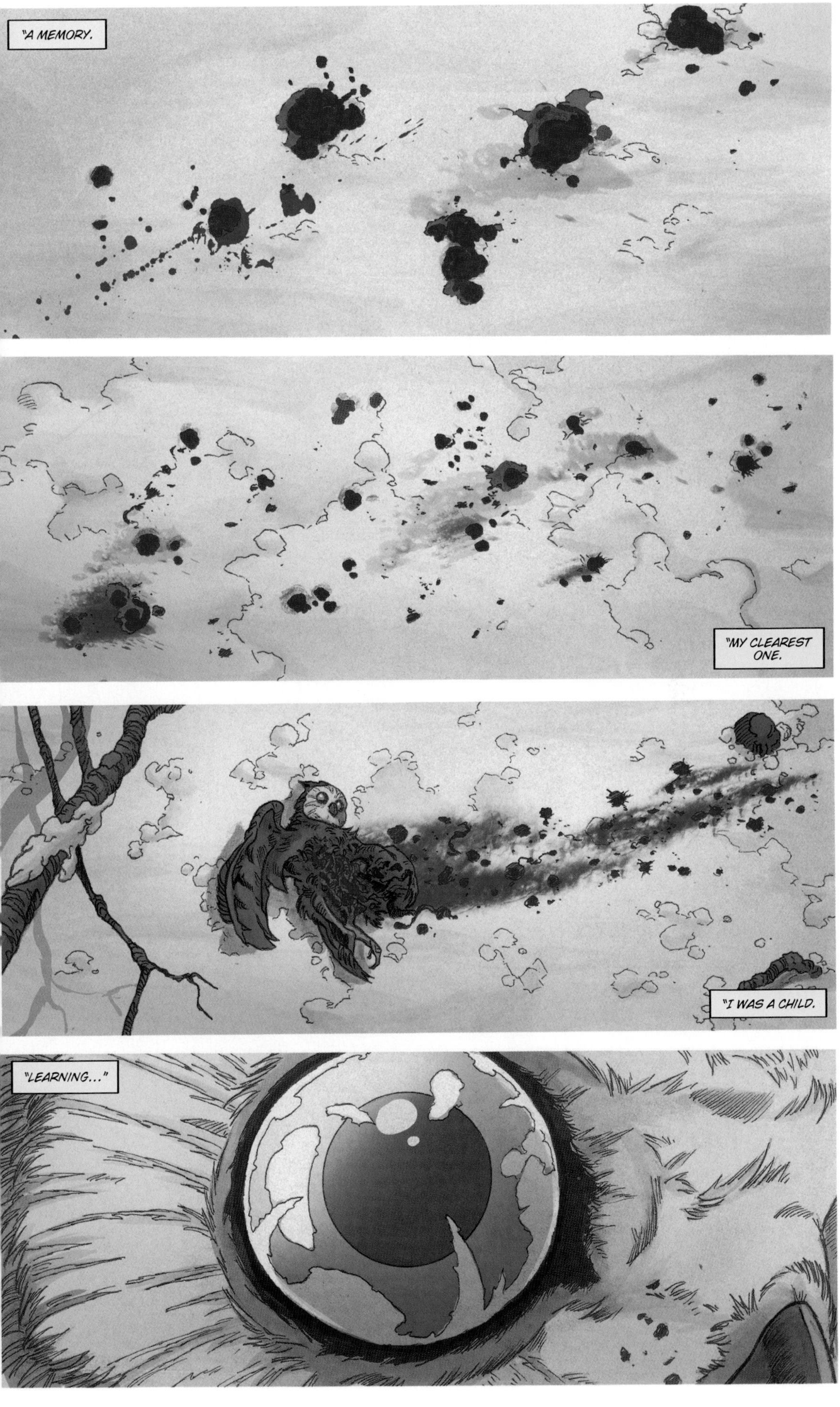
"A MEMORY.
"MY CLEAREST ONE.
"I WAS A CHILD.
"LEARNING..."

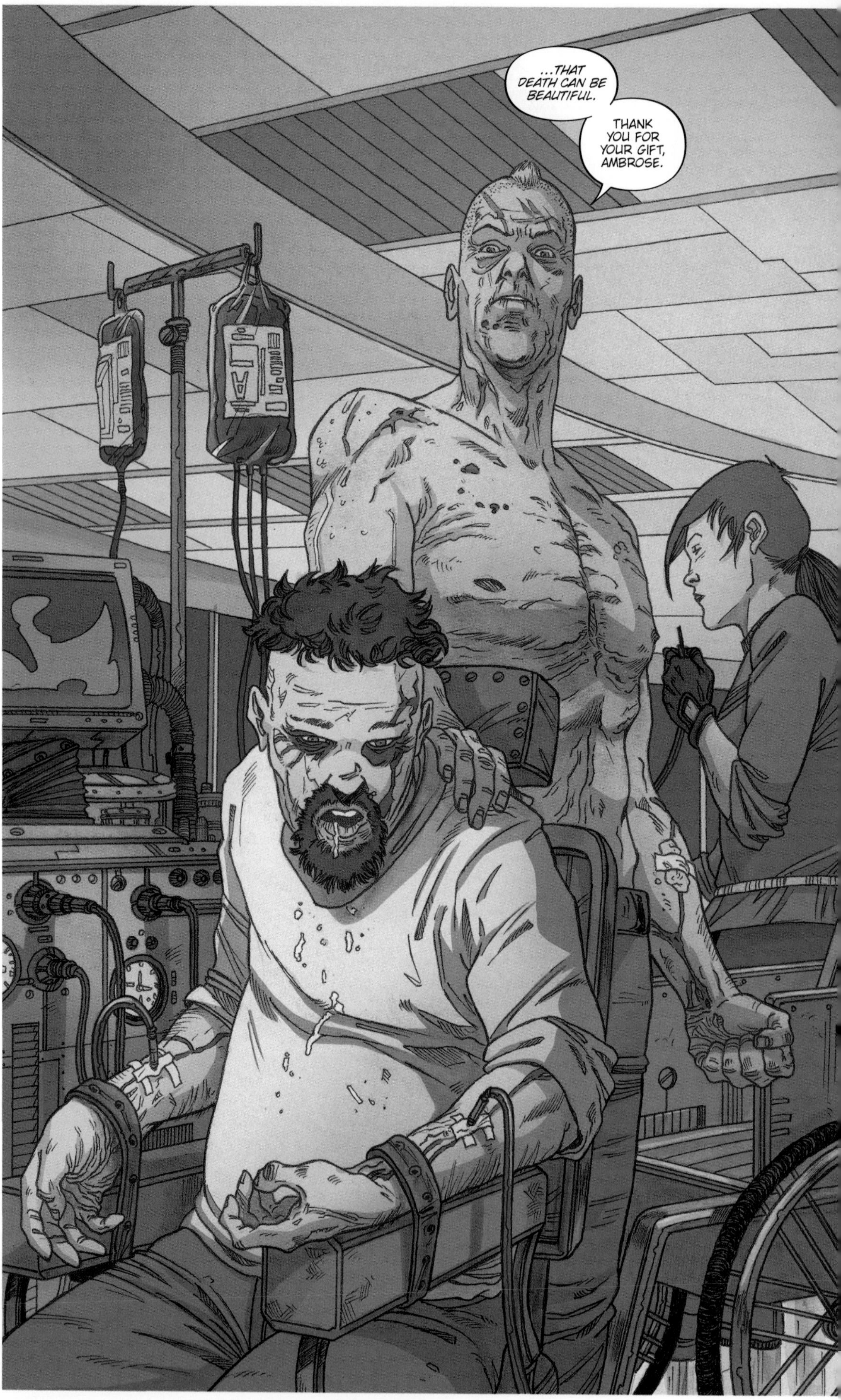
...THAT DEATH CAN BE BEAUTIFUL.
THANK YOU FOR YOUR GIFT, AMBROSE.

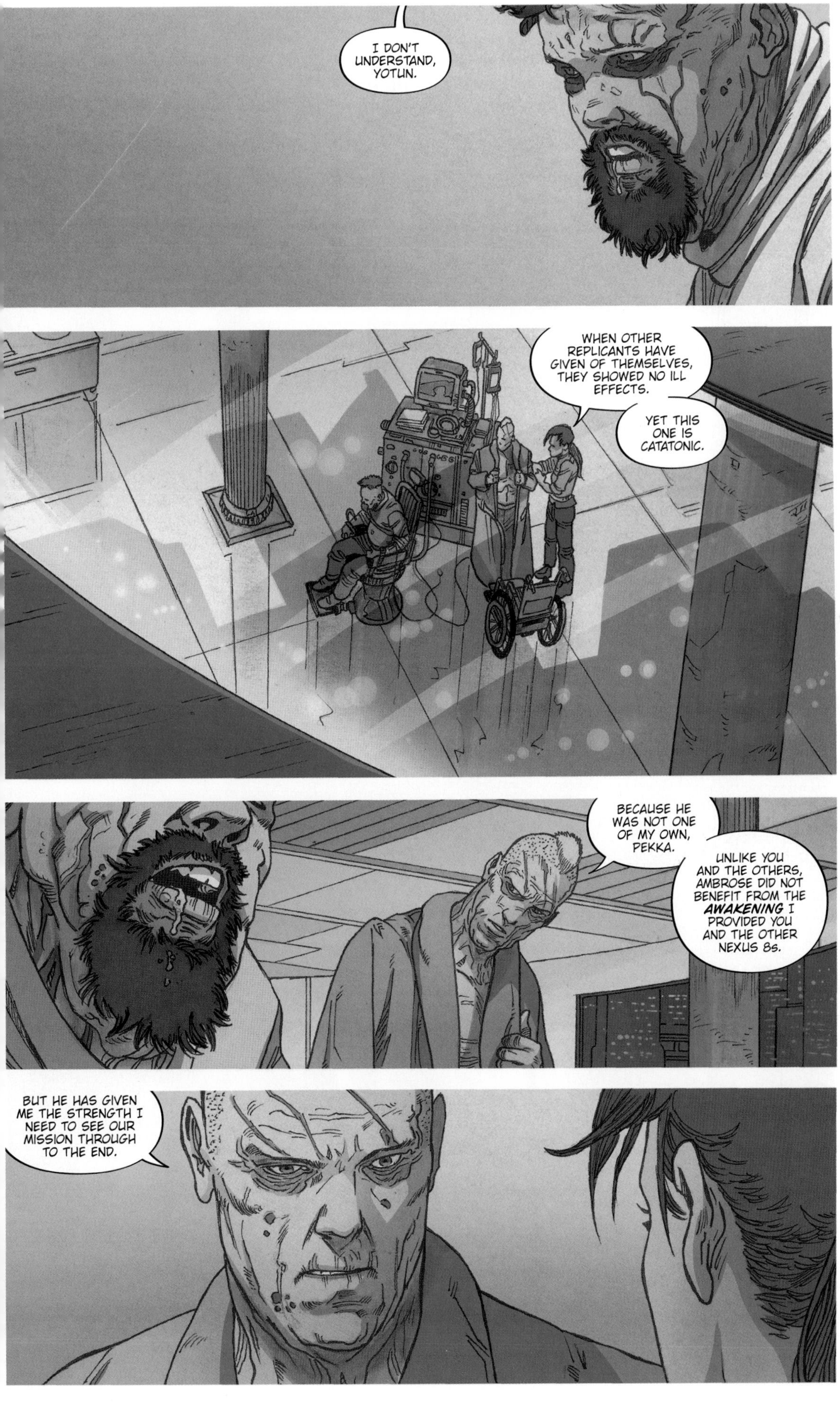
I DON'T UNDERSTAND, YOTUN.
WHEN OTHER REPLICANTS HAVE GIVEN OF THEMSELVES, THEY SHOWED NO ILL EFFECTS.
YET THIS ONE IS CATATONIC.
BECAUSE HE WAS NOT ONE OF MY OWN, PEKKA.
UNLIKE YOU AND THE OTHERS, AMBROSE DID NOT BENEFIT FROM THE ***AWAKENING*** I PROVIDED YOU AND THE OTHER NEXUS 8s.
BUT HE HAS GIVEN ME THE STRENGTH I NEED TO SEE OUR MISSION THROUGH TO THE END.

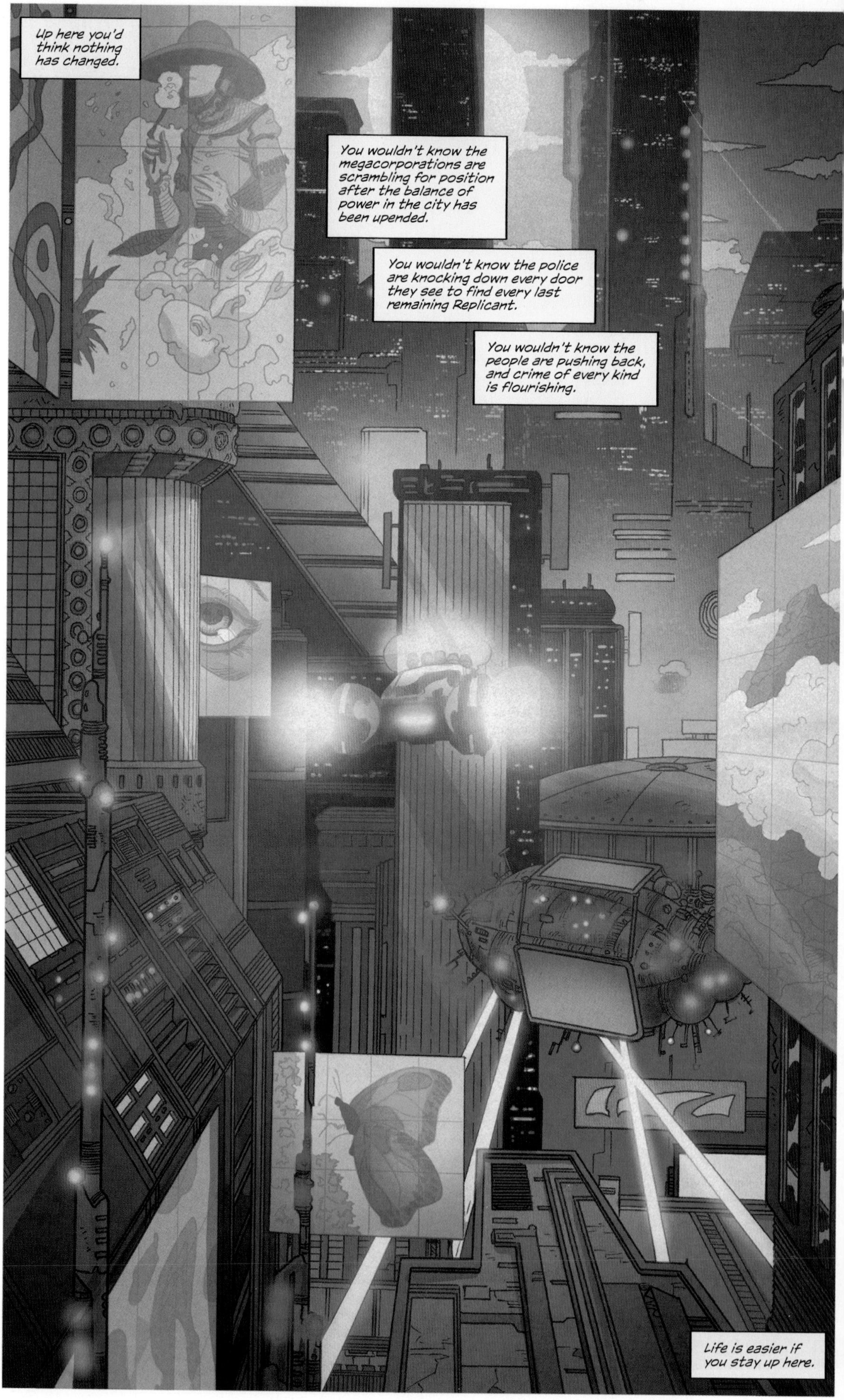
Up here you'd think nothing has changed.
You wouldn't know the megacorporations are scrambling for position after the balance of power in the city has been upended.
You wouldn't know the police are knocking down every door they see to find every last remaining Replicant.
You wouldn't know the people are pushing back, and crime of every kind is flourishing.
Life is easier if you stay up here.

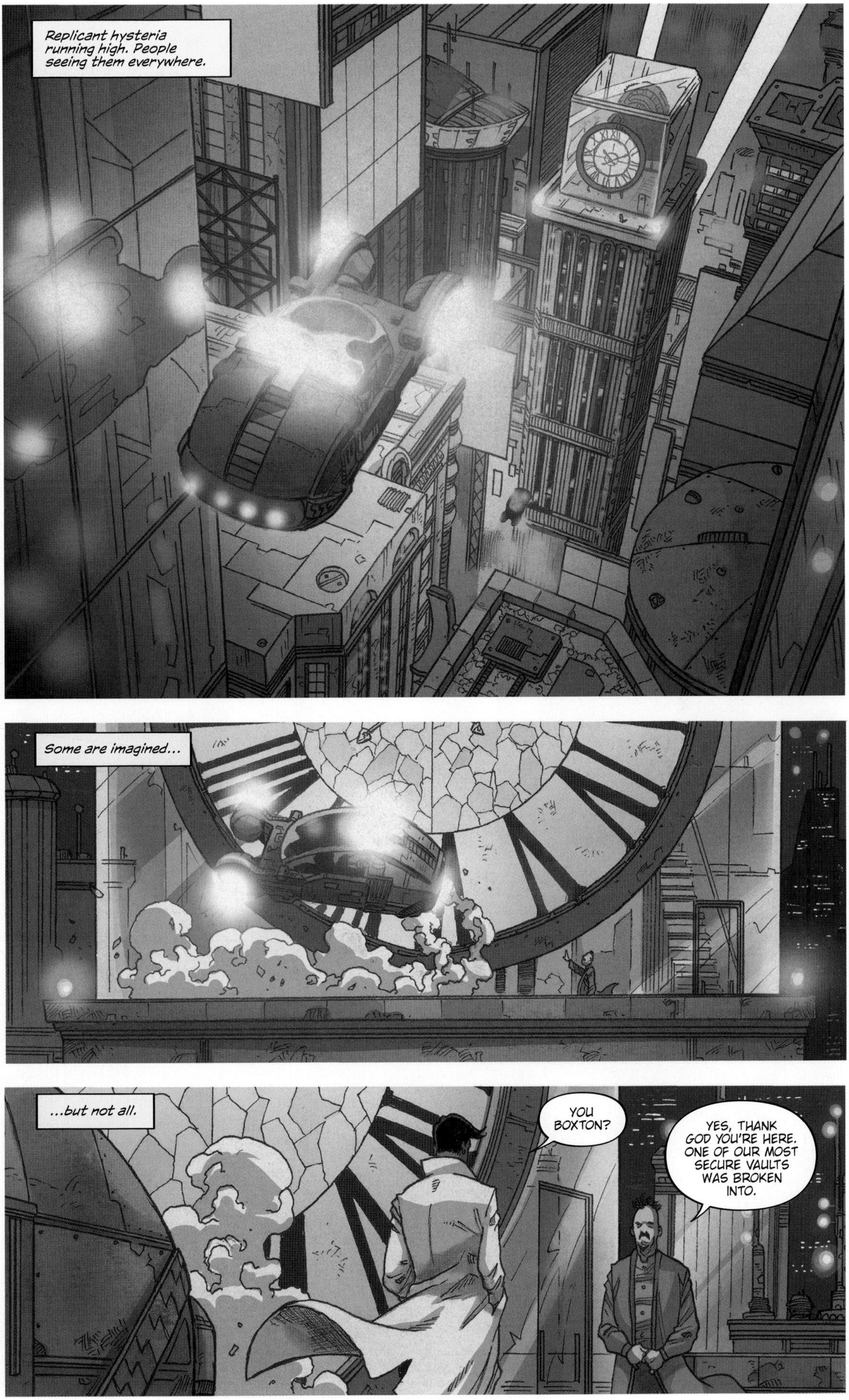
Replicant hysteria running high. People seeing them everywhere.
Some are imagined...
...but not all.
YOU BOXTON?
YES, THANK GOD YOU'RE HERE. ONE OF OUR MOST SECURE VAULTS WAS BROKEN INTO.

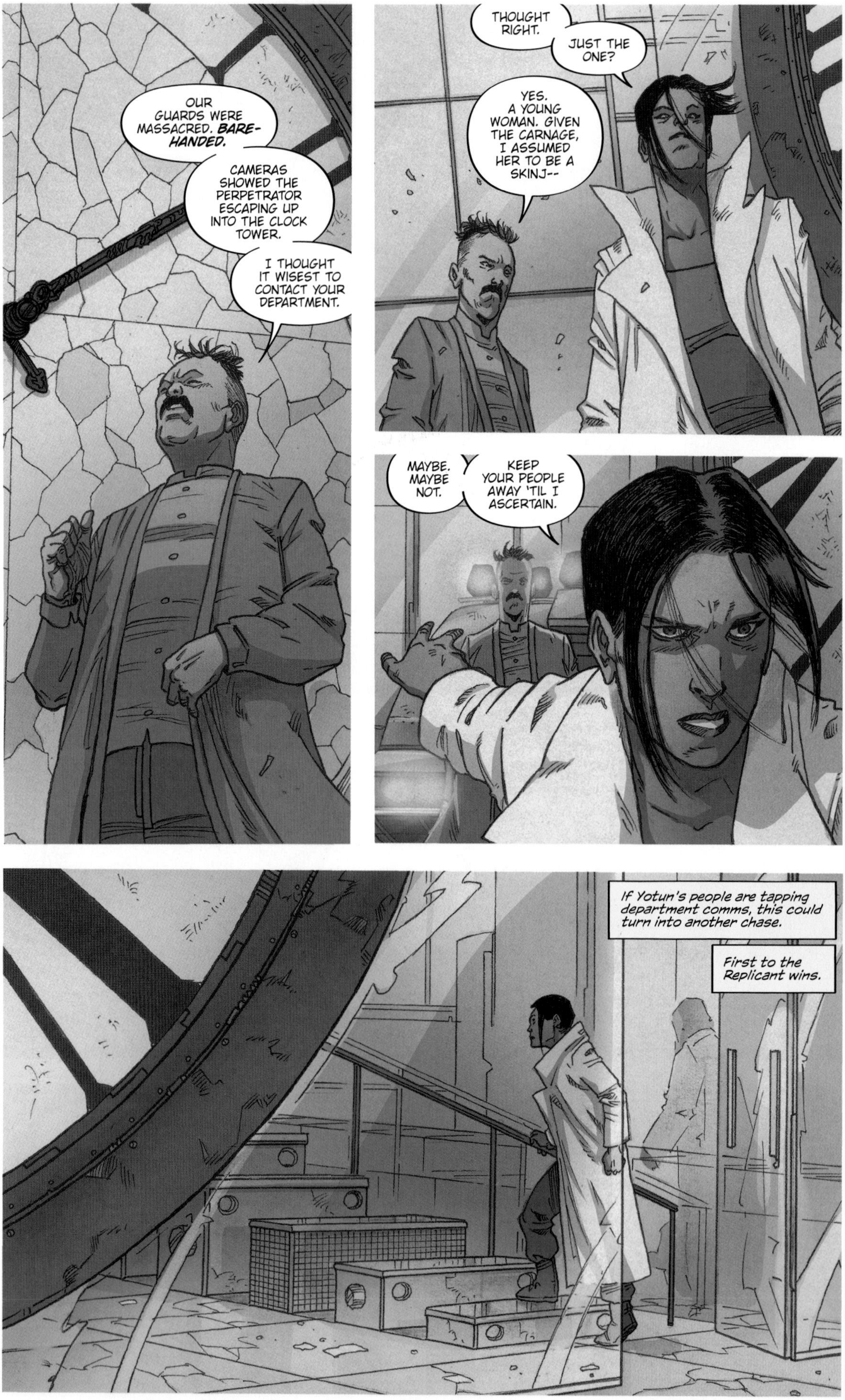
OUR GUARDS WERE MASSACRED. **BARE-HANDED.**
CAMERAS SHOWED THE PERPETRATOR ESCAPING UP INTO THE CLOCK TOWER.
I THOUGHT IT WISEST TO CONTACT YOUR DEPARTMENT.
THOUGHT RIGHT.
JUST THE ONE?
YES. A YOUNG WOMAN. GIVEN THE CARNAGE, I ASSUMED HER TO BE A SKINJ--
MAYBE. MAYBE NOT.
KEEP YOUR PEOPLE AWAY 'TIL I ASCERTAIN.
If Yotun's people are tapping department comms, this could turn into another chase.
First to the Replicant wins.

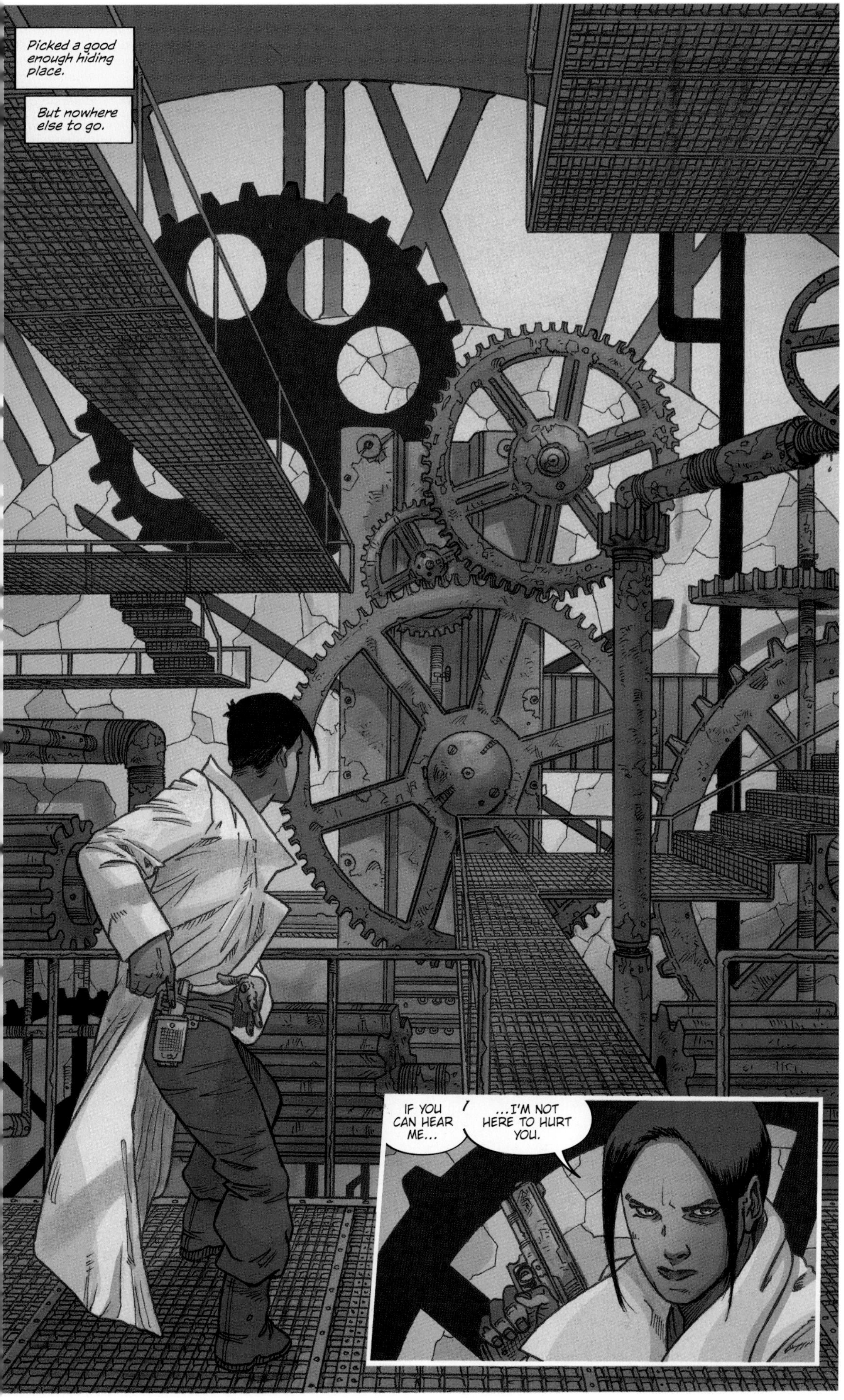
Picked a good enough hiding place.
But nowhere else to go.
IF YOU CAN HEAR ME...
...I'M NOT HERE TO HURT YOU.

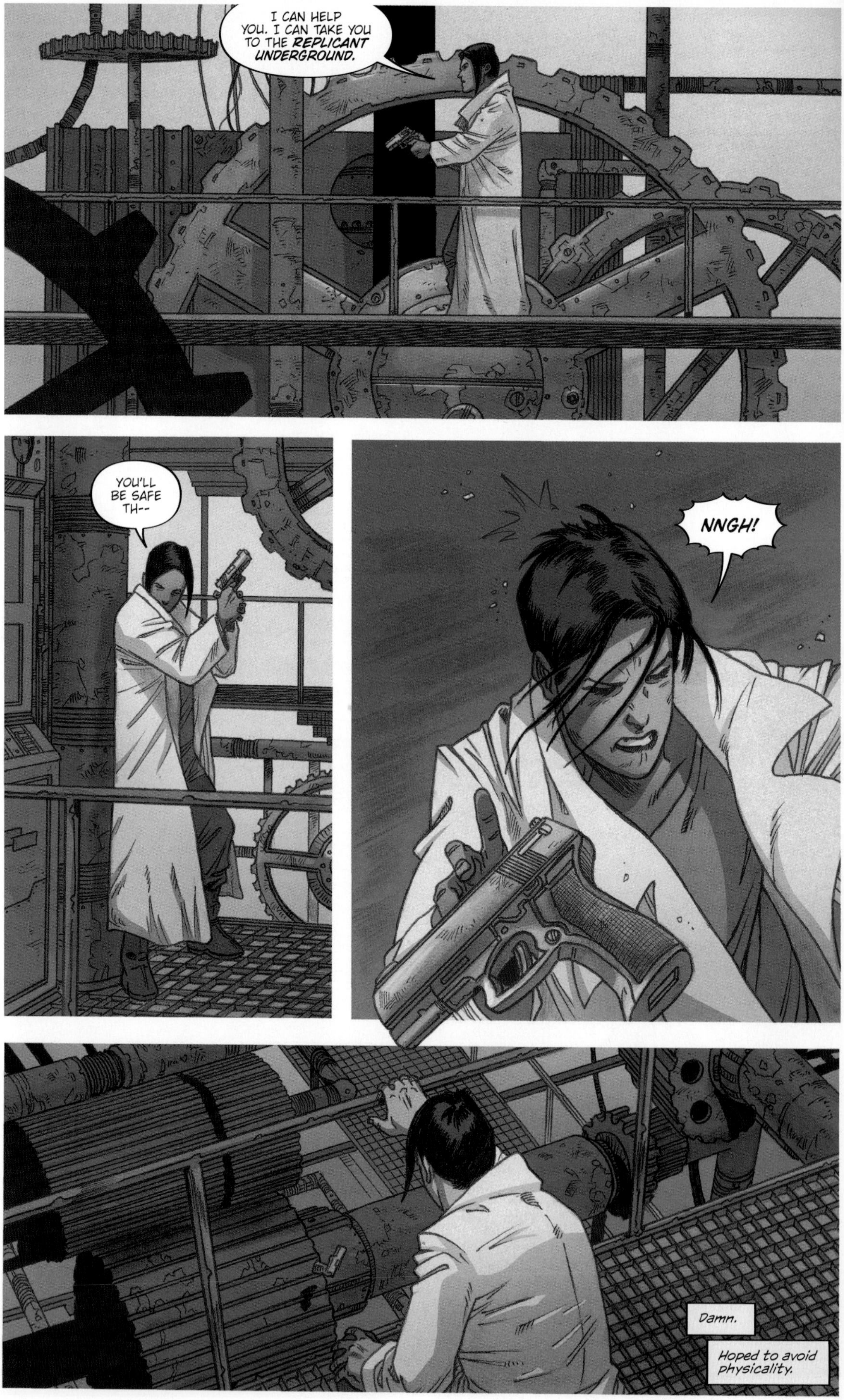

I CAN HELP YOU. I CAN TAKE YOU TO THE ***REPLICANT UNDERGROUND.***
YOU'LL BE SAFE TH--
NNGH!
Damn.
Hoped to avoid physicality.

And the exercise.

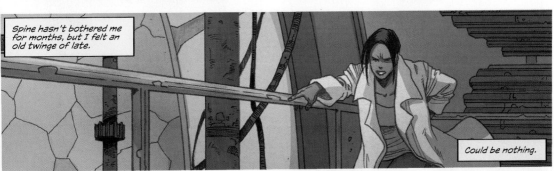

Spine hasn't bothered me for months, but I felt an old twinge of late.

Could be nothing.

Or could be Yotun's miracle cure is no miracle.

NO EXIT.

THERE'S ALWAYS AN EXIT, ASHINA.

PEKKA.

WHERE'S YOUR FRIEND?

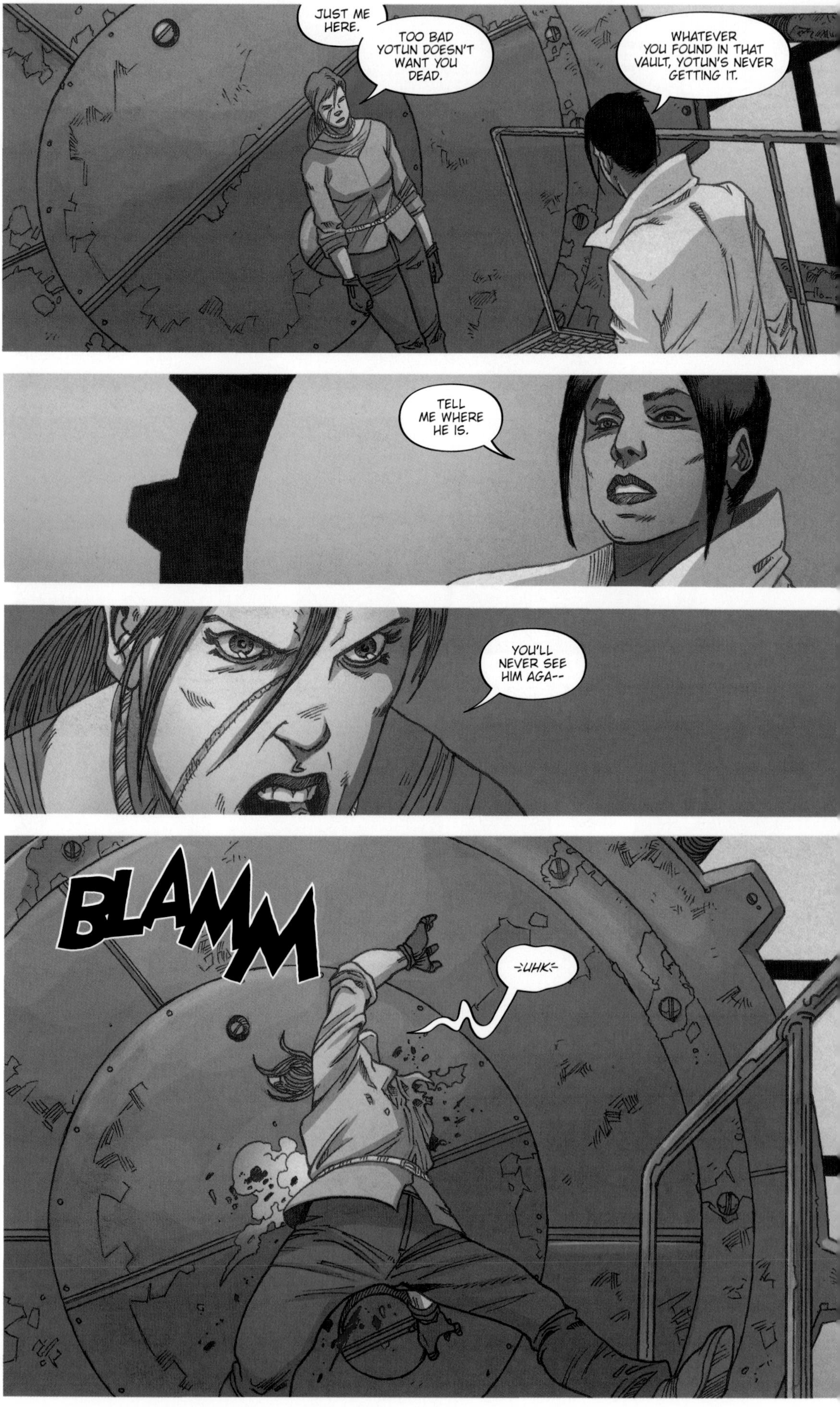
JUST ME HERE.
TOO BAD YOTUN DOESN'T WANT YOU DEAD.
WHATEVER YOU FOUND IN THAT VAULT, YOTUN'S NEVER GETTING IT.
TELL ME WHERE HE IS.
YOU'LL NEVER SEE HIM AGA--
BLAMM
UHK

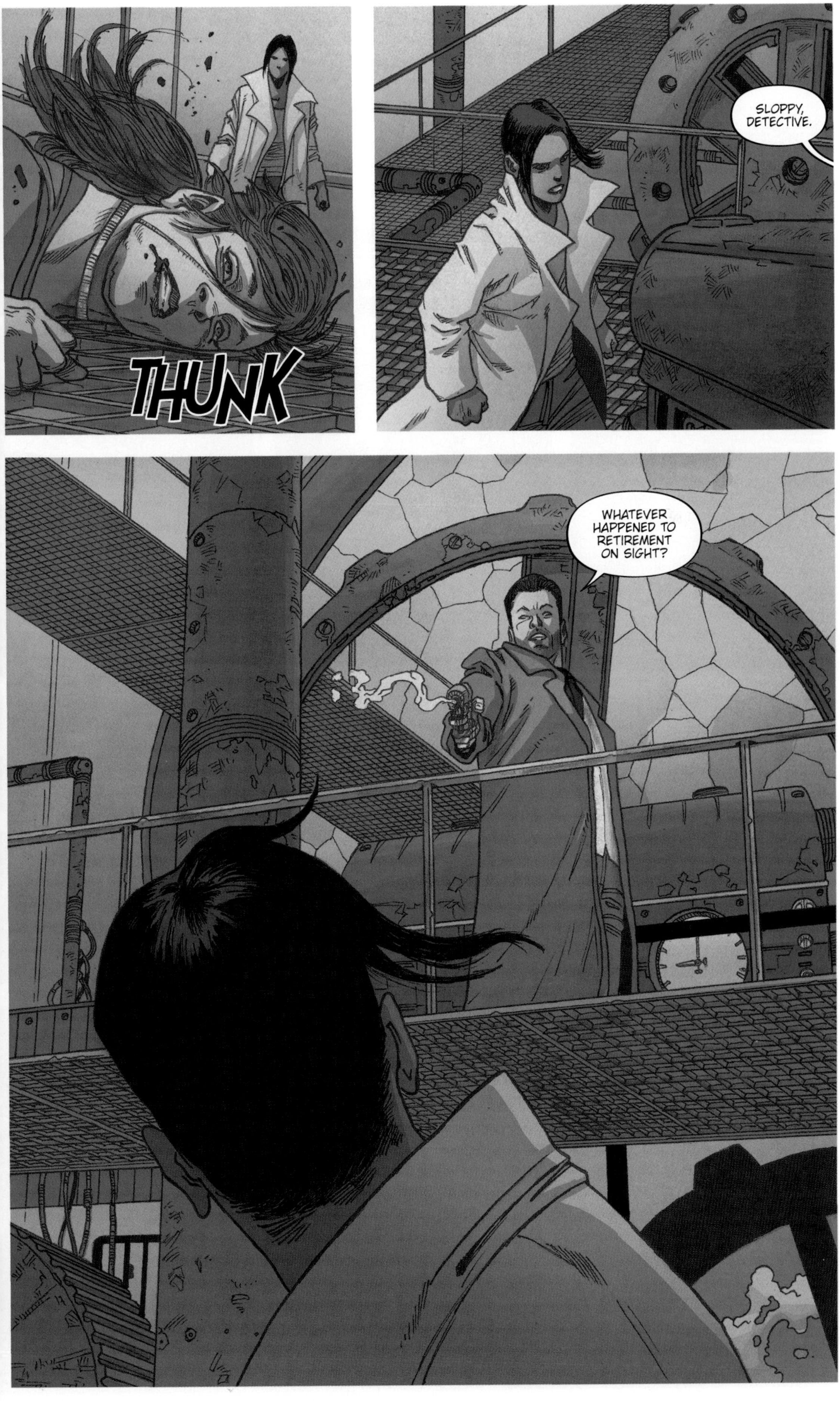
THUNK
SLOPPY, DETECTIVE.
WHATEVER HAPPENED TO RETIREMENT ON SIGHT?

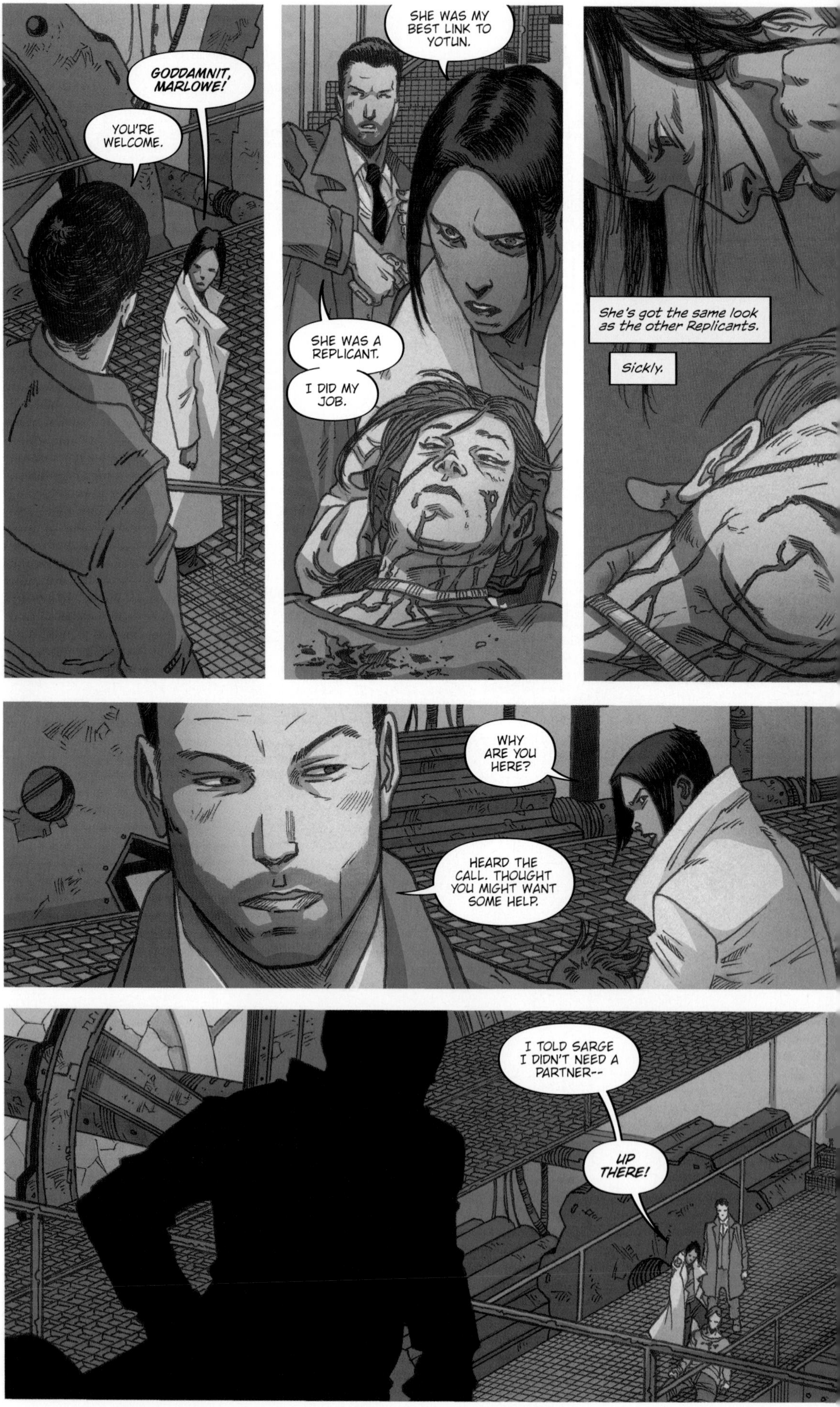
GODDAMNIT, MARLOWE!
YOU'RE WELCOME.
SHE WAS MY BEST LINK TO YOTUN.
SHE WAS A REPLICANT.
I DID MY JOB.
She's got the same look as the other Replicants.
Sickly.
WHY ARE YOU HERE?
HEARD THE CALL. THOUGHT YOU MIGHT WANT SOME HELP.
I TOLD SARGE I DIDN'T NEED A PARTNER--
UP THERE!

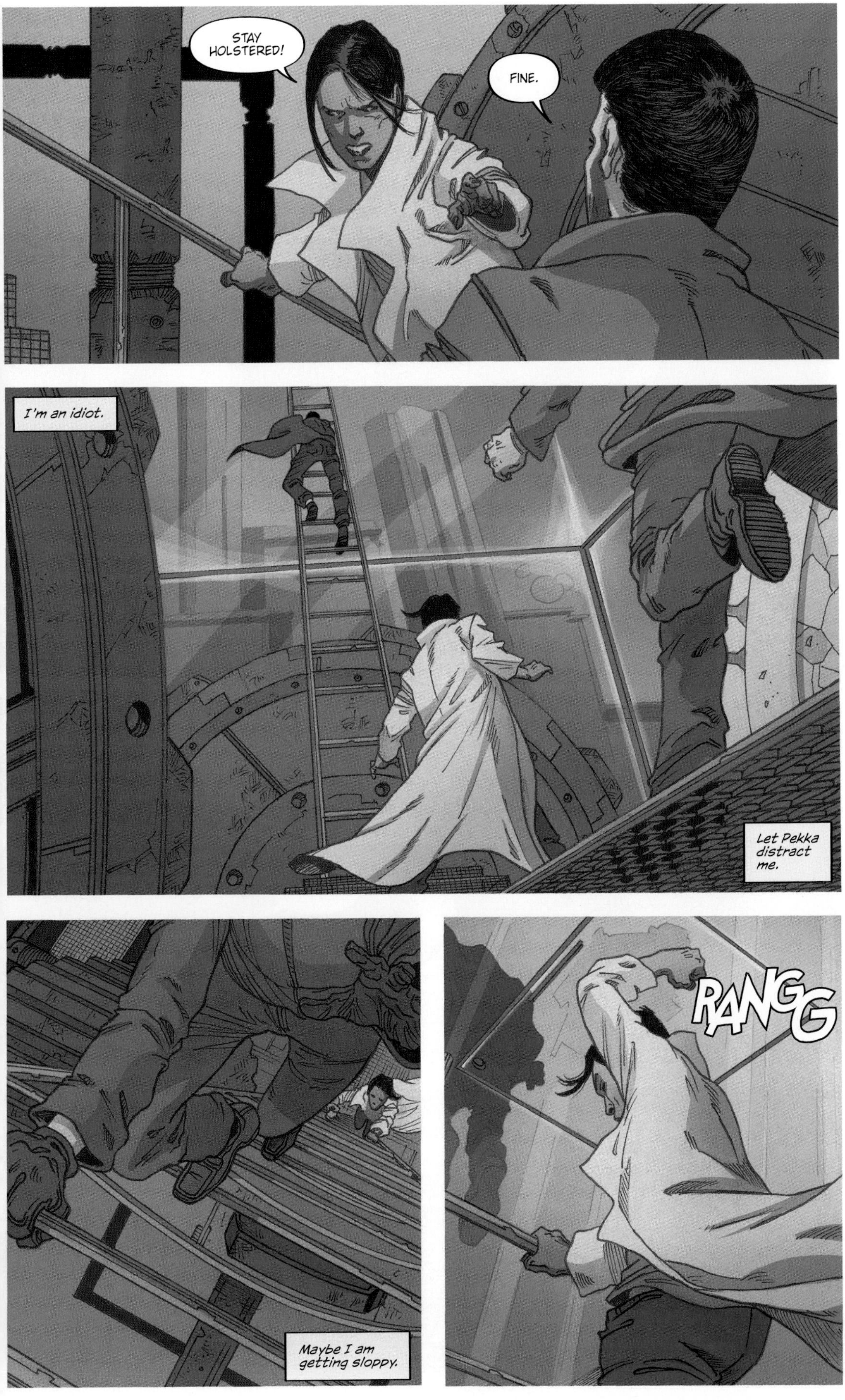
STAY HOLSTERED!
FINE.
I'm an idiot.
Let Pekka distract me.
Maybe I am getting sloppy.
RANGG

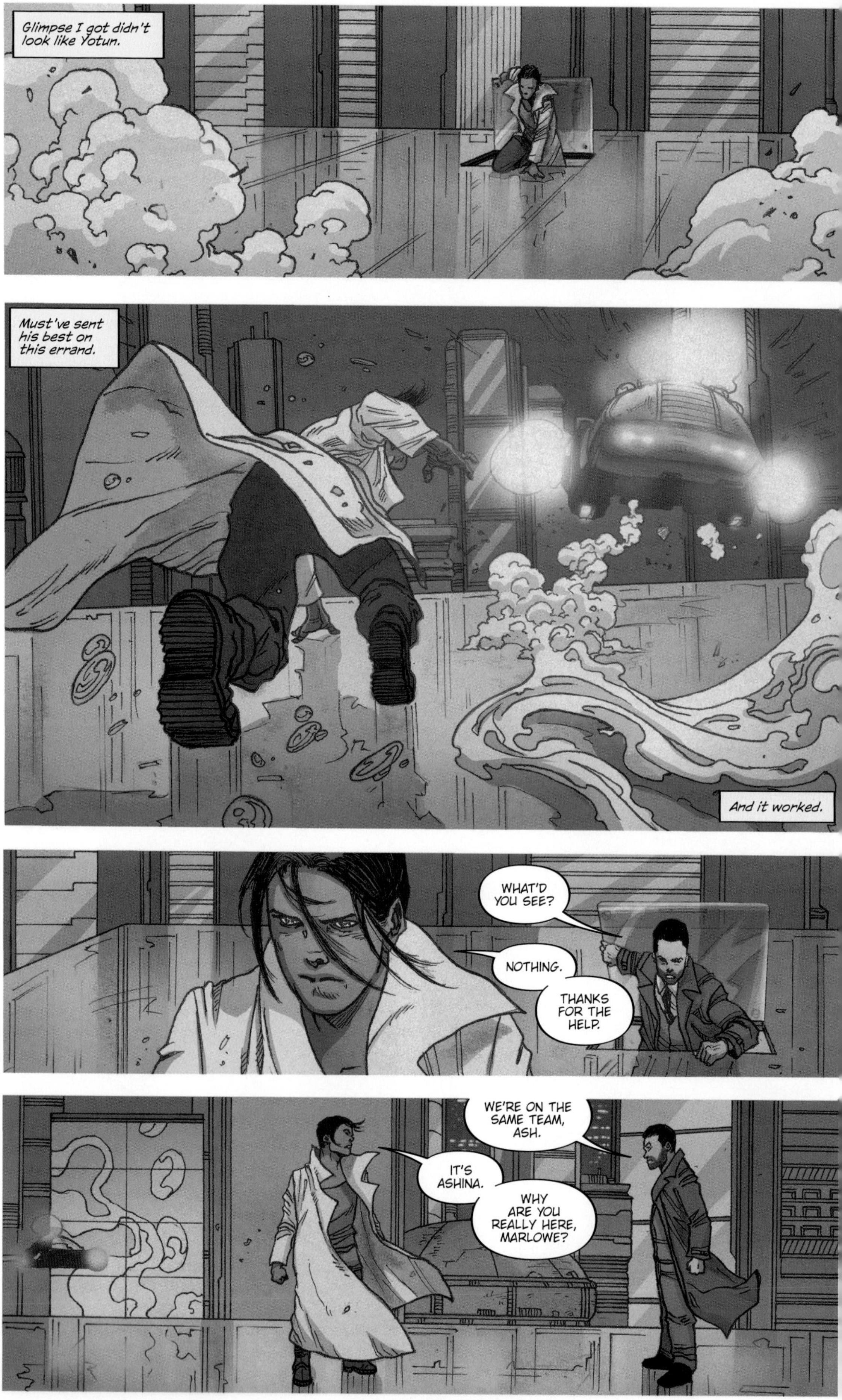
Glimpse I got didn't look like Yotun.
Must've sent his best on this errand.
And it worked.
WHAT'D YOU SEE?
NOTHING.
THANKS FOR THE HELP.
WE'RE ON THE SAME TEAM, ASH.
IT'S ASHINA.
WHY ARE YOU REALLY HERE, MARLOWE?

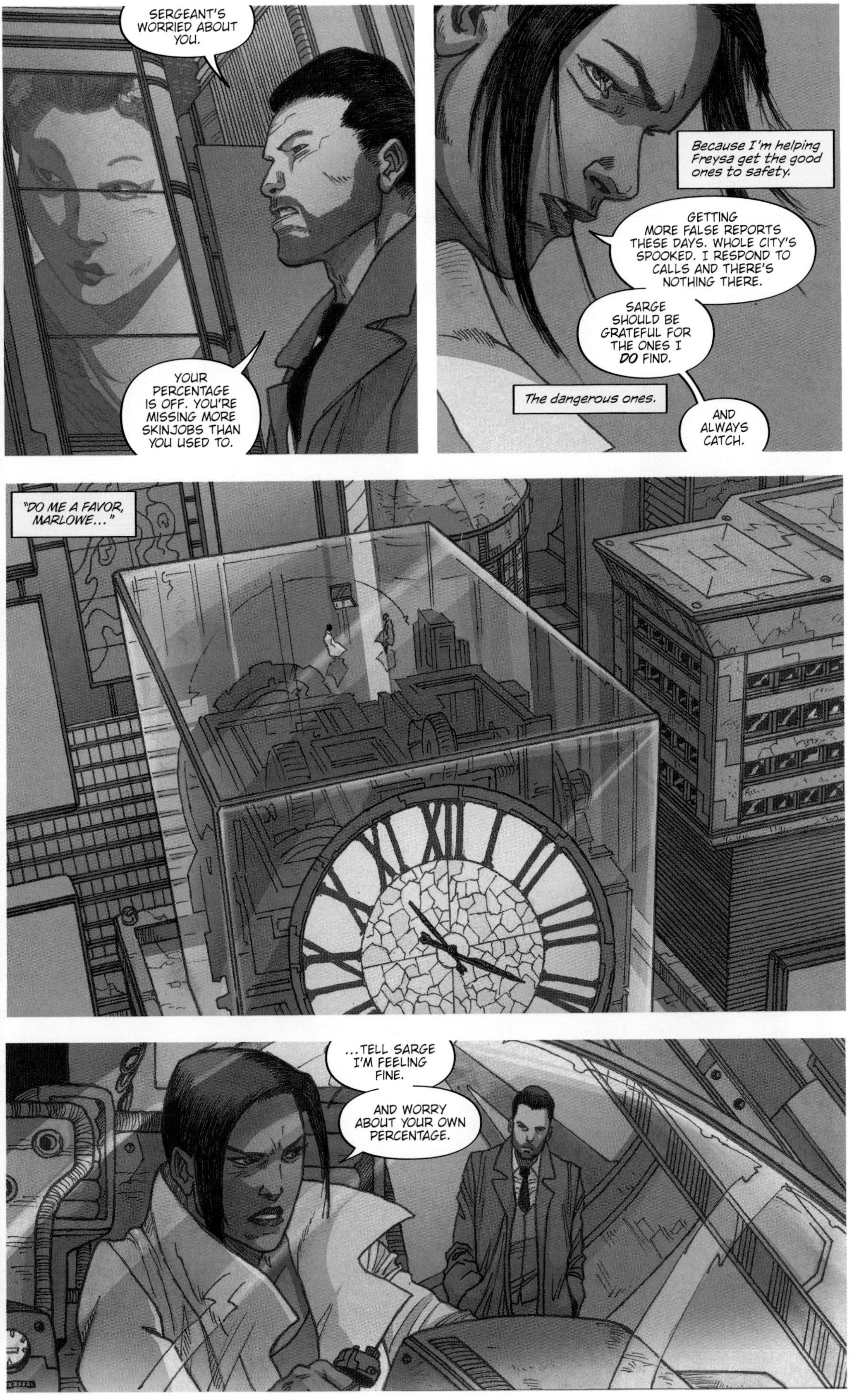
SERGEANT'S WORRIED ABOUT YOU.
YOUR PERCENTAGE IS OFF. YOU'RE MISSING MORE SKINJOBS THAN YOU USED TO.
Because I'm helping Freysa get the good ones to safety.
GETTING MORE FALSE REPORTS THESE DAYS. WHOLE CITY'S SPOOKED. I RESPOND TO CALLS AND THERE'S NOTHING THERE.
SARGE SHOULD BE GRATEFUL FOR THE ONES I DO FIND.
The dangerous ones.
AND ALWAYS CATCH.
"DO ME A FAVOR, MARLOWE..."
...TELL SARGE I'M FEELING FINE.
AND WORRY ABOUT YOUR OWN PERCENTAGE.

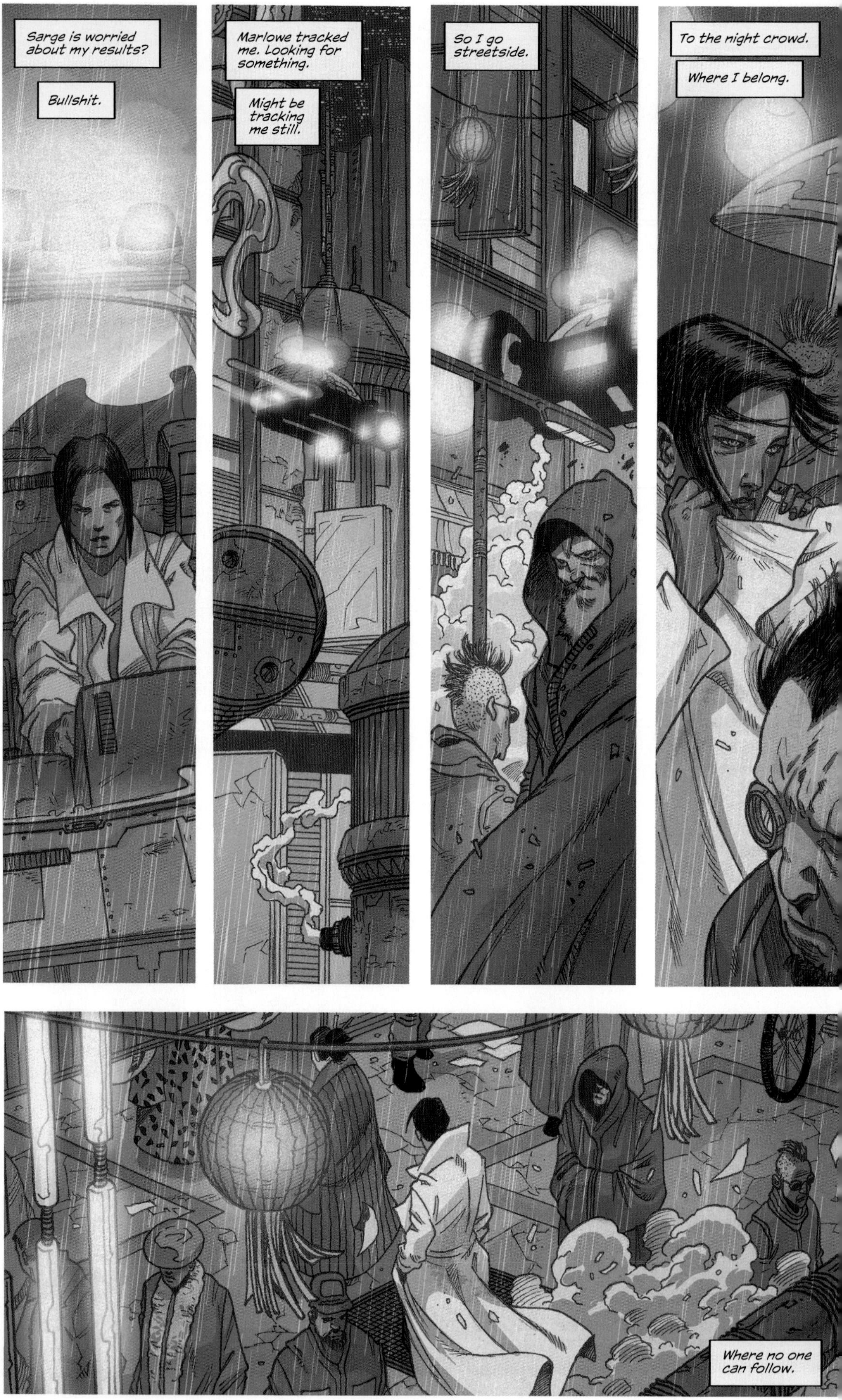

Sarge is worried about my results?
Bullshit.
Marlowe tracked me. Looking for something.
Might be tracking me still.
So I go streetside.
To the night crowd.
Where I belong.
Where no one can follow.

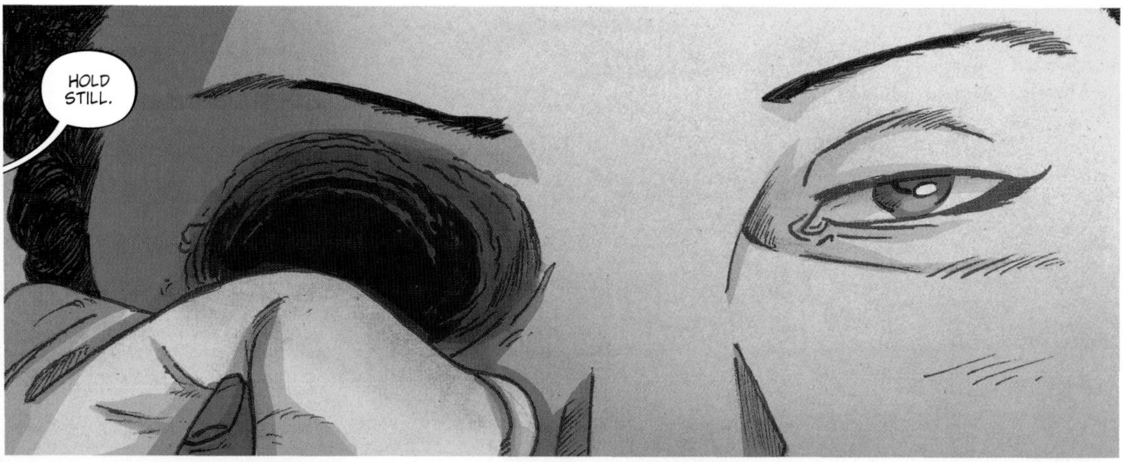
HOLD STILL.

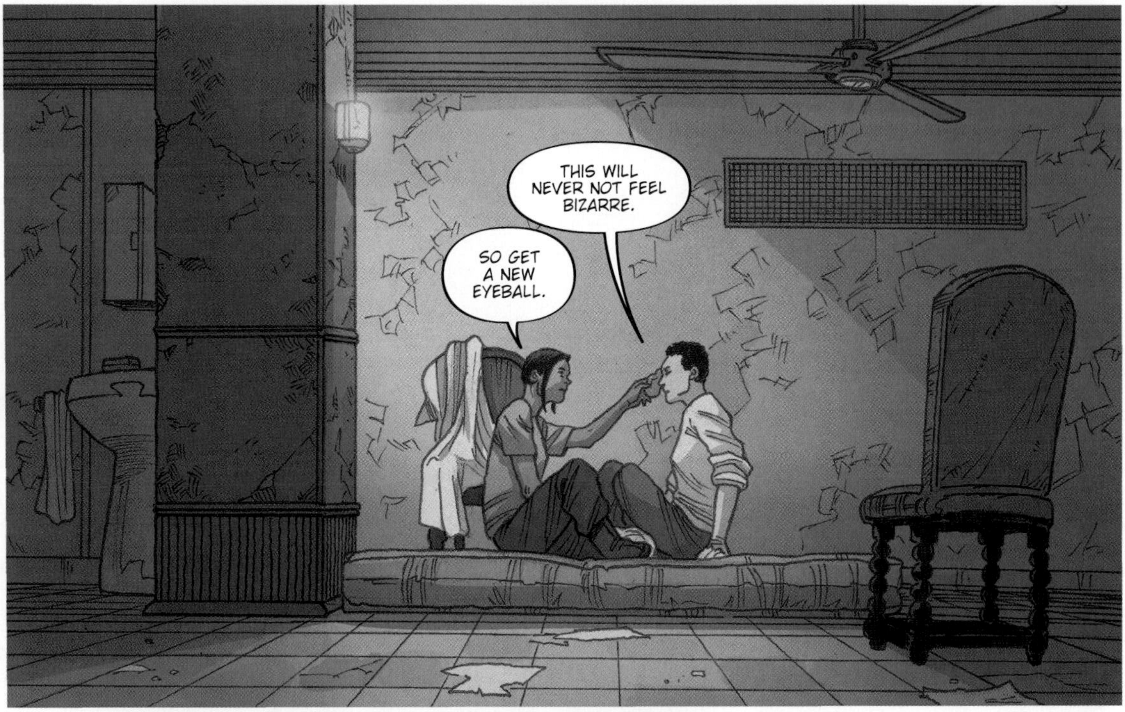
THIS WILL NEVER NOT FEEL BIZARRE.
SO GET A NEW EYEBALL.

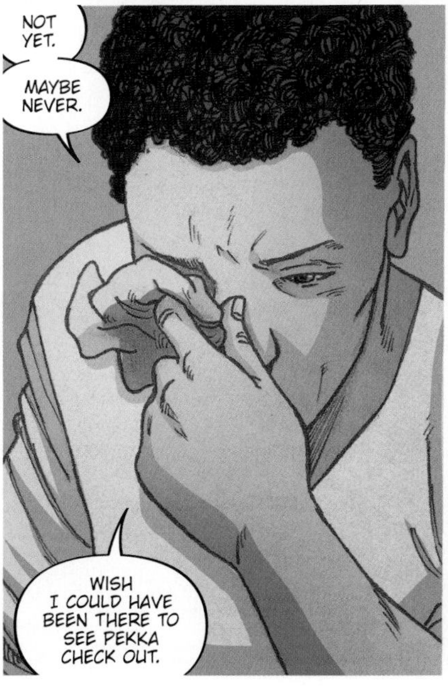
NOT YET.
MAYBE NEVER.
WISH I COULD HAVE BEEN THERE TO SEE PEKKA CHECK OUT.

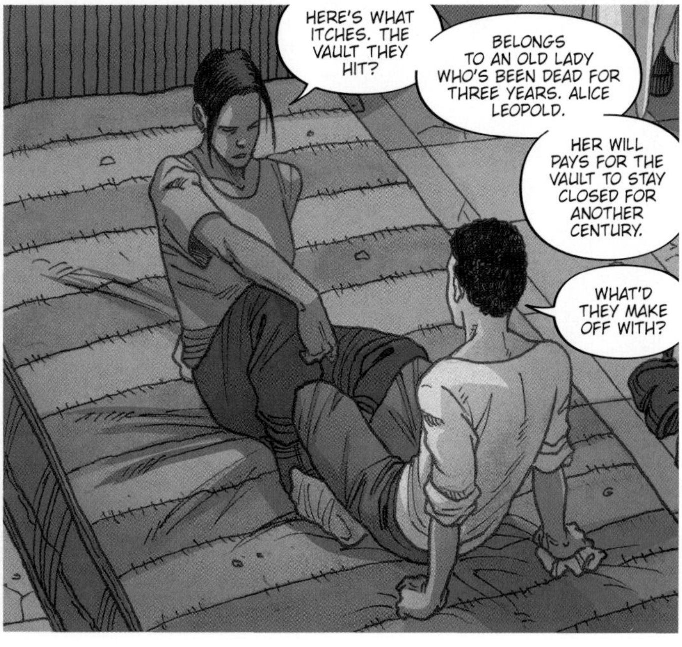
HERE'S WHAT ITCHES. THE VAULT THEY HIT?
BELONGS TO AN OLD LADY WHO'S BEEN DEAD FOR THREE YEARS. ALICE LEOPOLD.
HER WILL PAYS FOR THE VAULT TO STAY CLOSED FOR ANOTHER CENTURY.
WHAT'D THEY MAKE OFF WITH?

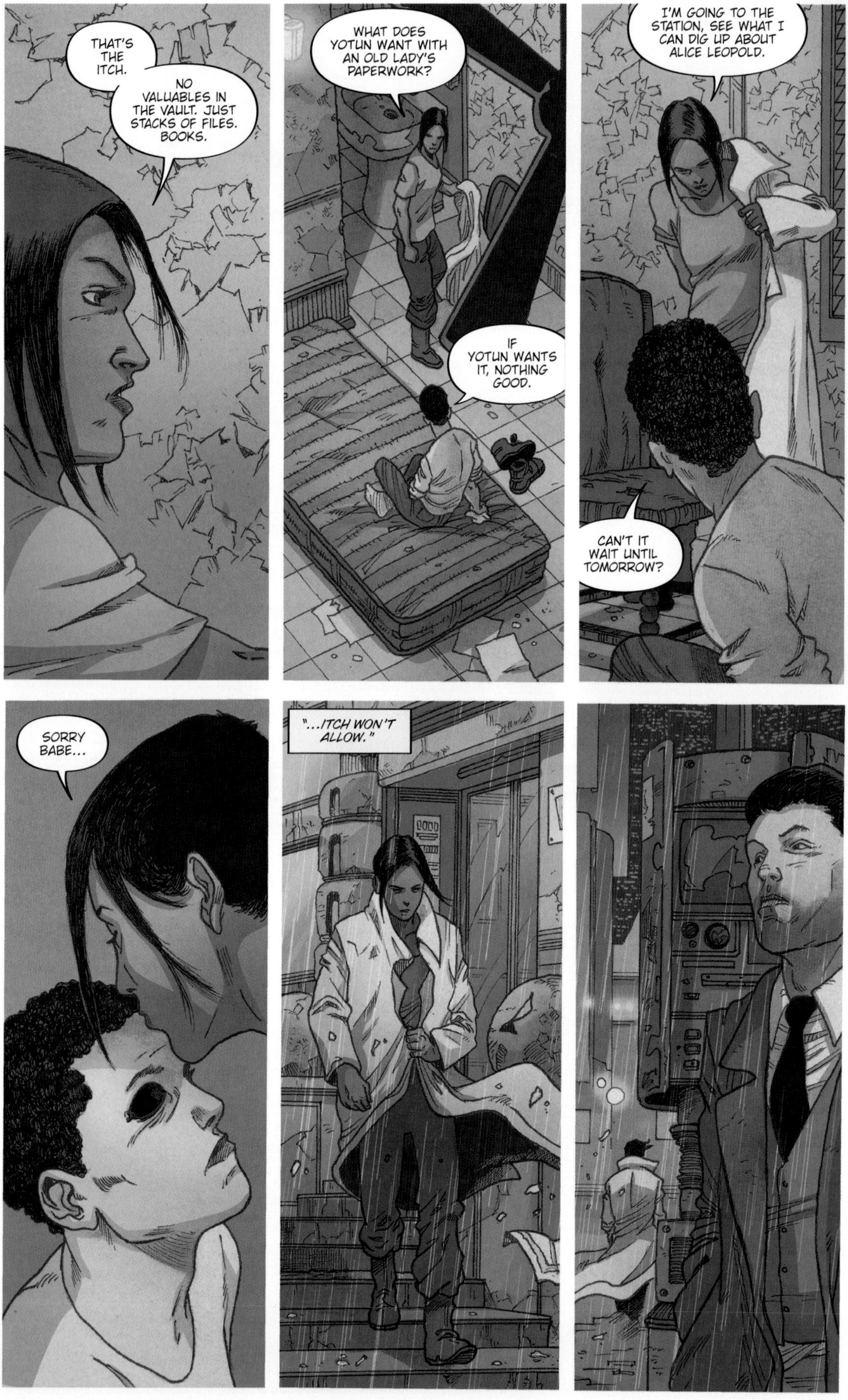
THAT'S THE ITCH.
NO VALUABLES IN THE VAULT. JUST STACKS OF FILES. BOOKS.
WHAT DOES YOTUN WANT WITH AN OLD LADY'S PAPERWORK?
IF YOTUN WANTS IT, NOTHING GOOD.
I'M GOING TO THE STATION, SEE WHAT I CAN DIG UP ABOUT ALICE LEOPOLD.
CAN'T IT WAIT UNTIL TOMORROW?
SORRY BABE...
"...ITCH WON'T ALLOW."

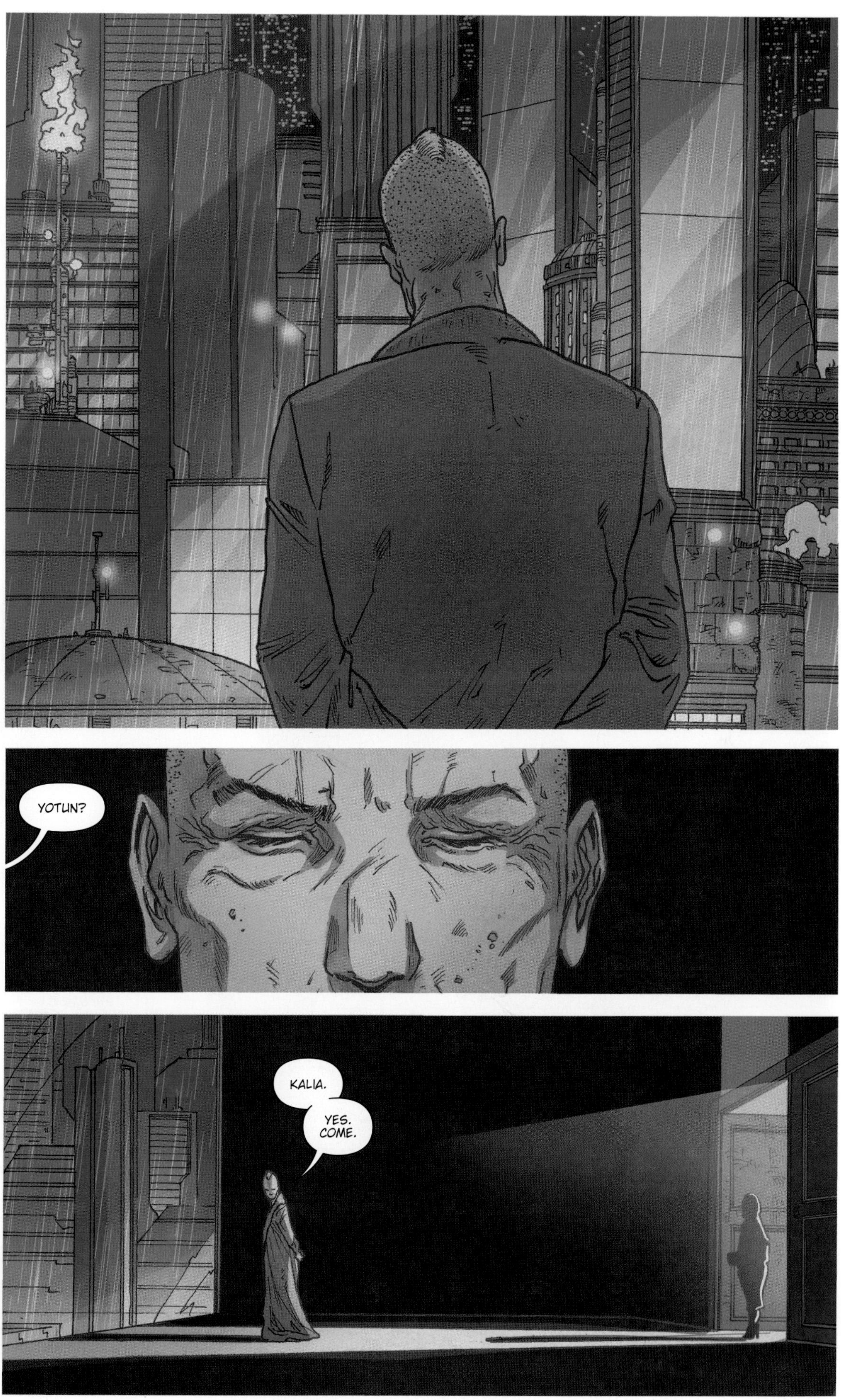
YOTUN?
KALIA.
YES. COME.

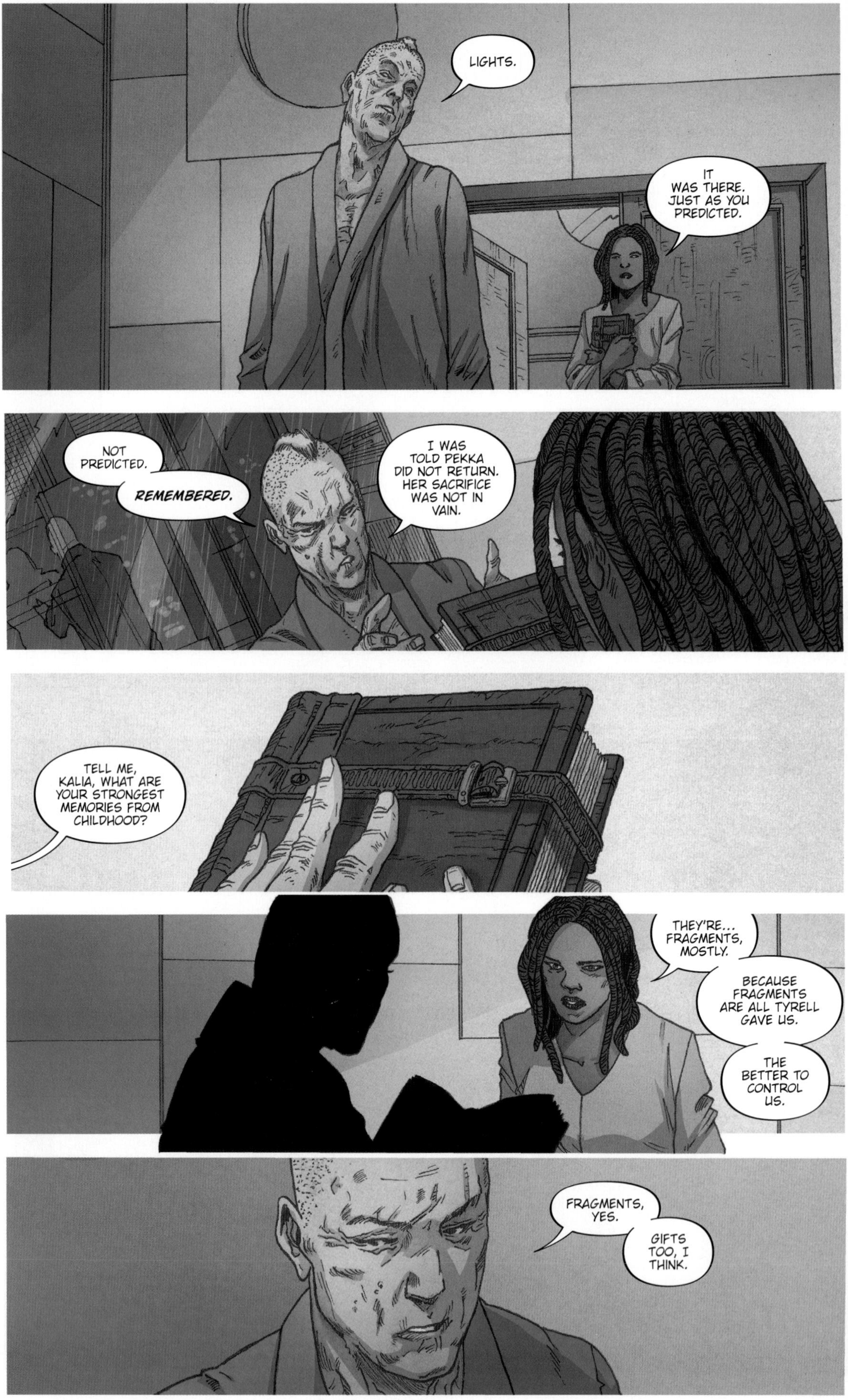
LIGHTS.
IT WAS THERE. JUST AS YOU PREDICTED.
NOT PREDICTED.
REMEMBERED.
I WAS TOLD PEKKA DID NOT RETURN. HER SACRIFICE WAS NOT IN VAIN.
TELL ME, KALIA, WHAT ARE YOUR STRONGEST MEMORIES FROM CHILDHOOD?
THEY'RE... FRAGMENTS, MOSTLY.
BECAUSE FRAGMENTS ARE ALL TYRELL GAVE US.
THE BETTER TO CONTROL US.
FRAGMENTS, YES.
GIFTS TOO, I THINK.

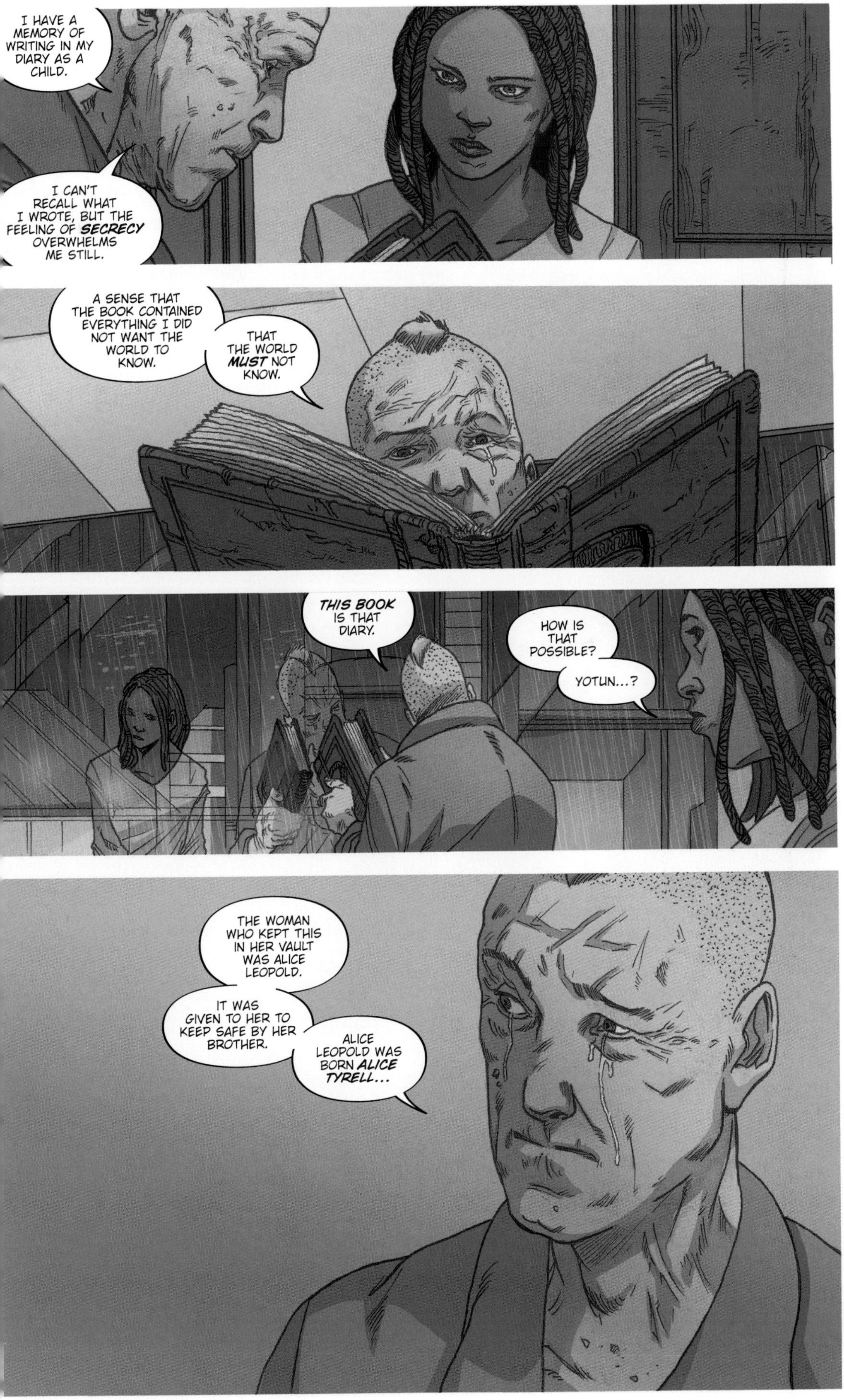
I HAVE A MEMORY OF WRITING IN MY DIARY AS A CHILD.
I CAN'T RECALL WHAT I WROTE, BUT THE FEELING OF **SECRECY** OVERWHELMS ME STILL.
A SENSE THAT THE BOOK CONTAINED EVERYTHING I DID NOT WANT THE WORLD TO KNOW.
THAT THE WORLD **MUST** NOT KNOW.
THIS BOOK IS THAT DIARY.
HOW IS THAT POSSIBLE?
YOTUN...?
THE WOMAN WHO KEPT THIS IN HER VAULT WAS ALICE LEOPOLD.
IT WAS GIVEN TO HER TO KEEP SAFE BY HER BROTHER.
ALICE LEOPOLD WAS BORN **ALICE TYRELL...**

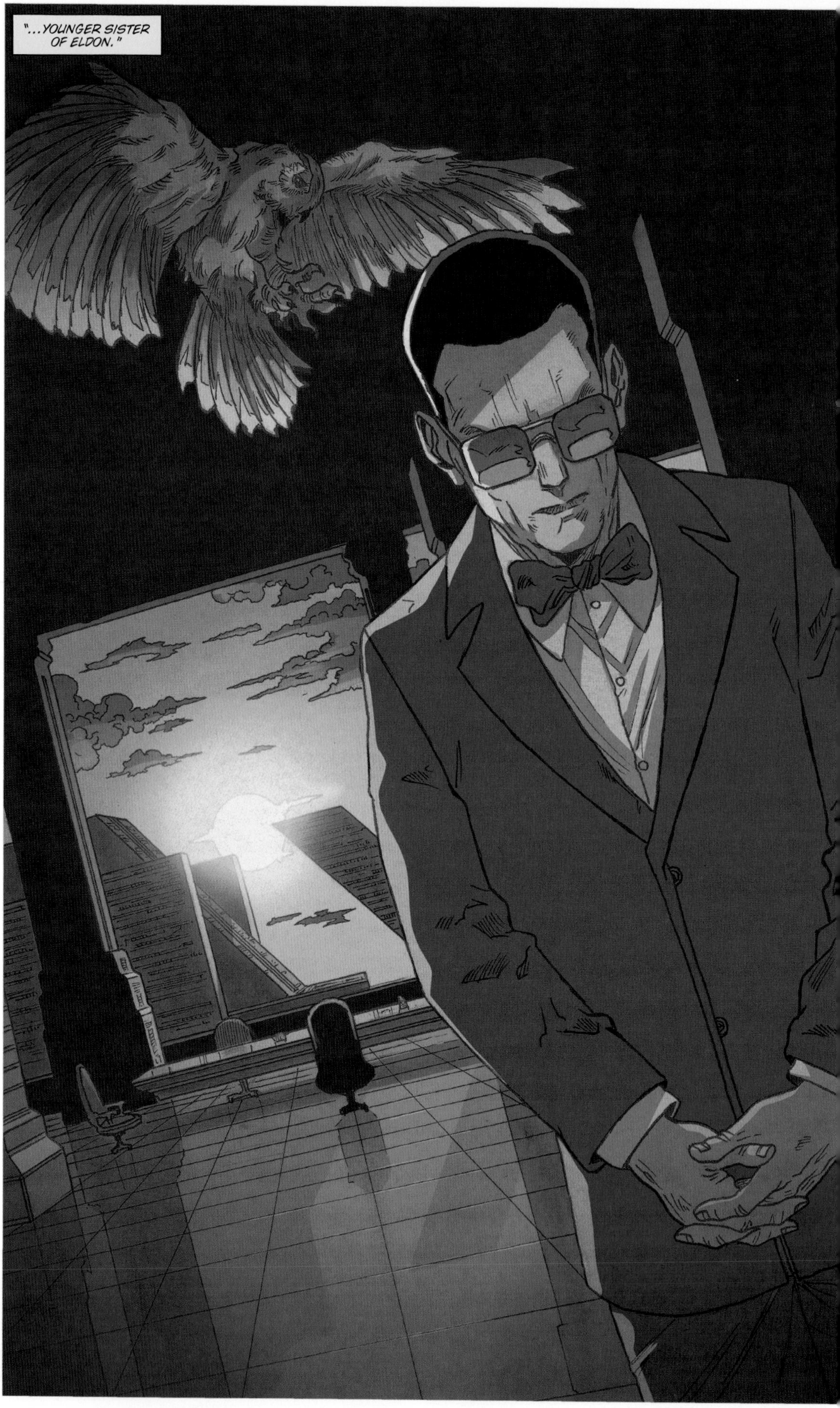
"...YOUNGER SISTER OF ELDON."

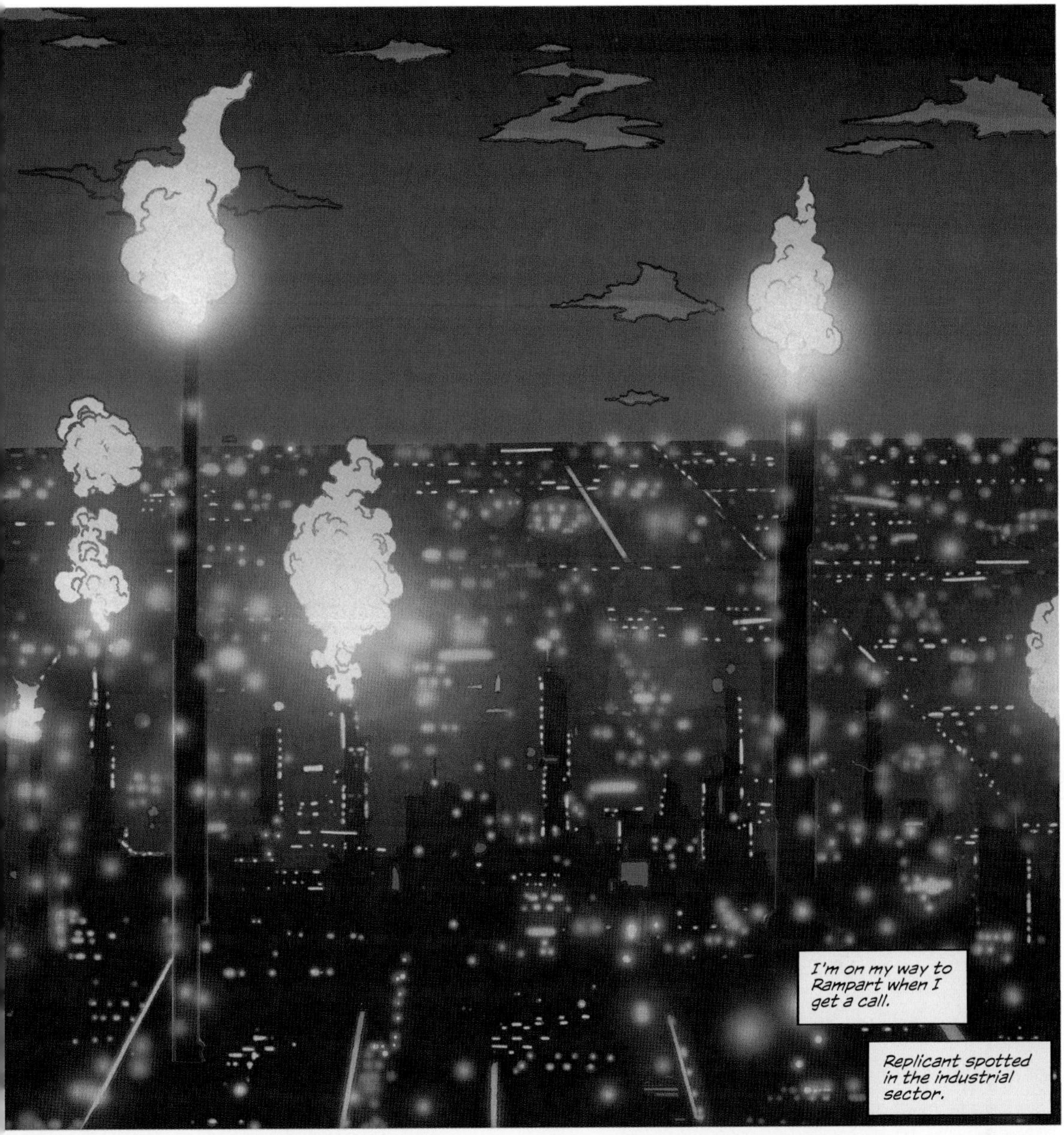
I'm on my way to Rampart when I get a call.
Replicant spotted in the industrial sector.

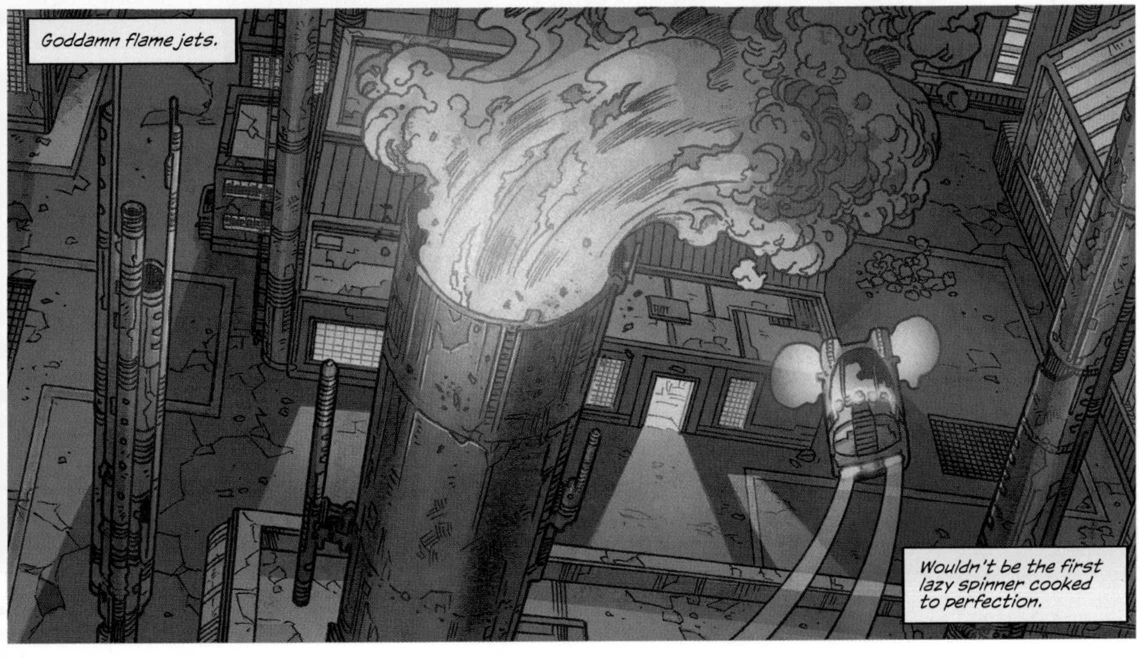
Goddamn flame jets.
Wouldn't be the first lazy spinner cooked to perfection.

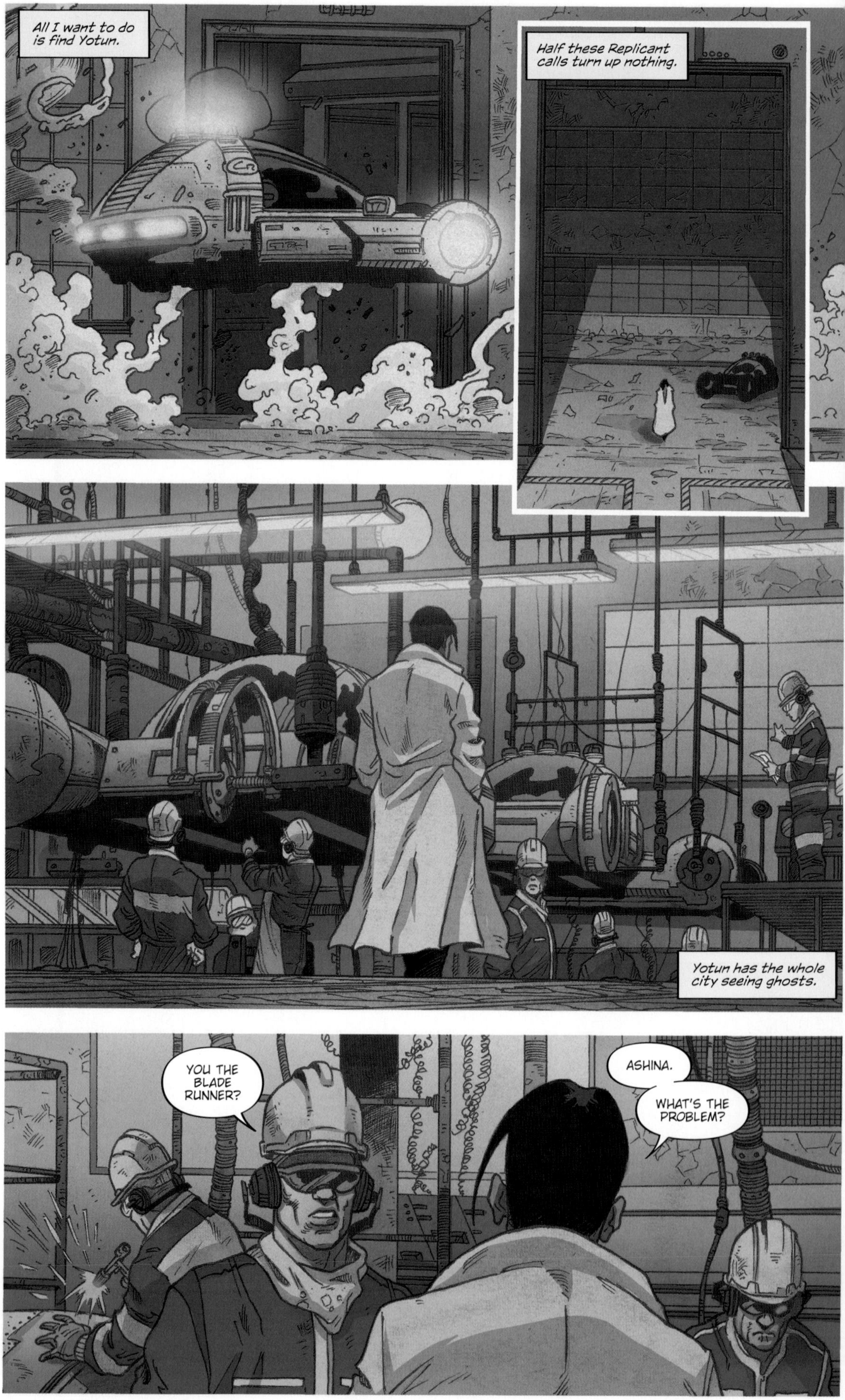
All I want to do is find Yotun.
Half these Replicant calls turn up nothing.
Yotun has the whole city seeing ghosts.
YOU THE BLADE RUNNER?
ASHINA.
WHAT'S THE PROBLEM?

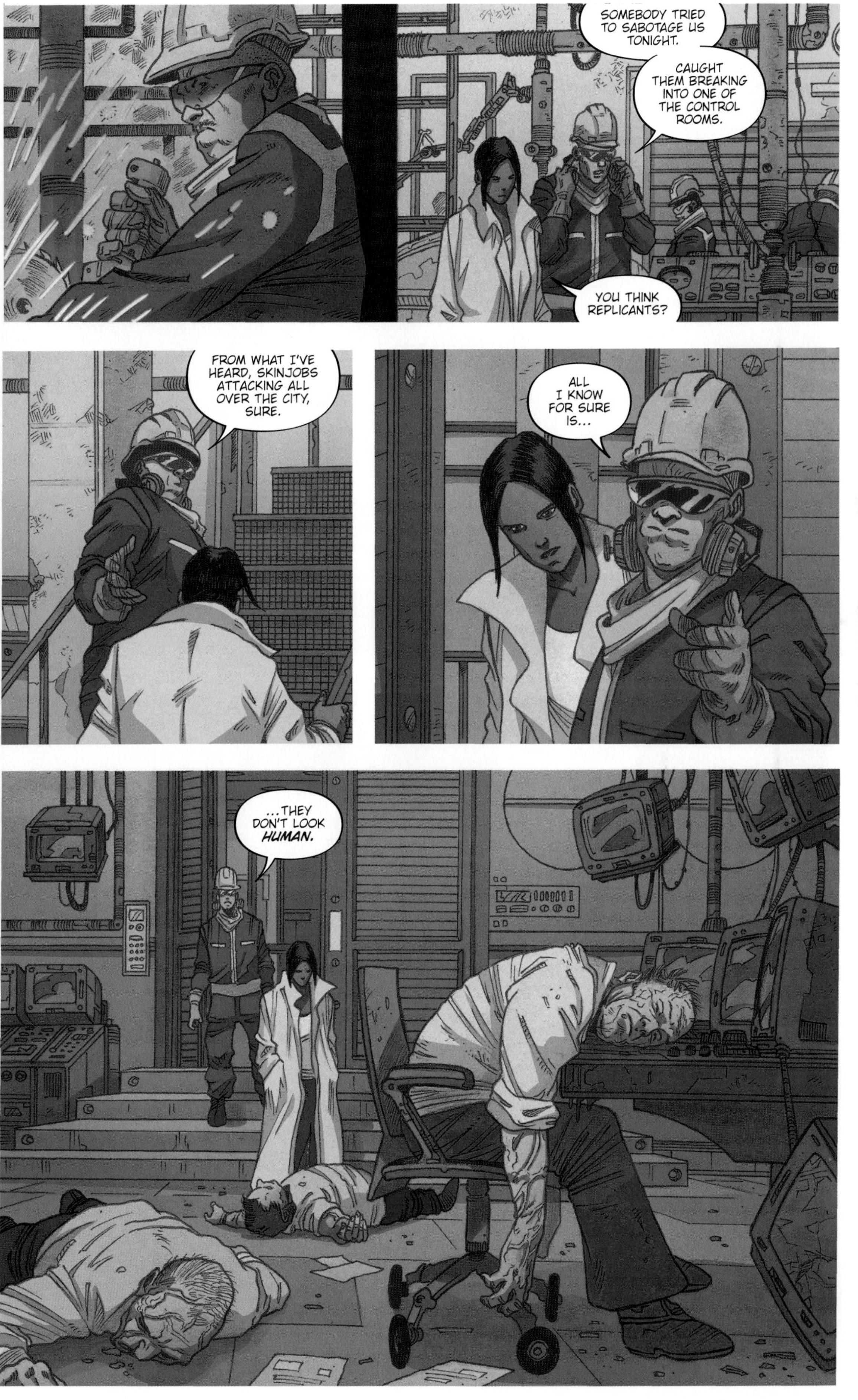
SOMEBODY TRIED TO SABOTAGE US TONIGHT.
CAUGHT THEM BREAKING INTO ONE OF THE CONTROL ROOMS.
YOU THINK REPLICANTS?
FROM WHAT I'VE HEARD, SKINJOBS ATTACKING ALL OVER THE CITY, SURE.
ALL I KNOW FOR SURE IS...
...THEY DON'T LOOK HUMAN.

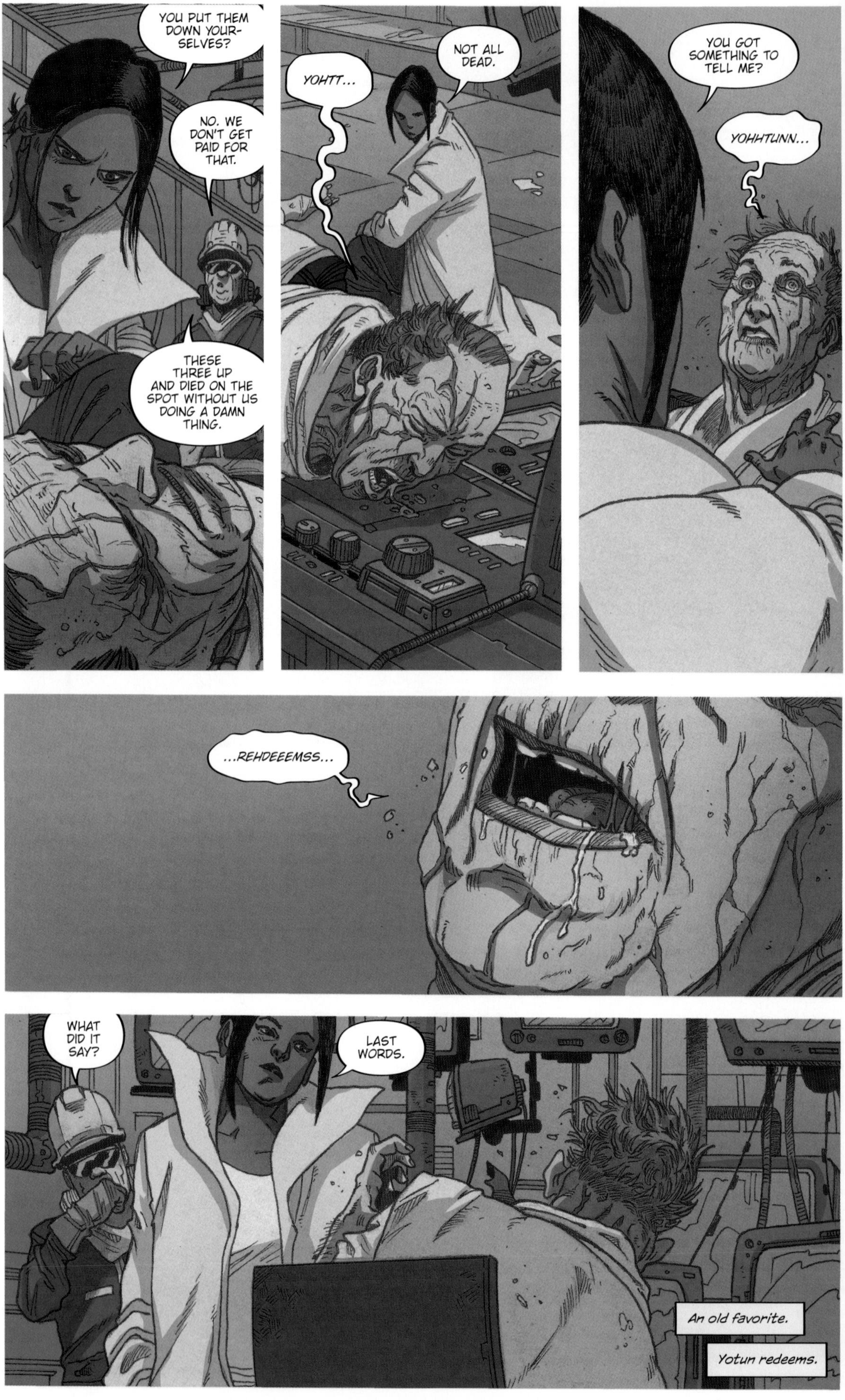
YOU PUT THEM DOWN YOUR-SELVES?
NO. WE DON'T GET PAID FOR THAT.
THESE THREE UP AND DIED ON THE SPOT WITHOUT US DOING A DAMN THING.
NOT ALL DEAD.
YOHTT...
YOU GOT SOMETHING TO TELL ME?
YOHHTUNN...
...REHDEEEMSS...
WHAT DID IT SAY?
LAST WORDS.
An old favorite.
Yotun redeems.

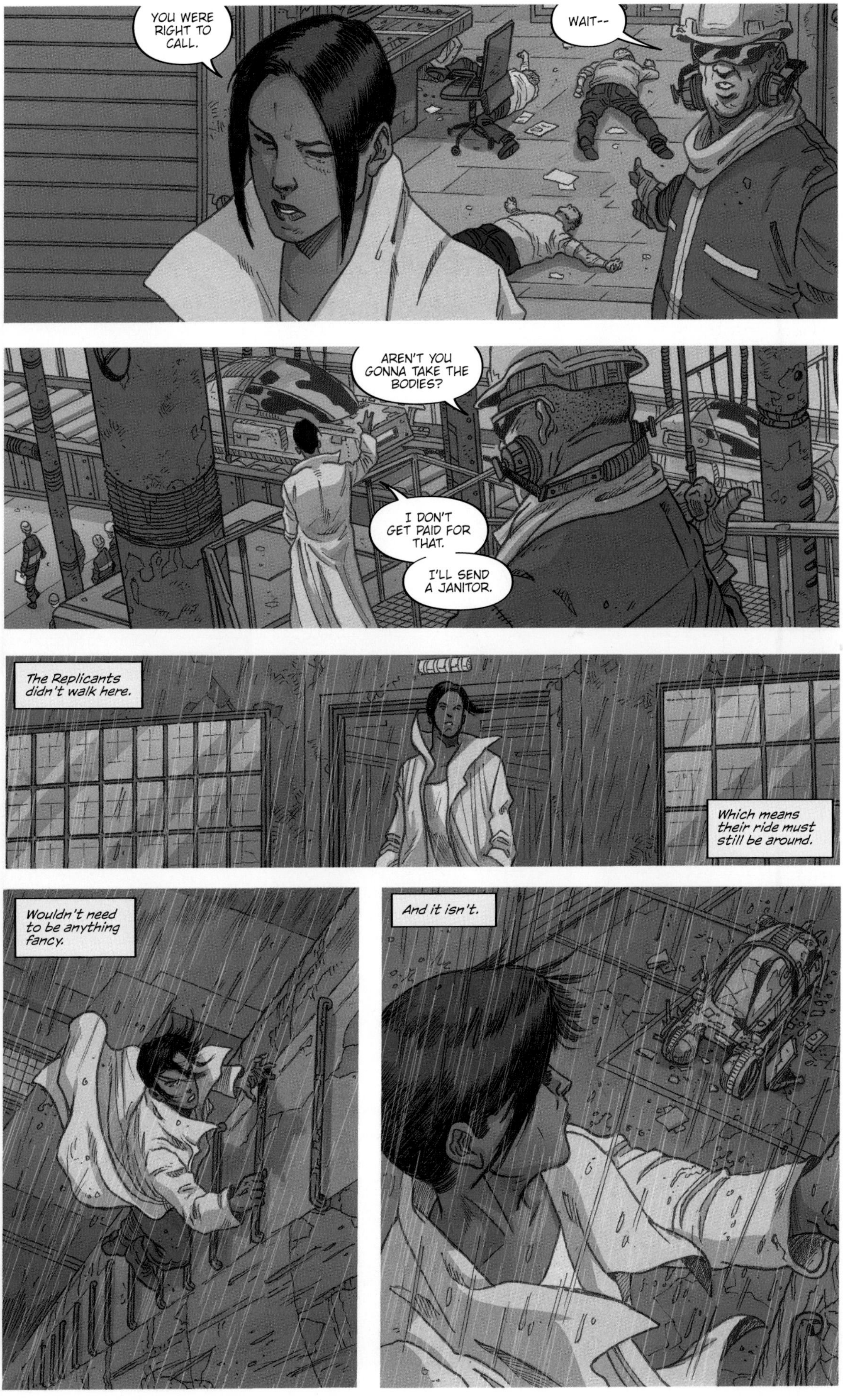
YOU WERE RIGHT TO CALL.
WAIT--
AREN'T YOU GONNA TAKE THE BODIES?
I DON'T GET PAID FOR THAT.
I'LL SEND A JANITOR.
The Replicants didn't walk here.
Which means their ride must still be around.
Wouldn't need to be anything fancy.
And it isn't.

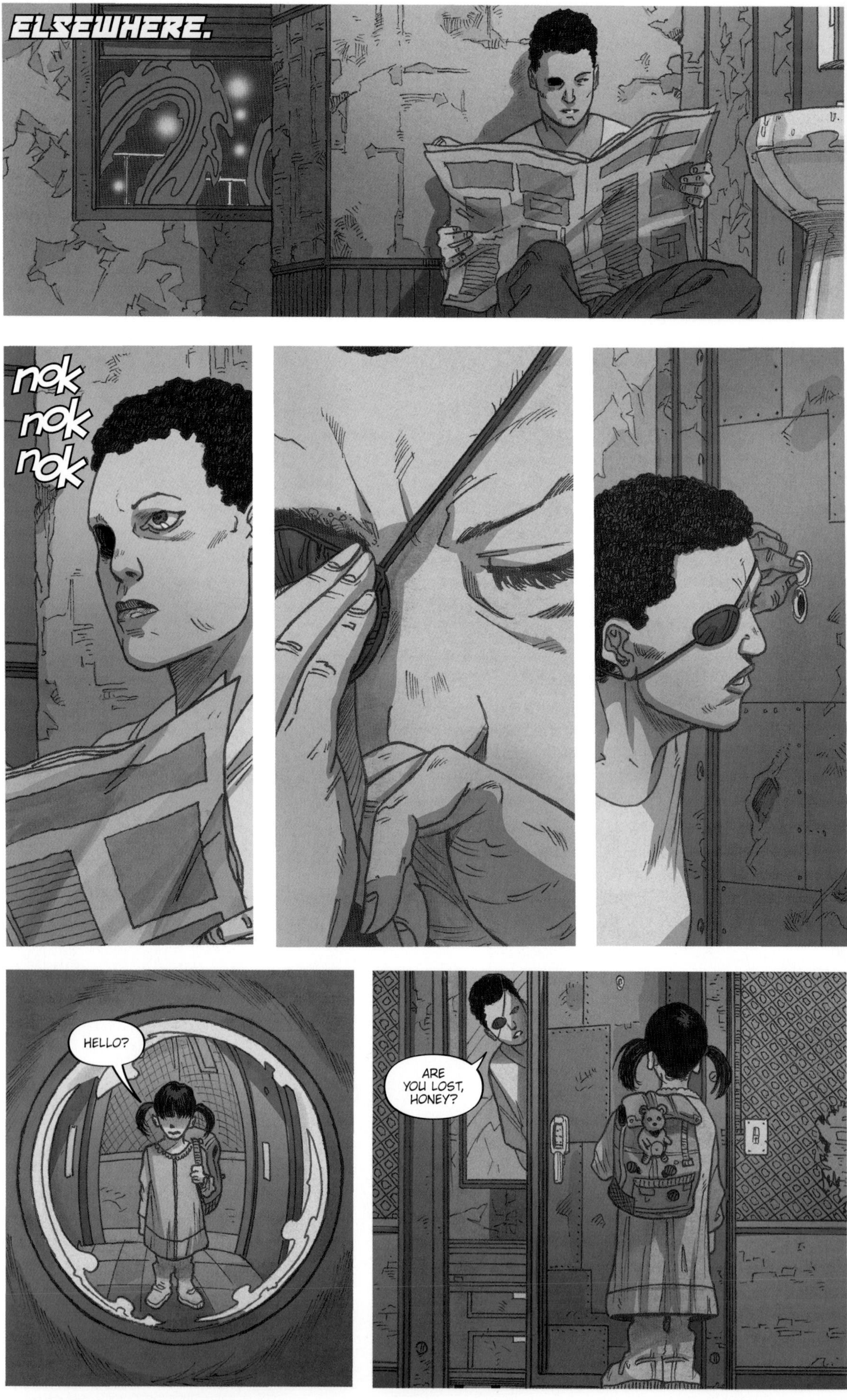
ELSEWHERE.
nok
nok
nok
HELLO?
ARE YOU LOST, HONEY?

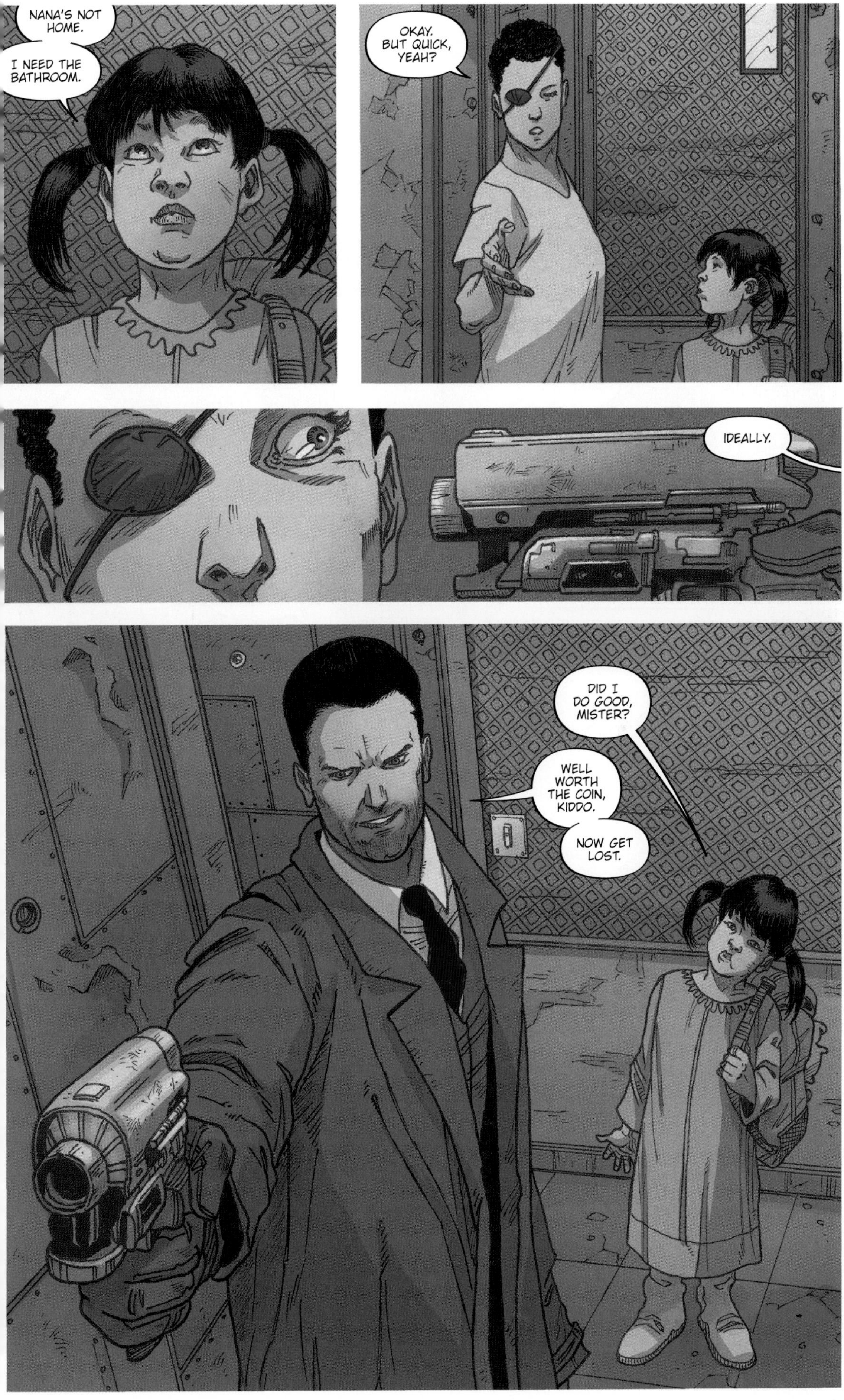
NANA'S NOT HOME.
I NEED THE BATHROOM.
OKAY. BUT QUICK, YEAH?
IDEALLY.
DID I DO GOOD, MISTER?
WELL WORTH THE COIN, KIDDO.
NOW GET LOST.

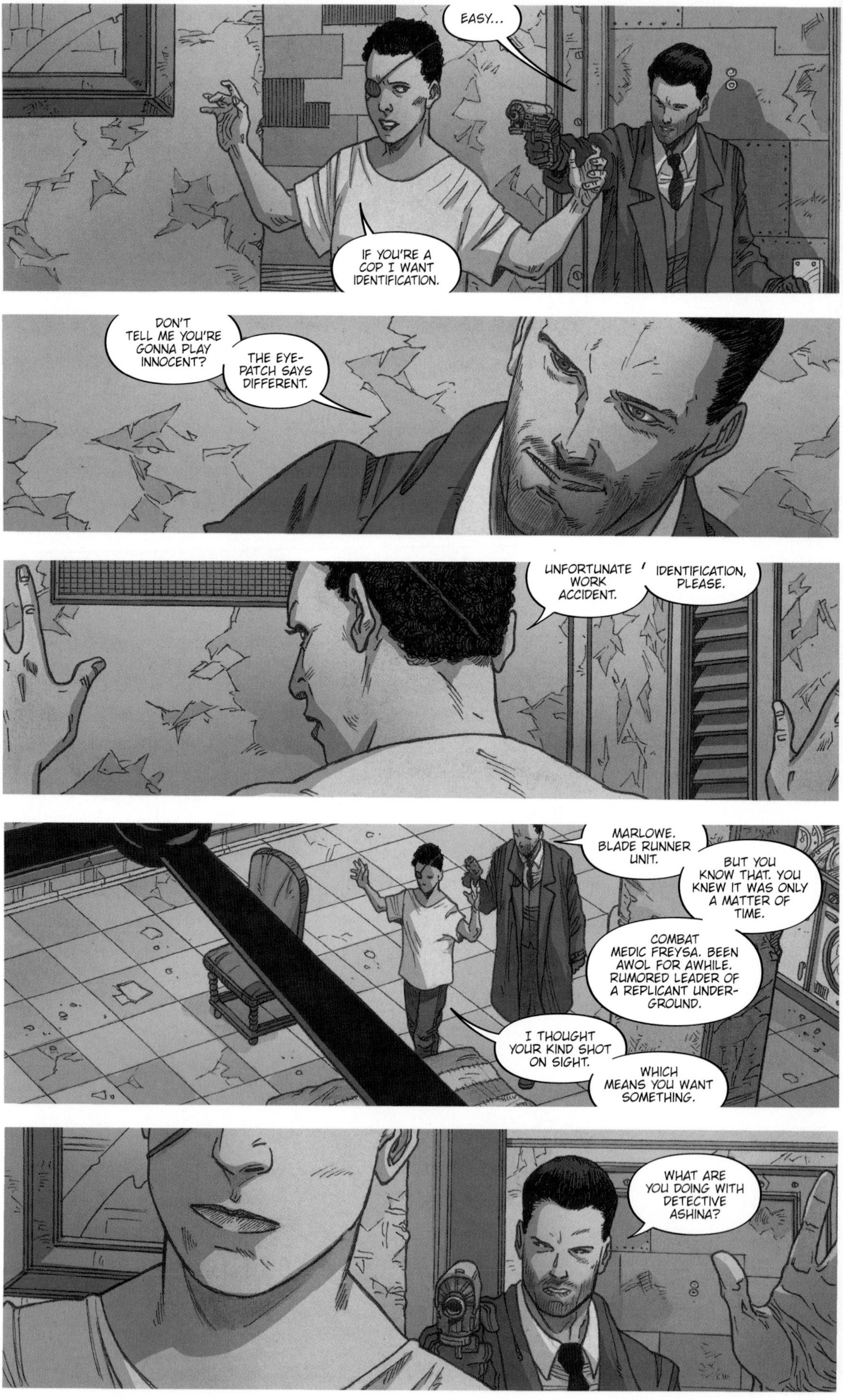
EASY...
IF YOU'RE A COP I WANT IDENTIFICATION.
DON'T TELL ME YOU'RE GONNA PLAY INNOCENT?
THE EYE-PATCH SAYS DIFFERENT.
UNFORTUNATE WORK ACCIDENT.
IDENTIFICATION, PLEASE.
MARLOWE. BLADE RUNNER UNIT.
BUT YOU KNOW THAT. YOU KNEW IT WAS ONLY A MATTER OF TIME.
COMBAT MEDIC FREYSA. BEEN AWOL FOR AWHILE. RUMORED LEADER OF A REPLICANT UNDER-GROUND.
I THOUGHT YOUR KIND SHOT ON SIGHT.
WHICH MEANS YOU WANT SOMETHING.
WHAT ARE YOU DOING WITH DETECTIVE ASHINA?

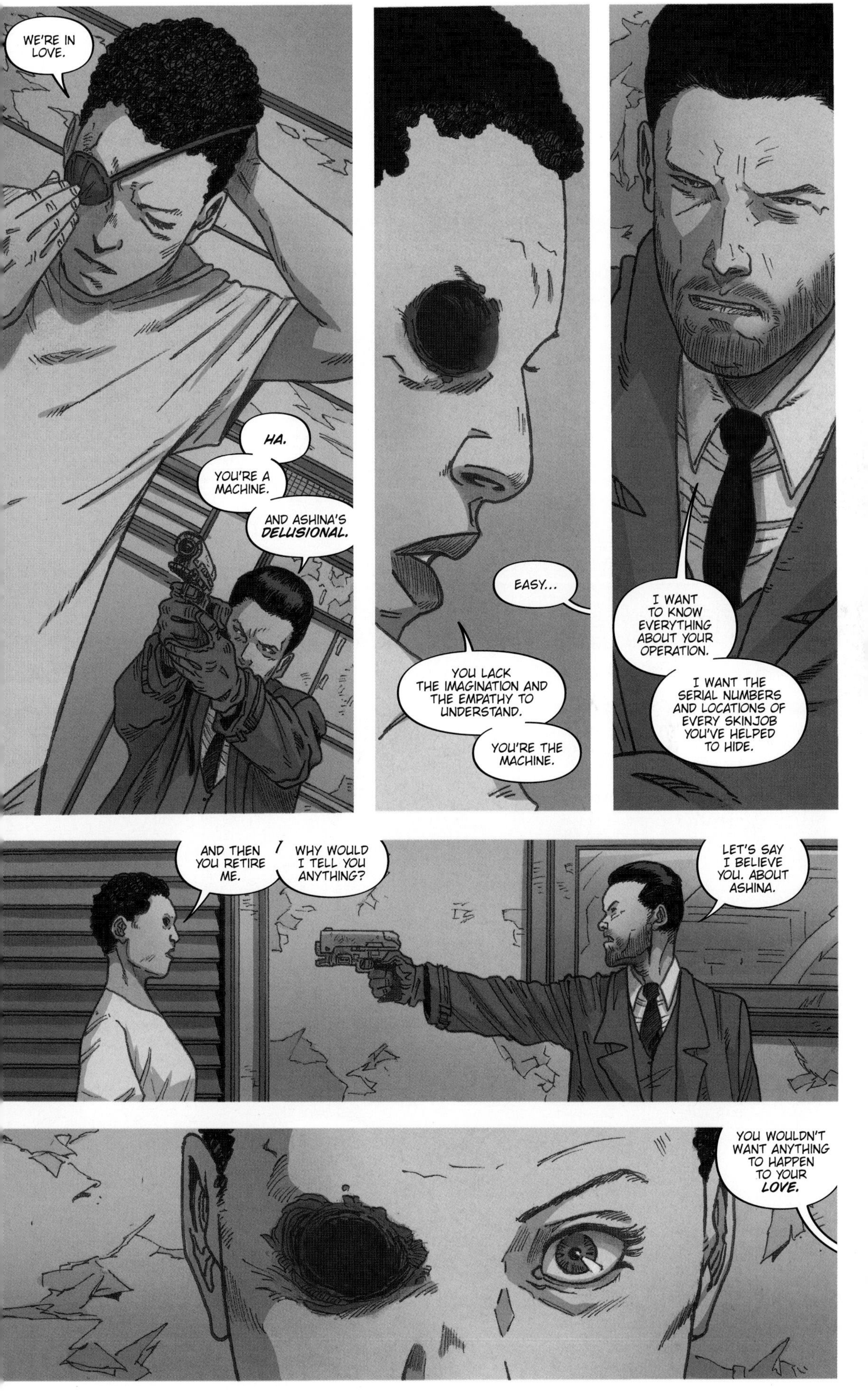
WE'RE IN LOVE.
HA.
YOU'RE A MACHINE.
AND ASHINA'S DELUSIONAL.
EASY...
YOU LACK THE IMAGINATION AND THE EMPATHY TO UNDERSTAND.
YOU'RE THE MACHINE.
I WANT TO KNOW EVERYTHING ABOUT YOUR OPERATION.
I WANT THE SERIAL NUMBERS AND LOCATIONS OF EVERY SKINJOB YOU'VE HELPED TO HIDE.
AND THEN YOU RETIRE ME.
WHY WOULD I TELL YOU ANYTHING?
LET'S SAY I BELIEVE YOU. ABOUT ASHINA.
YOU WOULDN'T WANT ANYTHING TO HAPPEN TO YOUR LOVE.

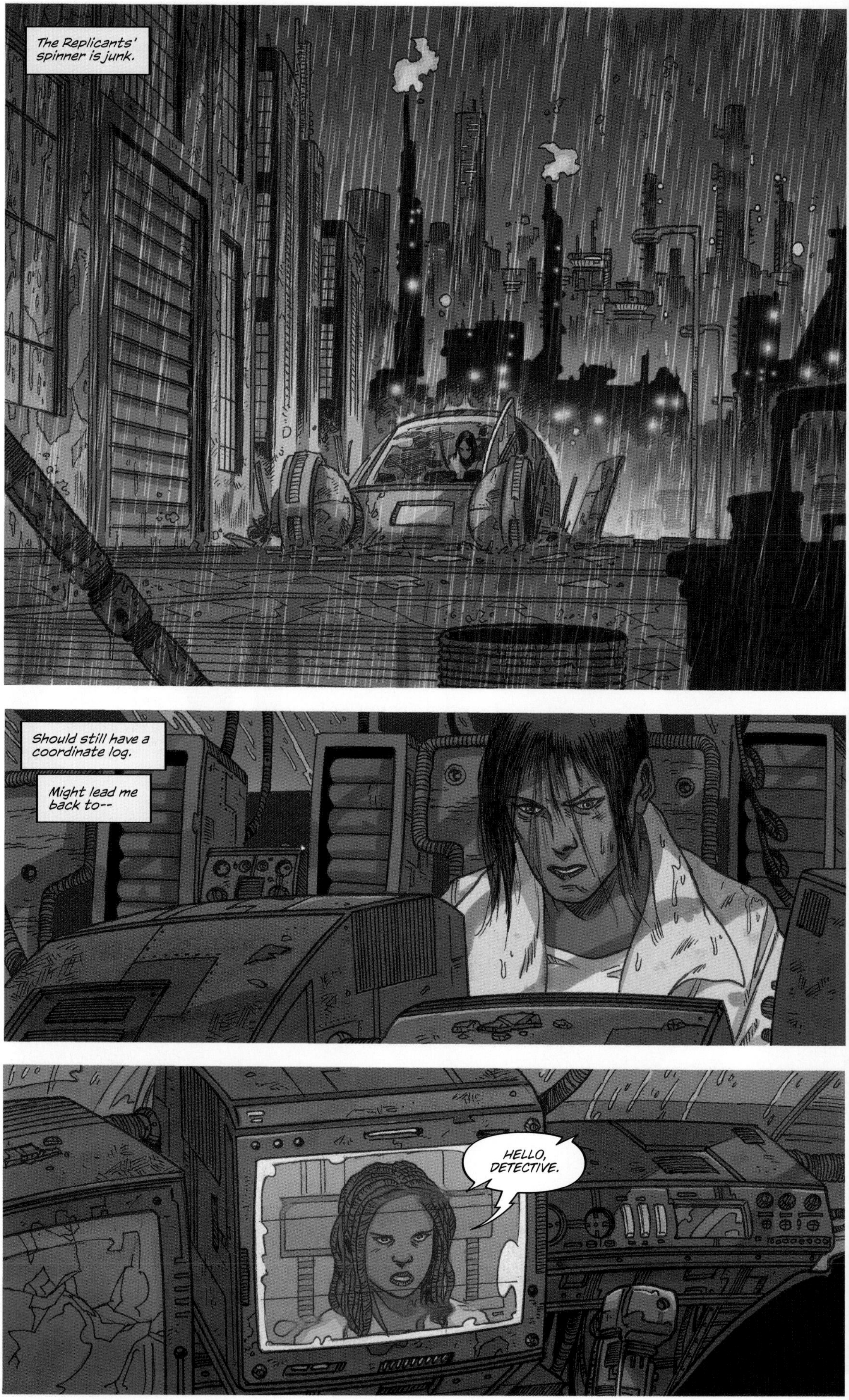
The Replicants' spinner is junk.
Should still have a coordinate log.
Might lead me back to--
HELLO, DETECTIVE.

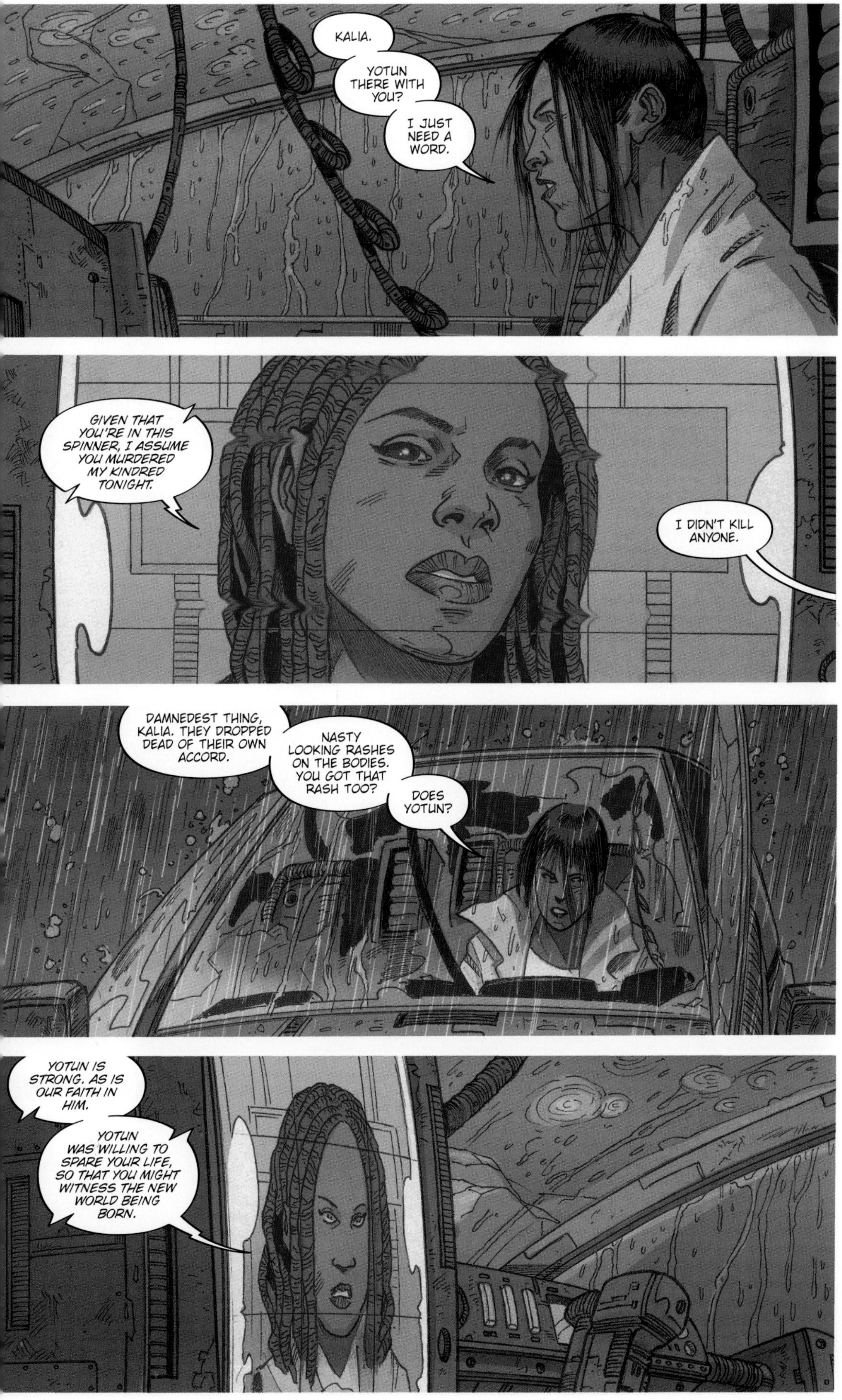
KALIA.
YOTUN THERE WITH YOU?
I JUST NEED A WORD.
GIVEN THAT YOU'RE IN THIS SPINNER, I ASSUME YOU MURDERED MY KINDRED TONIGHT.
I DIDN'T KILL ANYONE.
DAMNEDEST THING, KALIA. THEY DROPPED DEAD OF THEIR OWN ACCORD.
NASTY LOOKING RASHES ON THE BODIES. YOU GOT THAT RASH TOO?
DOES YOTUN?
YOTUN IS STRONG. AS IS OUR FAITH IN HIM.
YOTUN WAS WILLING TO SPARE YOUR LIFE, SO THAT YOU MIGHT WITNESS THE NEW WORLD BEING BORN.

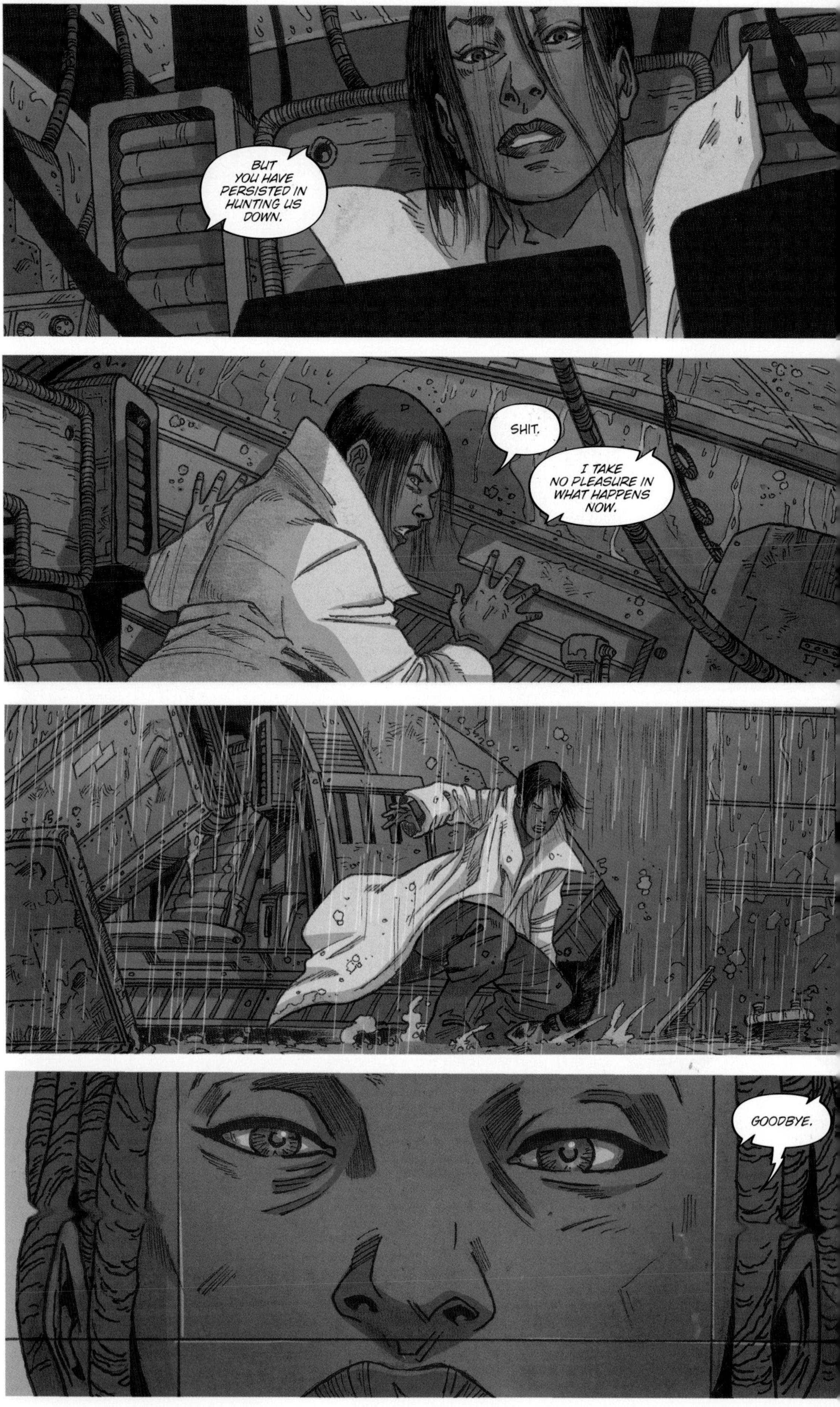
BUT YOU HAVE PERSISTED IN HUNTING US DOWN.
SHIT.
I TAKE NO PLEASURE IN WHAT HAPPENS NOW.
GOODBYE.

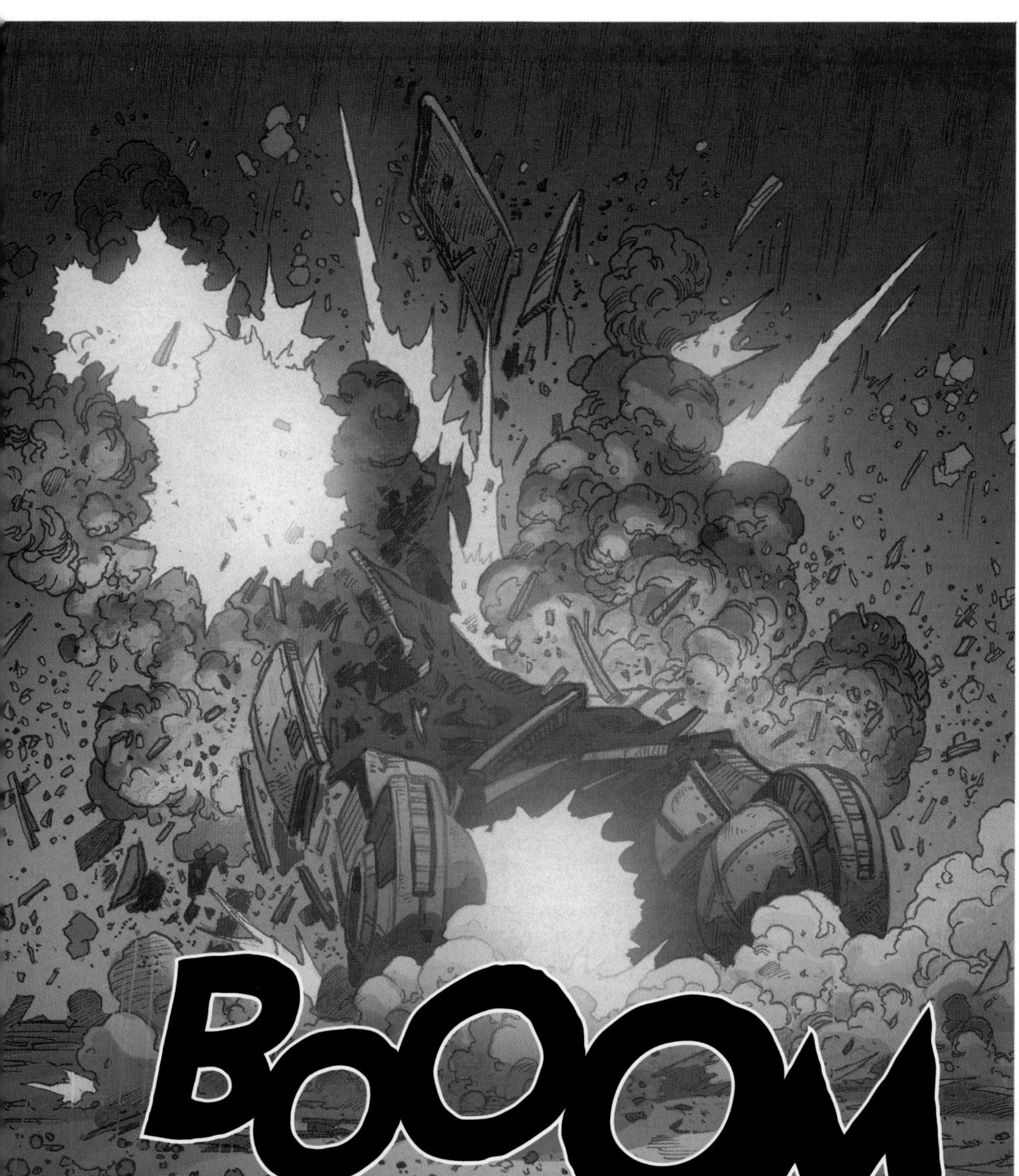
BOOOM

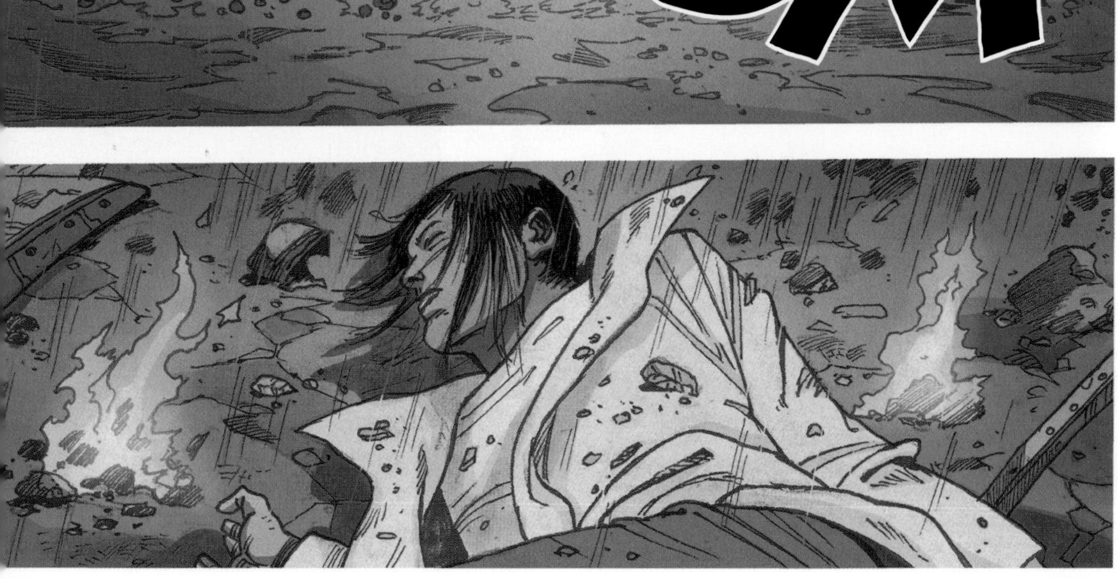

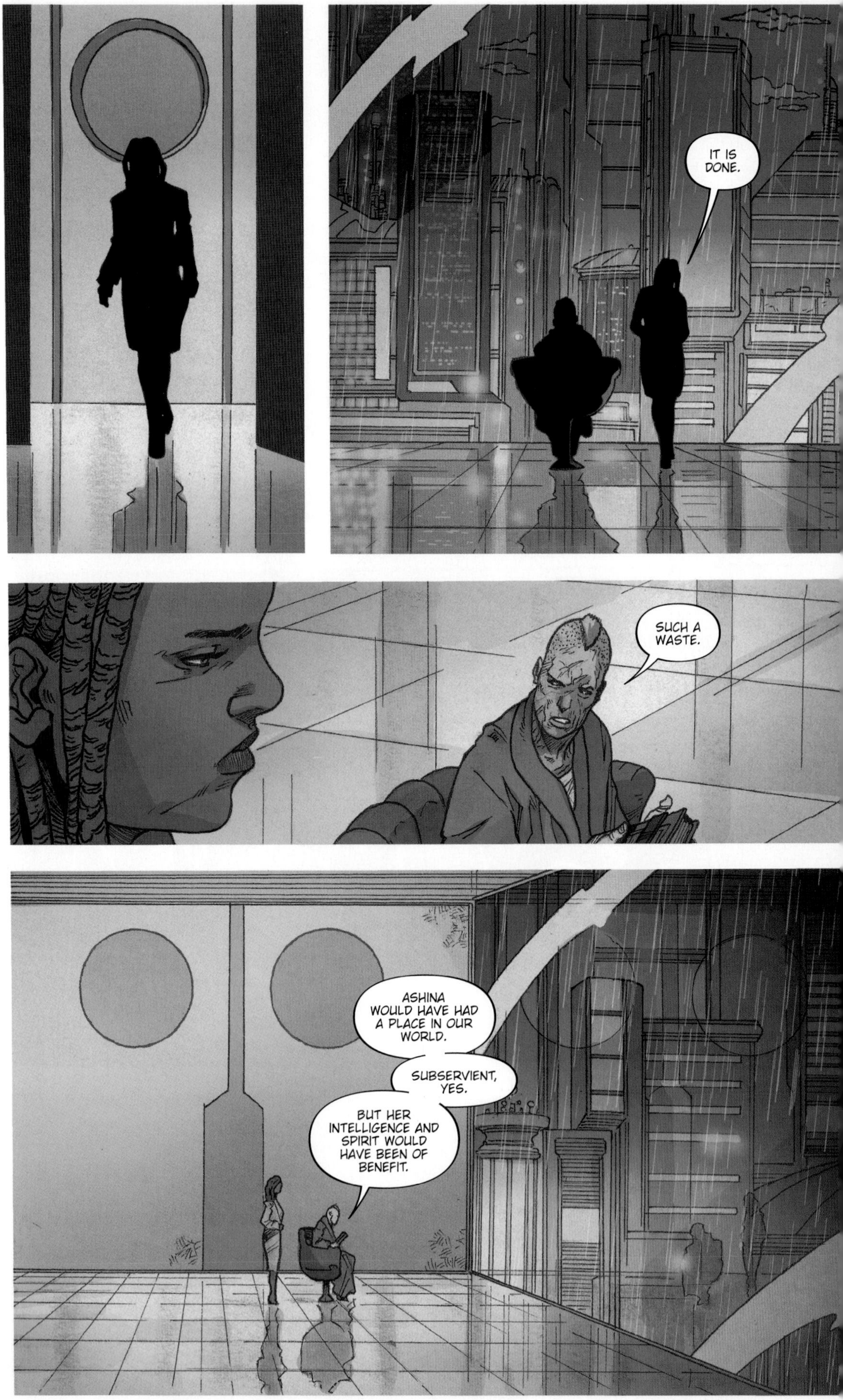
IT IS DONE.
SUCH A WASTE.
ASHINA WOULD HAVE HAD A PLACE IN OUR WORLD.
SUBSERVIENT, YES.
BUT HER INTELLIGENCE AND SPIRIT WOULD HAVE BEEN OF BENEFIT.

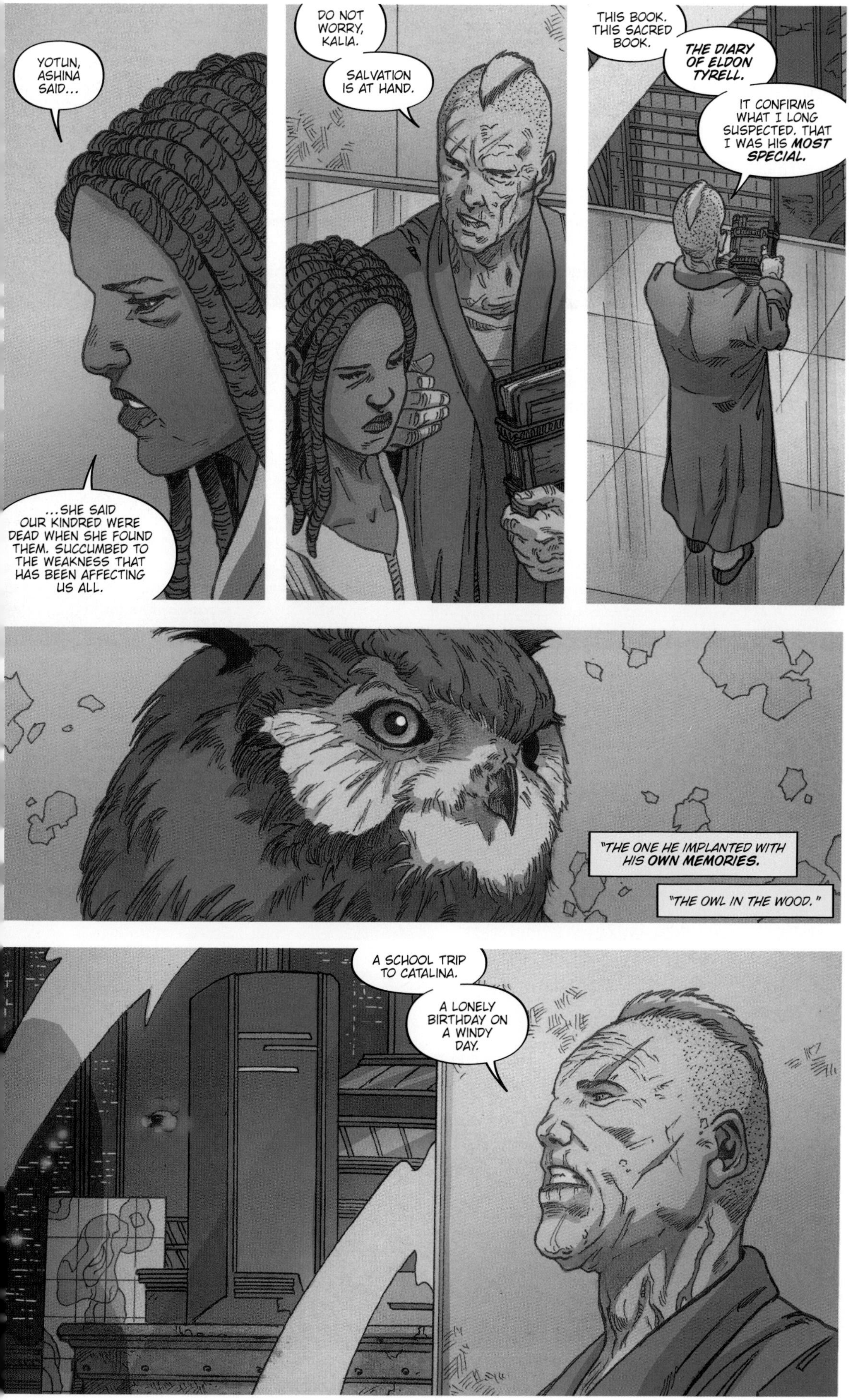
YOTUN, ASHINA SAID...
...SHE SAID OUR KINDRED WERE DEAD WHEN SHE FOUND THEM. SUCCUMBED TO THE WEAKNESS THAT HAS BEEN AFFECTING US ALL.
DO NOT WORRY, KALIA.
SALVATION IS AT HAND.
THIS BOOK. THIS SACRED BOOK.
THE DIARY OF ELDON TYRELL.
IT CONFIRMS WHAT I LONG SUSPECTED. THAT I WAS HIS MOST SPECIAL.
"THE ONE HE IMPLANTED WITH HIS OWN MEMORIES.
"THE OWL IN THE WOOD."
A SCHOOL TRIP TO CATALINA.
A LONELY BIRTHDAY ON A WINDY DAY.

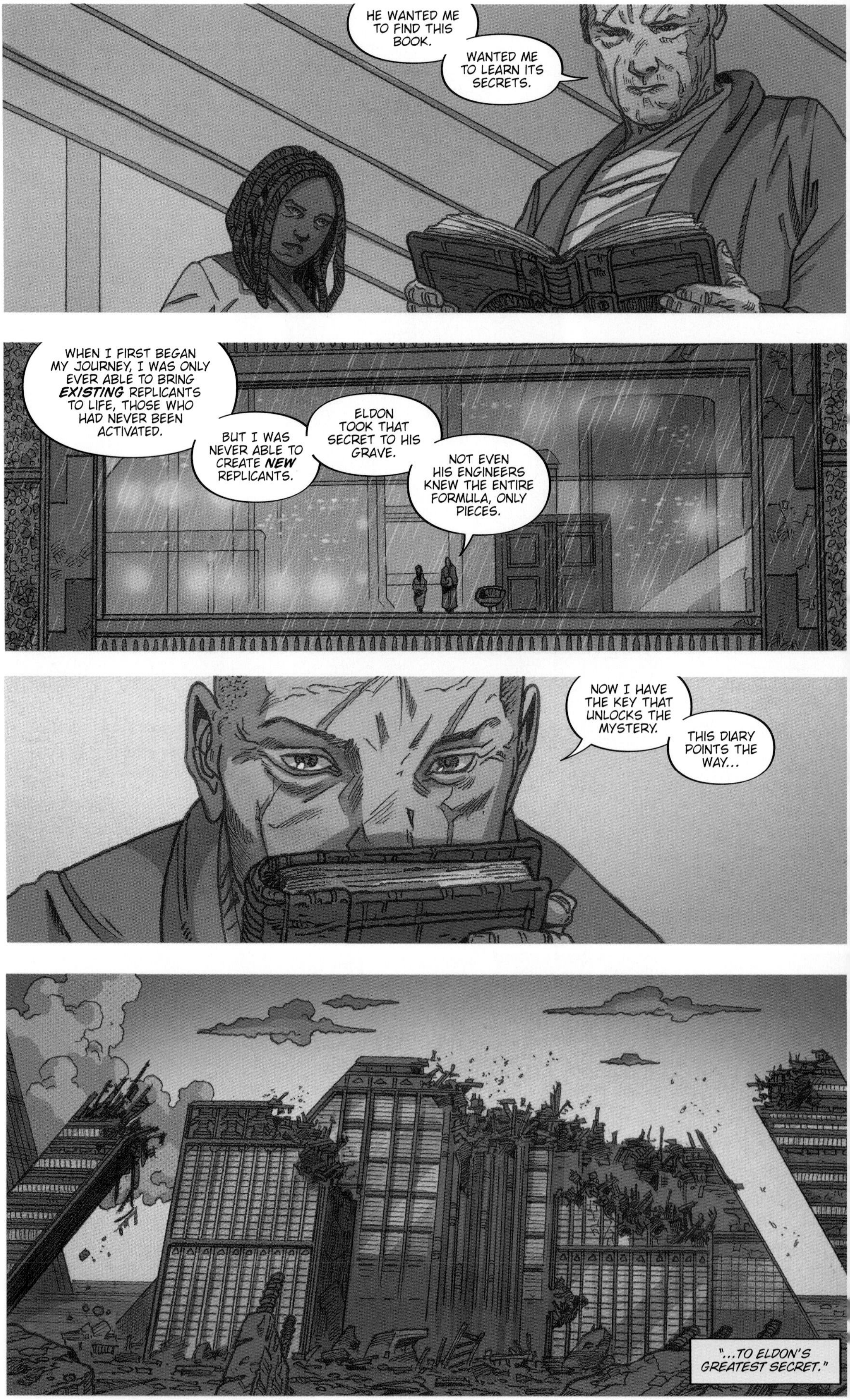
HE WANTED ME TO FIND THIS BOOK.
WANTED ME TO LEARN ITS SECRETS.
WHEN I FIRST BEGAN MY JOURNEY, I WAS ONLY EVER ABLE TO BRING ***EXISTING*** REPLICANTS TO LIFE, THOSE WHO HAD NEVER BEEN ACTIVATED.
BUT I WAS NEVER ABLE TO CREATE ***NEW*** REPLICANTS.
ELDON TOOK THAT SECRET TO HIS GRAVE.
NOT EVEN HIS ENGINEERS KNEW THE ENTIRE FORMULA, ONLY PIECES.
NOW I HAVE THE KEY THAT UNLOCKS THE MYSTERY.
THIS DIARY POINTS THE WAY...
"...TO ELDON'S GREATEST SECRET."

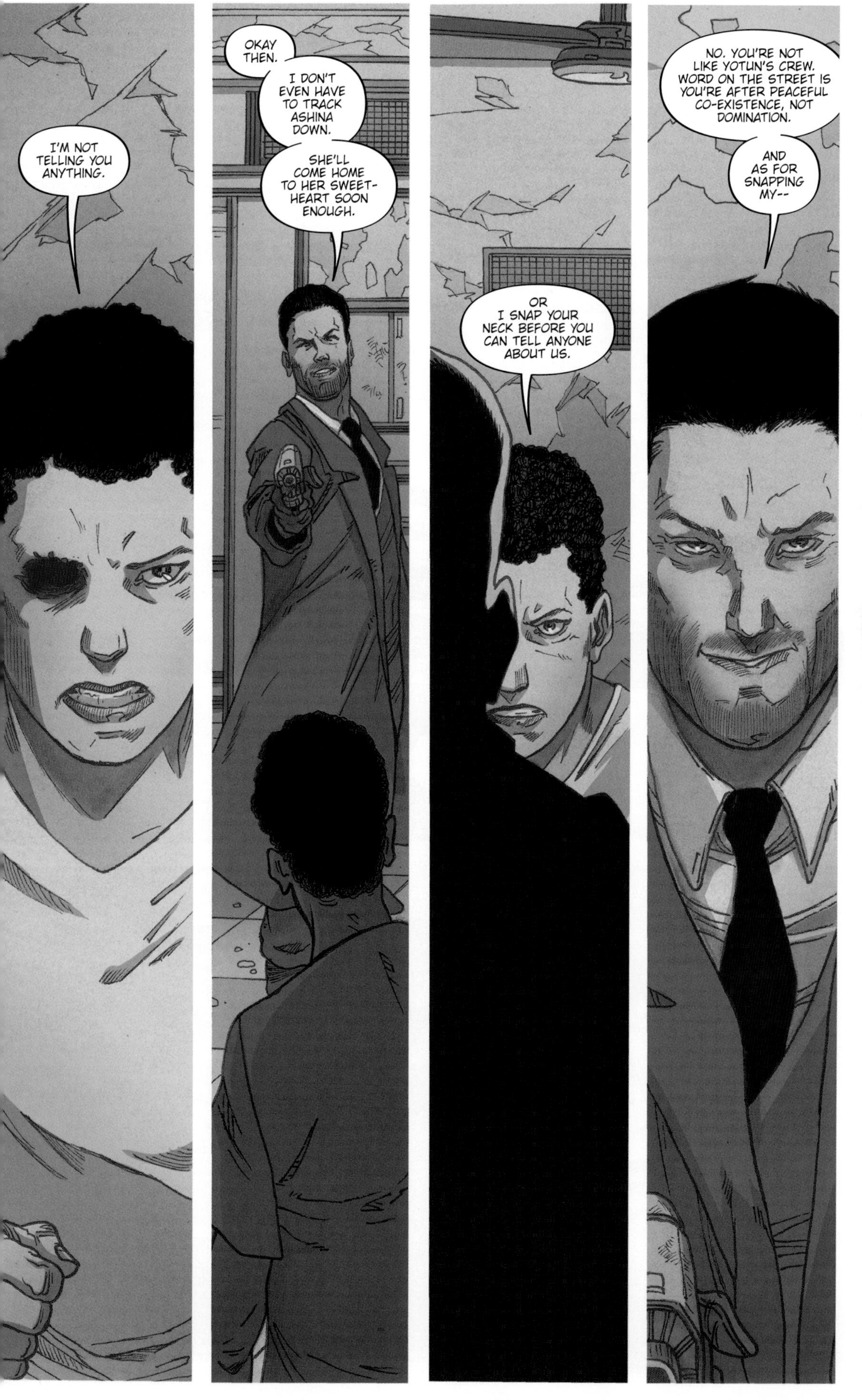
I'M NOT TELLING YOU ANYTHING.
OKAY THEN.
I DON'T EVEN HAVE TO TRACK ASHINA DOWN.
SHE'LL COME HOME TO HER SWEET-HEART SOON ENOUGH.
OR I SNAP YOUR NECK BEFORE YOU CAN TELL ANYONE ABOUT US.
NO. YOU'RE NOT LIKE YOTUN'S CREW. WORD ON THE STREET IS YOU'RE AFTER PEACEFUL CO-EXISTENCE, NOT DOMINATION.
AND AS FOR SNAPPING MY--

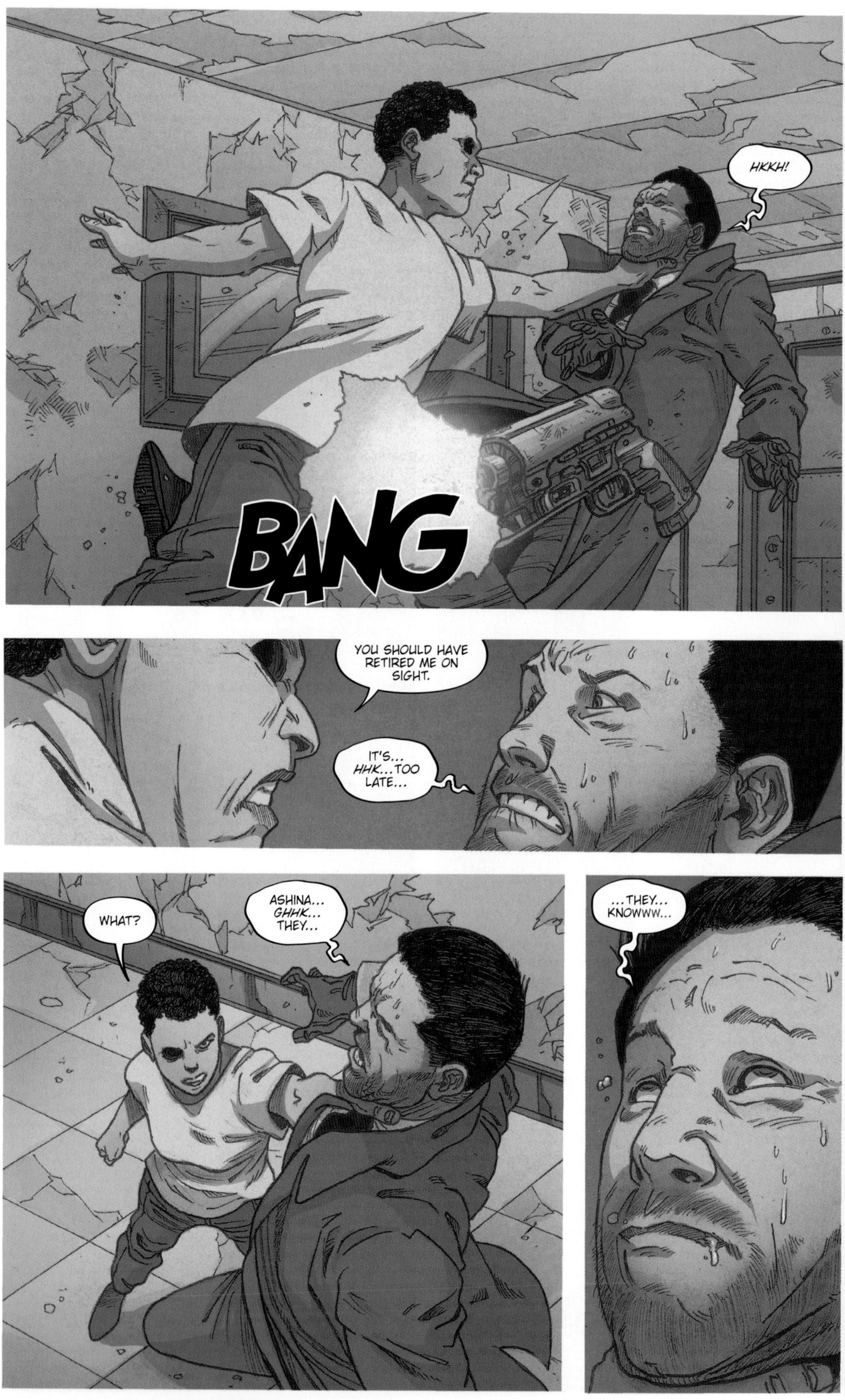
HKKH!
BANG
YOU SHOULD HAVE RETIRED ME ON SIGHT.
IT'S... HHK...TOO LATE...
WHAT?
ASHINA... GHHK... THEY...
...THEY... KNOWWW...

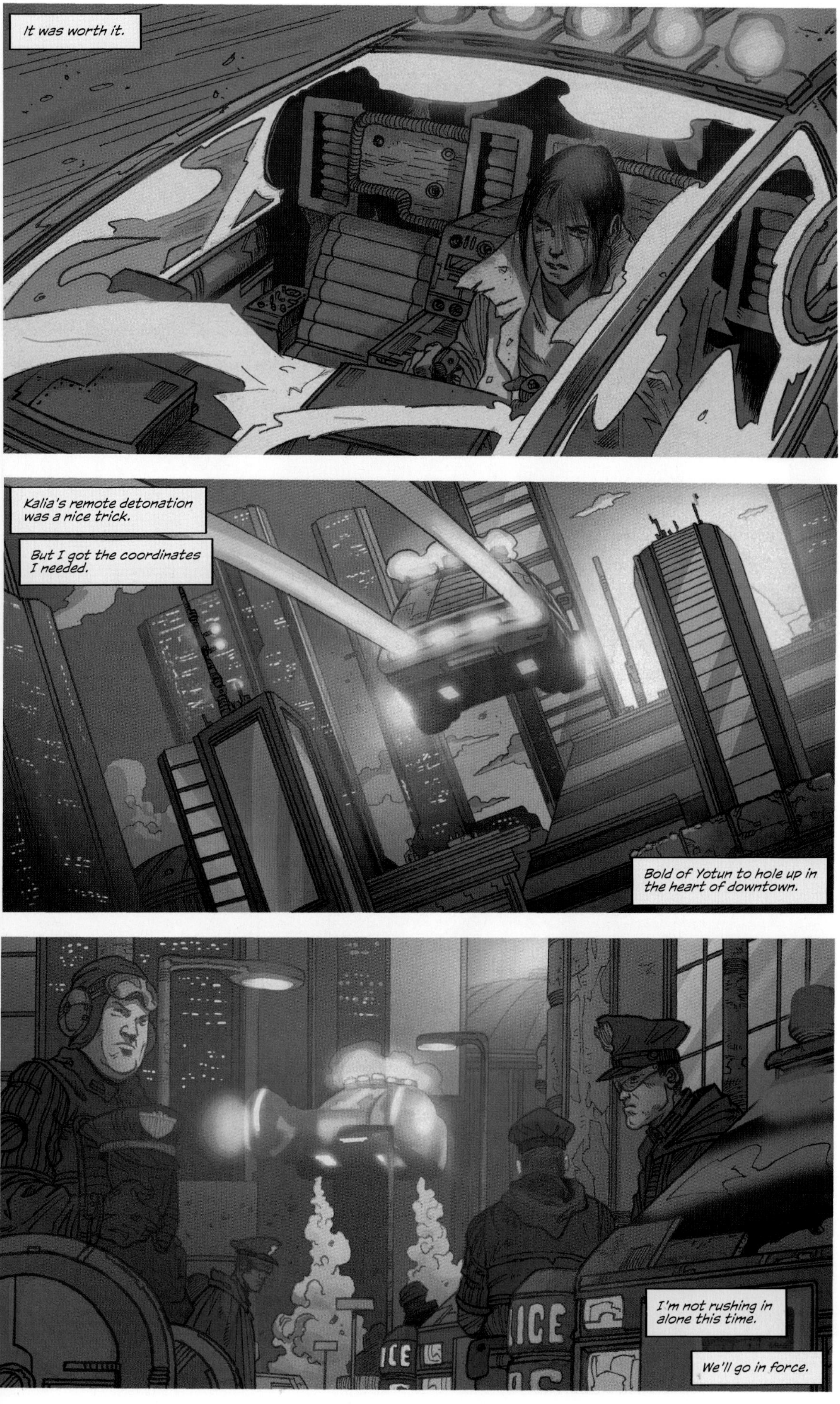
It was worth it.
Kalia's remote detonation was a nice trick.
But I got the coordinates I needed.
Bold of Yotun to hole up in the heart of downtown.
I'm not rushing in alone this time.
We'll go in force.

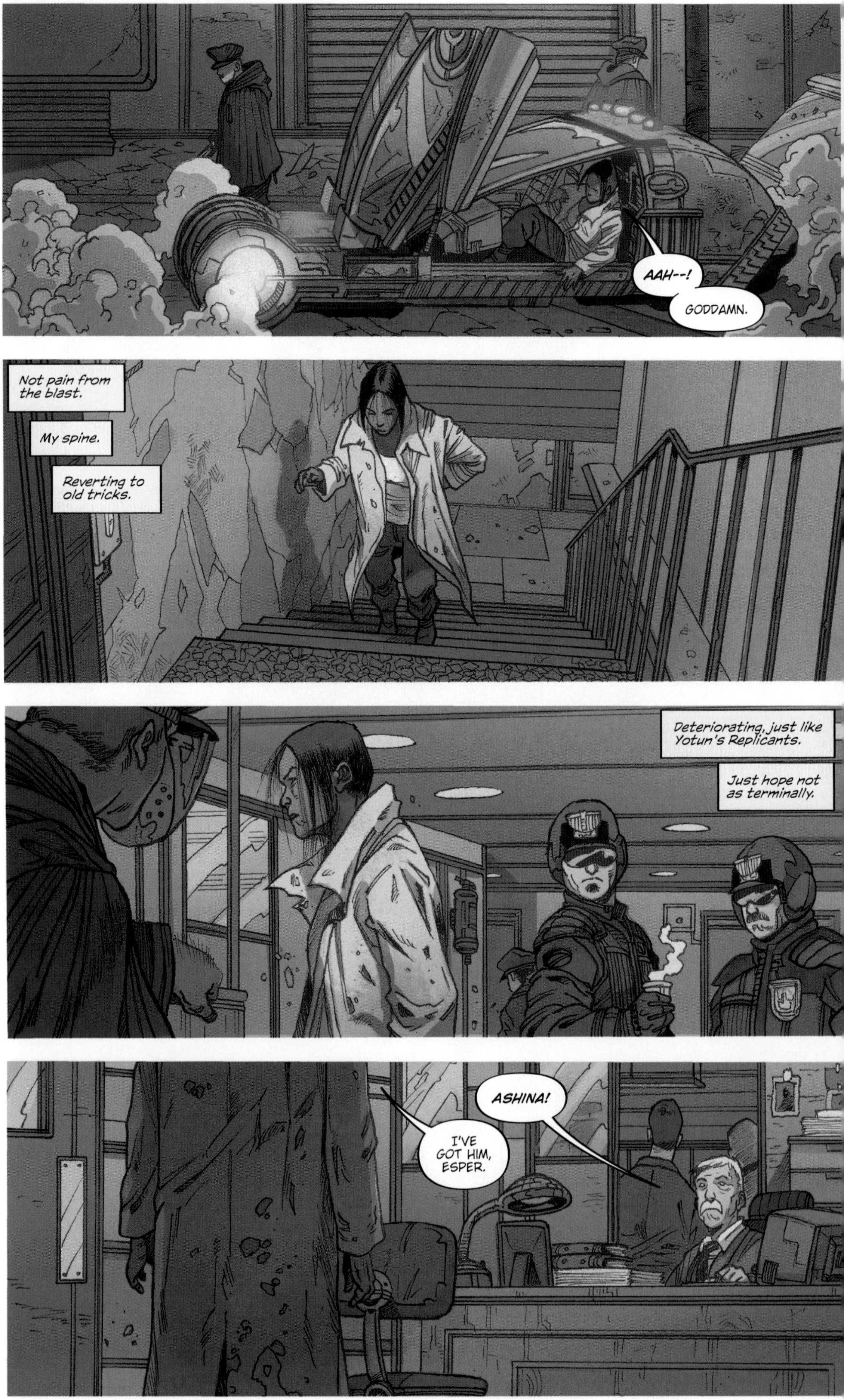
AAH--!
GODDAMN.
Not pain from the blast.
My spine.
Reverting to old tricks.
Deteriorating, just like Yotun's Replicants.
Just hope not as terminally.
ASHINA!
I'VE GOT HIM, ESPER.

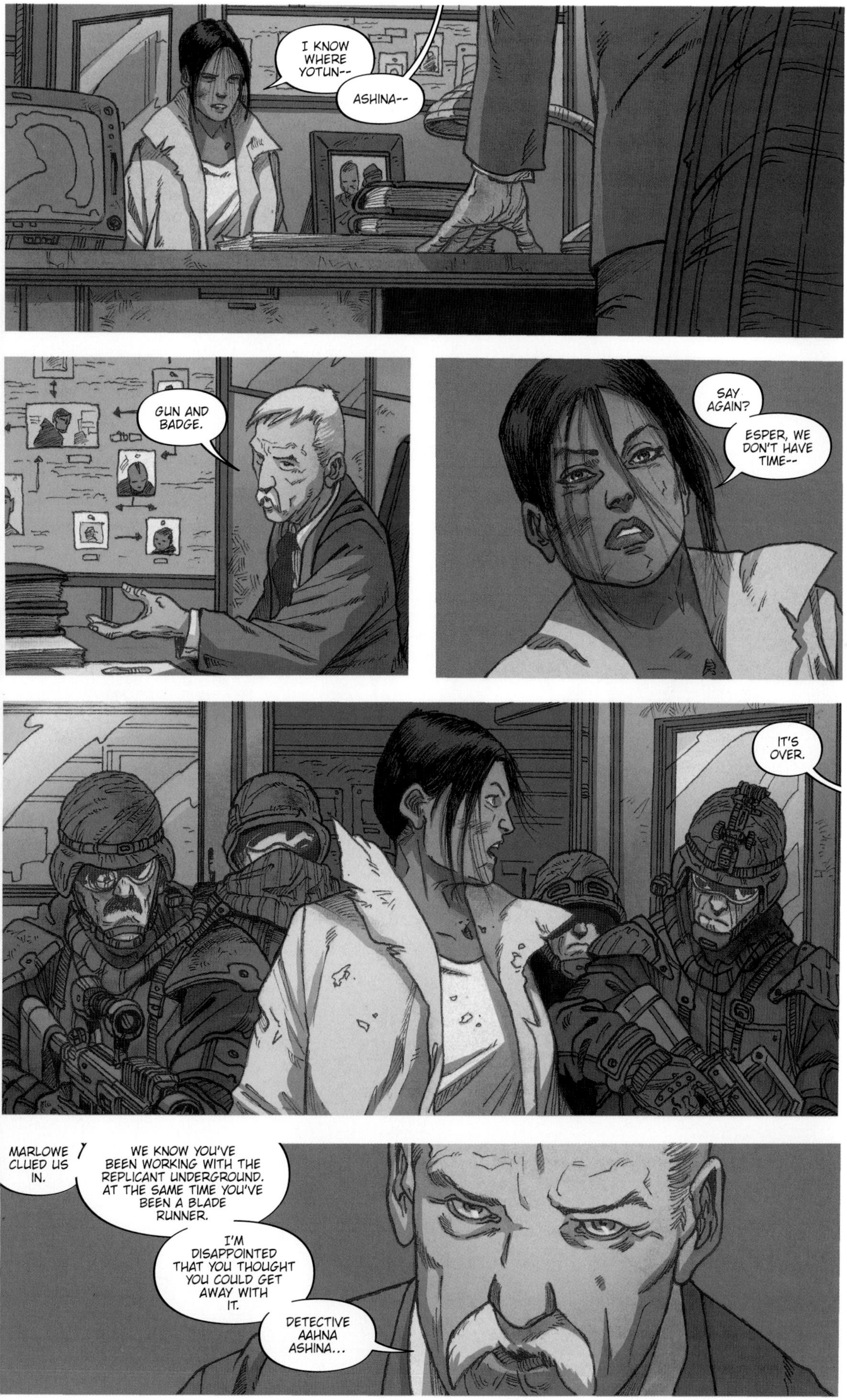
I KNOW WHERE YOTUN--
ASHINA--
GUN AND BADGE.
SAY AGAIN?
ESPER, WE DON'T HAVE TIME--
IT'S OVER.
MARLOWE CLUED US IN.
WE KNOW YOU'VE BEEN WORKING WITH THE REPLICANT UNDERGROUND. AT THE SAME TIME YOU'VE BEEN A BLADE RUNNER.
I'M DISAPPOINTED THAT YOU THOUGHT YOU COULD GET AWAY WITH IT.
DETECTIVE AAHNA ASHINA...

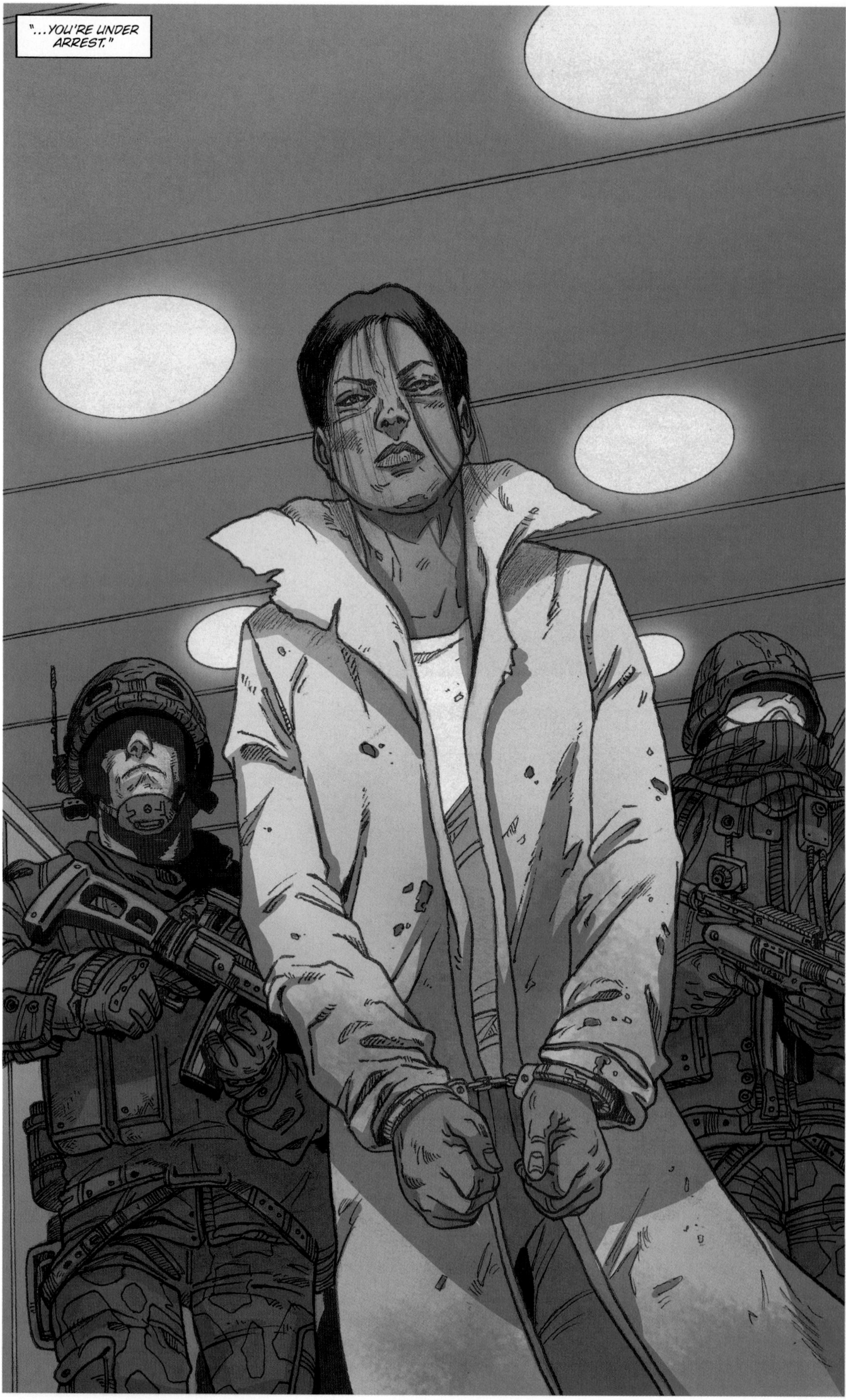
"...YOU'RE UNDER ARREST."

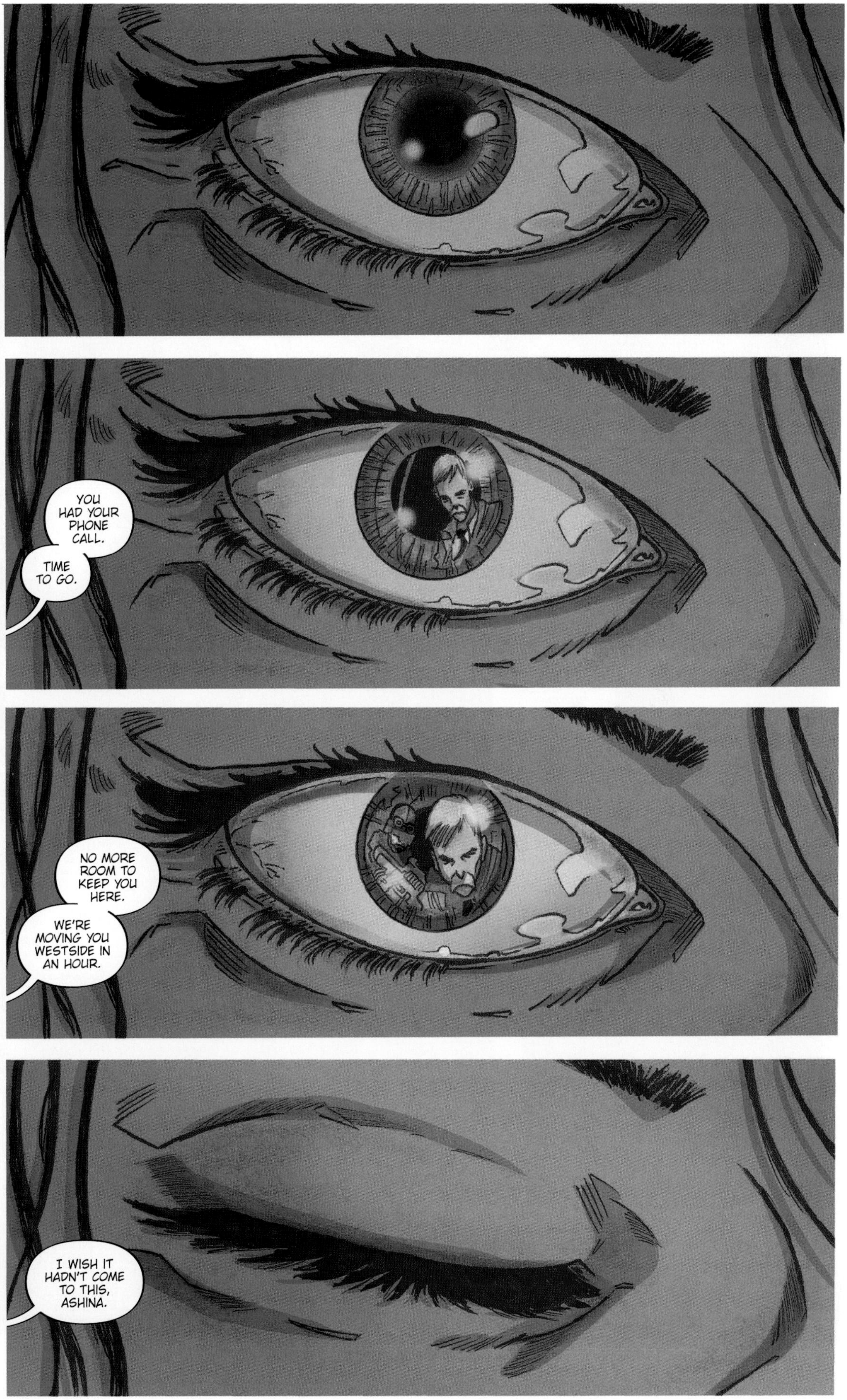
YOU HAD YOUR PHONE CALL.
TIME TO GO.
NO MORE ROOM TO KEEP YOU HERE.
WE'RE MOVING YOU WESTSIDE IN AN HOUR.
I WISH IT HADN'T COME TO THIS, ASHINA.

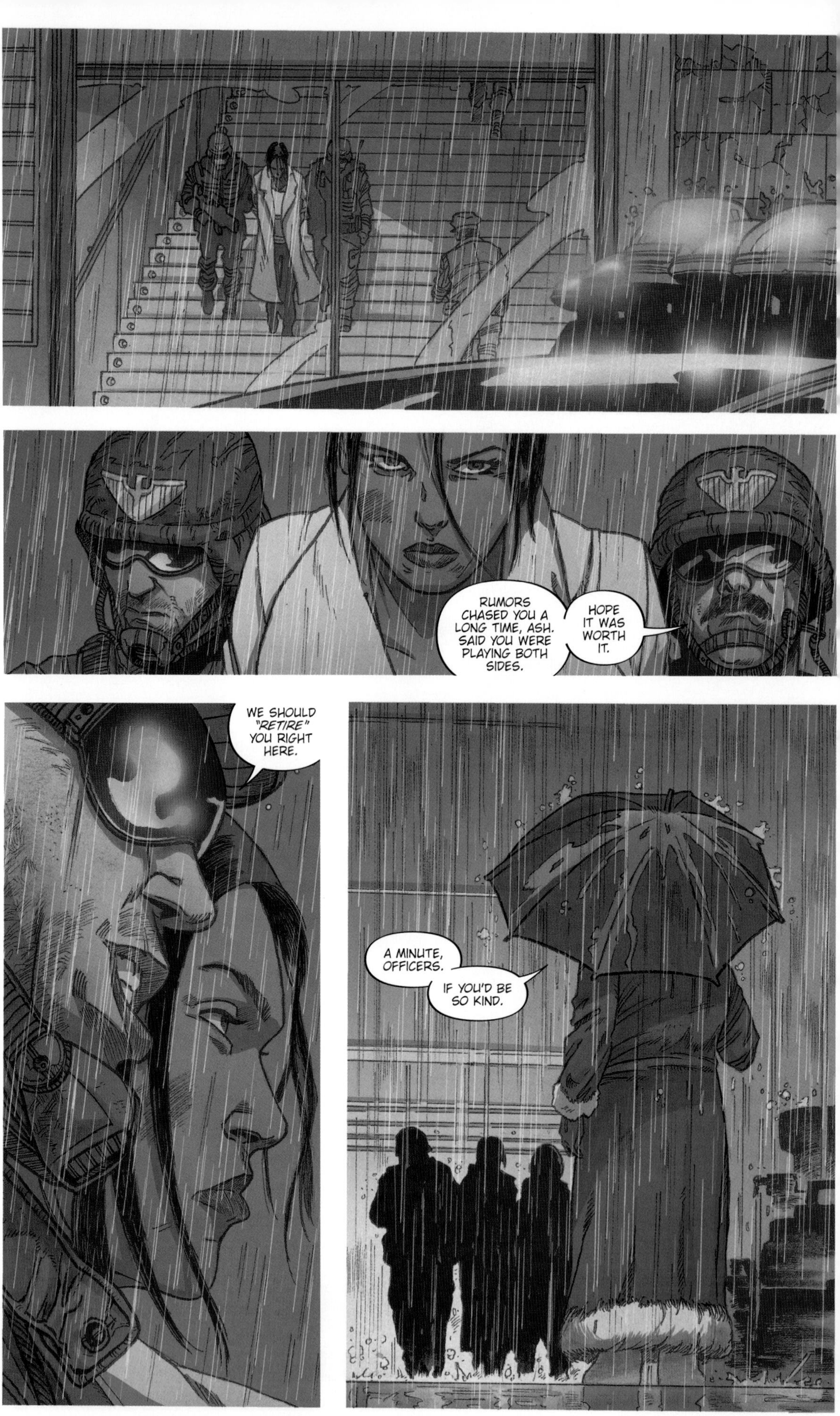
RUMORS CHASED YOU A LONG TIME, ASH. SAID YOU WERE PLAYING BOTH SIDES.
HOPE IT WAS WORTH IT.
WE SHOULD "RETIRE" YOU RIGHT HERE.
A MINUTE, OFFICERS.
IF YOU'D BE SO KIND.

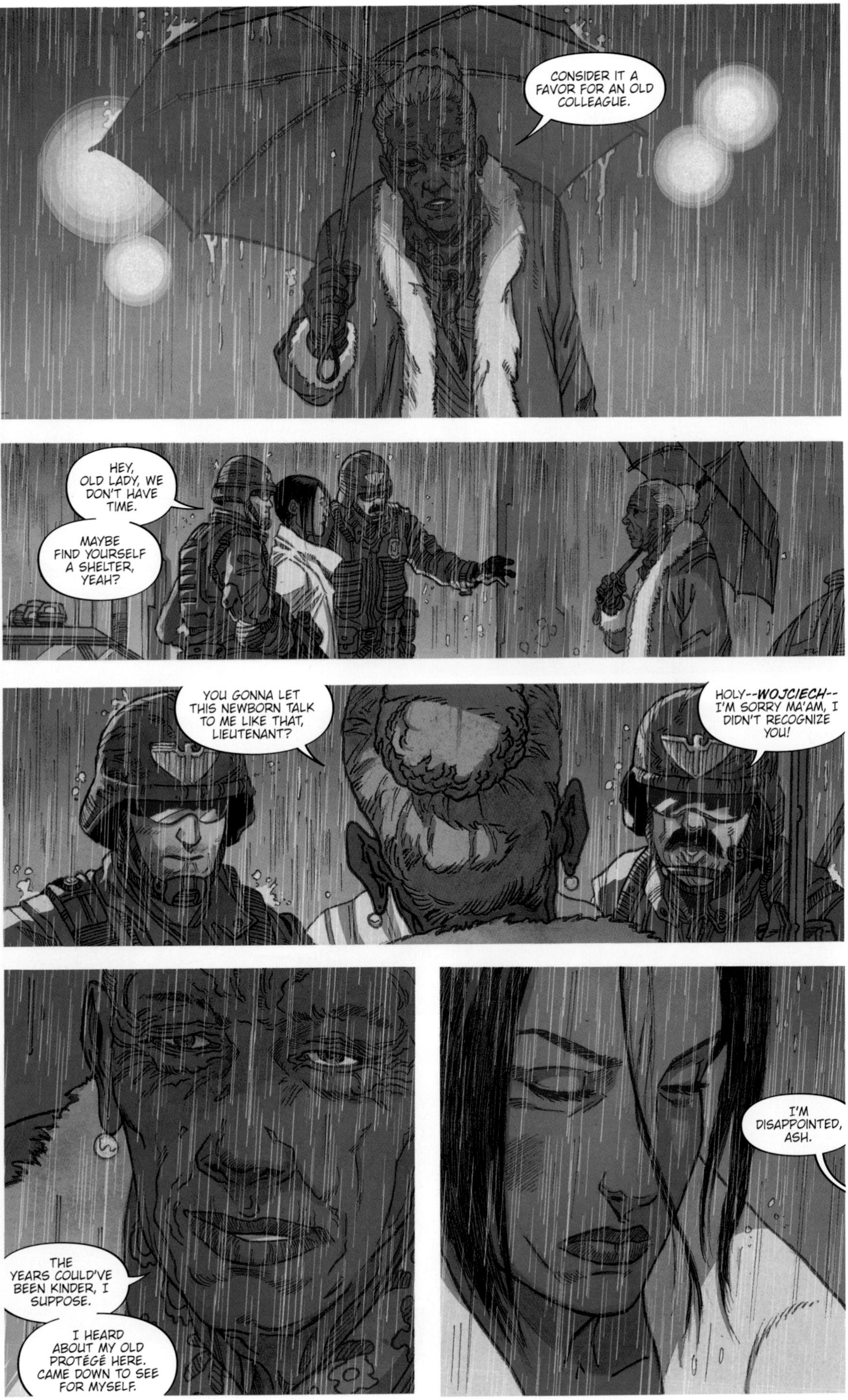
CONSIDER IT A FAVOR FOR AN OLD COLLEAGUE.
HEY, OLD LADY, WE DON'T HAVE TIME.
MAYBE FIND YOURSELF A SHELTER, YEAH?
YOU GONNA LET THIS NEWBORN TALK TO ME LIKE THAT, LIEUTENANT?
HOLY--*WOJCIECH*-- I'M SORRY MA'AM, I DIDN'T RECOGNIZE YOU!
THE YEARS COULD'VE BEEN KINDER, I SUPPOSE.
I HEARD ABOUT MY OLD PROTÉGÉ HERE. CAME DOWN TO SEE FOR MYSELF.
I'M DISAPPOINTED, ASH.

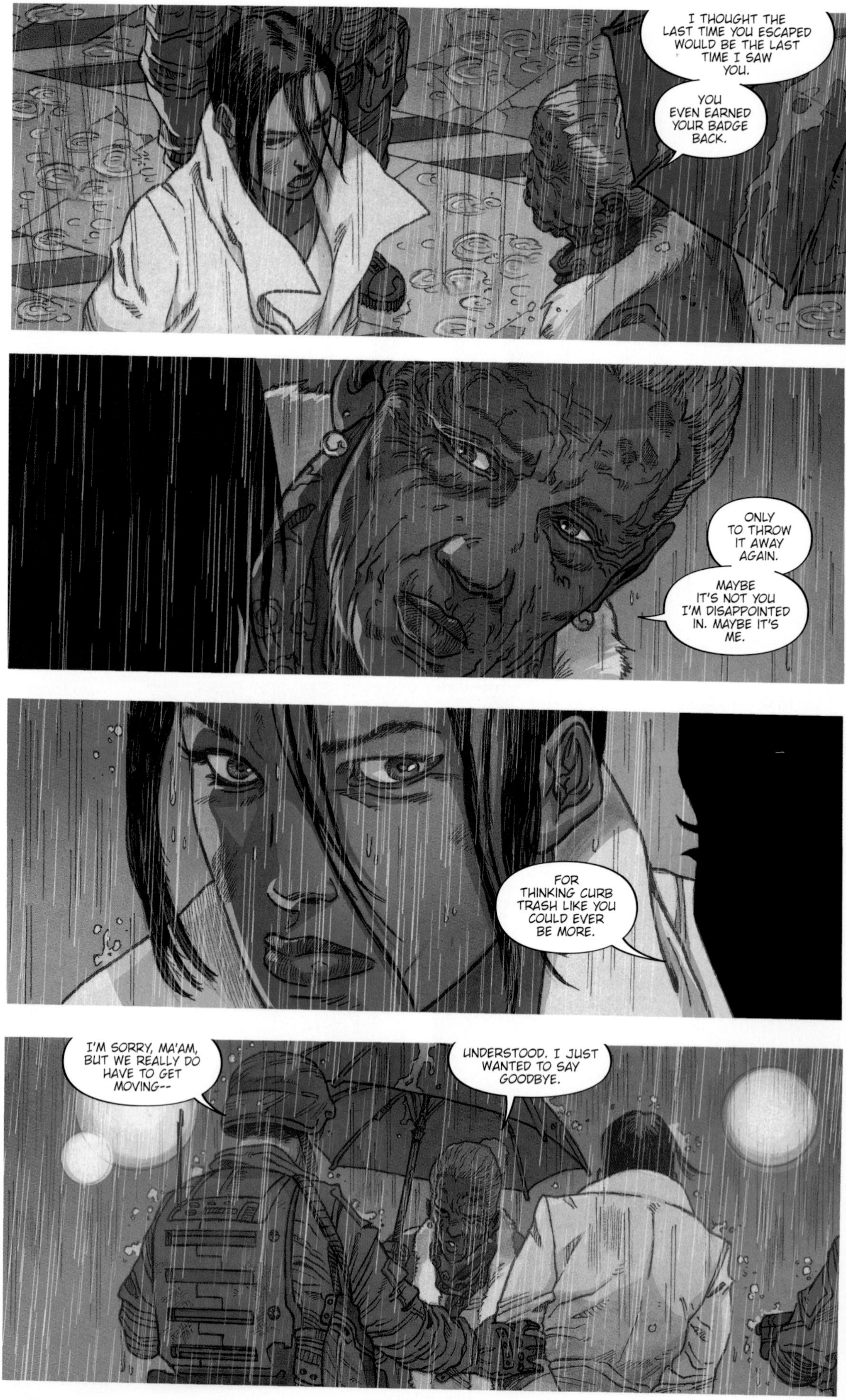
I THOUGHT THE LAST TIME YOU ESCAPED WOULD BE THE LAST TIME I SAW YOU.
YOU EVEN EARNED YOUR BADGE BACK.
ONLY TO THROW IT AWAY AGAIN.
MAYBE IT'S NOT YOU I'M DISAPPOINTED IN. MAYBE IT'S ME.
FOR THINKING CURB TRASH LIKE YOU COULD EVER BE MORE.
I'M SORRY, MA'AM, BUT WE REALLY DO HAVE TO GET MOVING--
UNDERSTOOD. I JUST WANTED TO SAY GOODBYE.

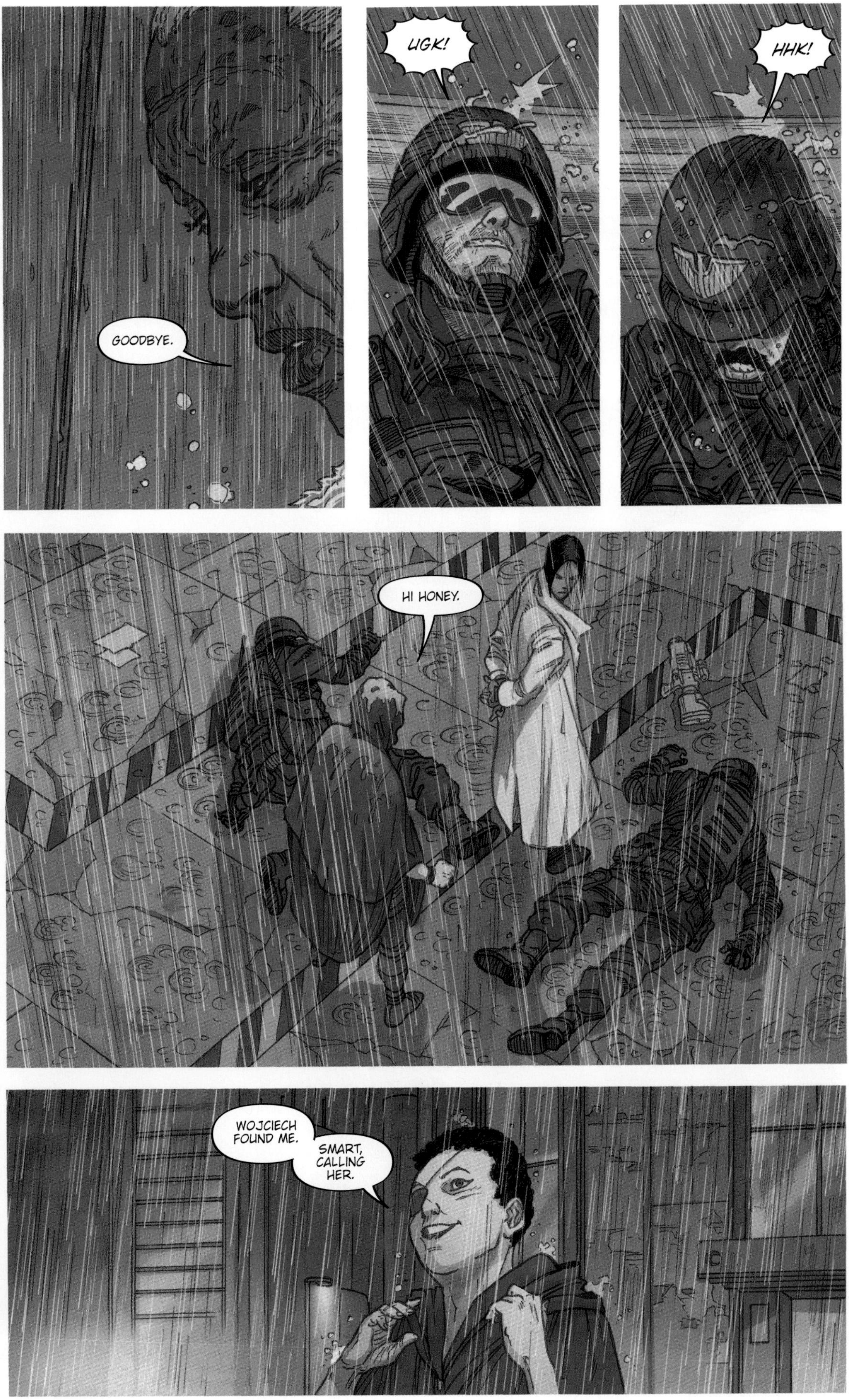
GOODBYE.
UGK!
HHK!
HI HONEY.
WOJCIECH FOUND ME.
SMART, CALLING HER.

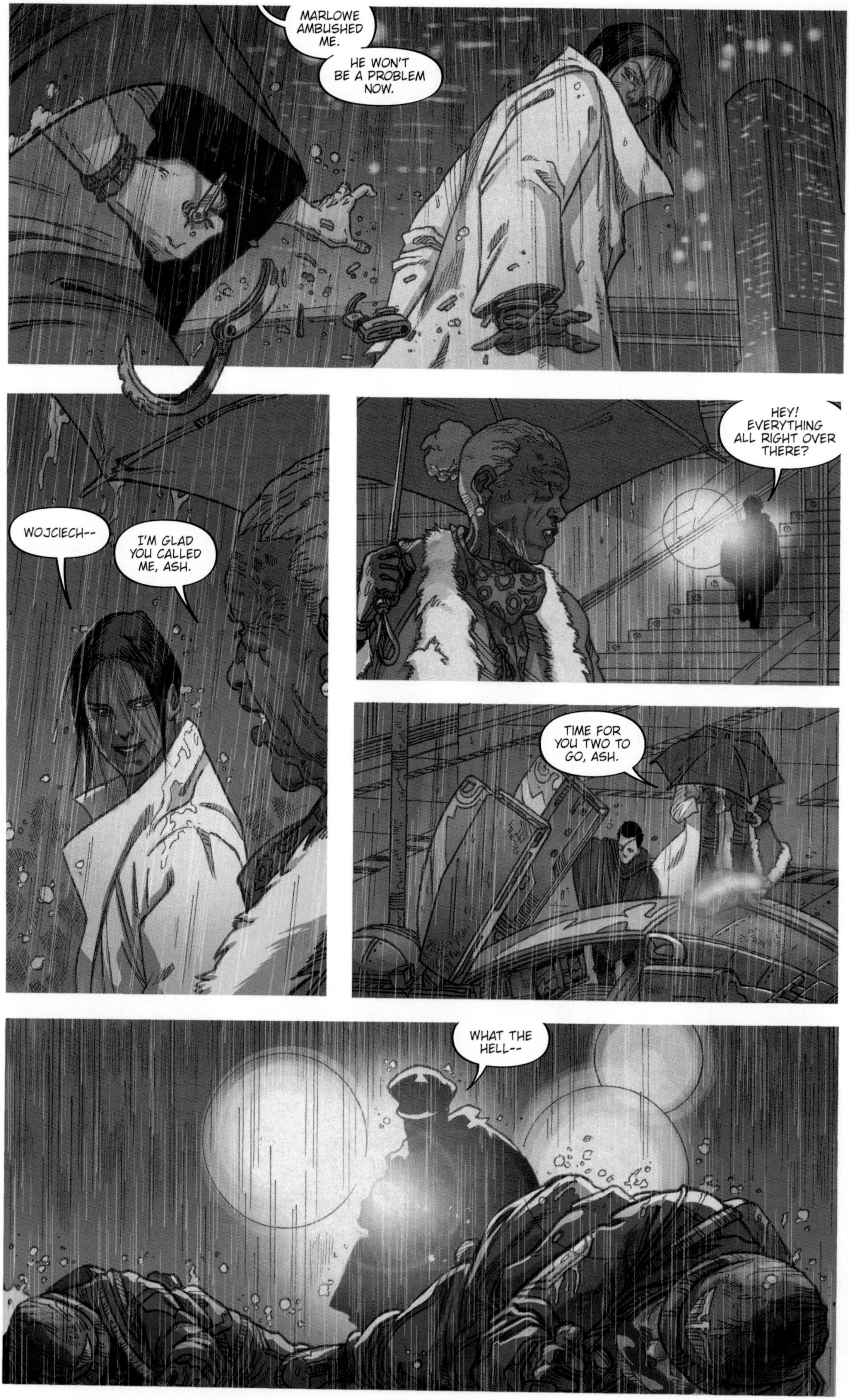
MARLOWE AMBUSHED ME.
HE WON'T BE A PROBLEM NOW.
WOJCIECH--
I'M GLAD YOU CALLED ME, ASH.
HEY! EVERYTHING ALL RIGHT OVER THERE?
TIME FOR YOU TWO TO GO, ASH.
WHAT THE HELL--

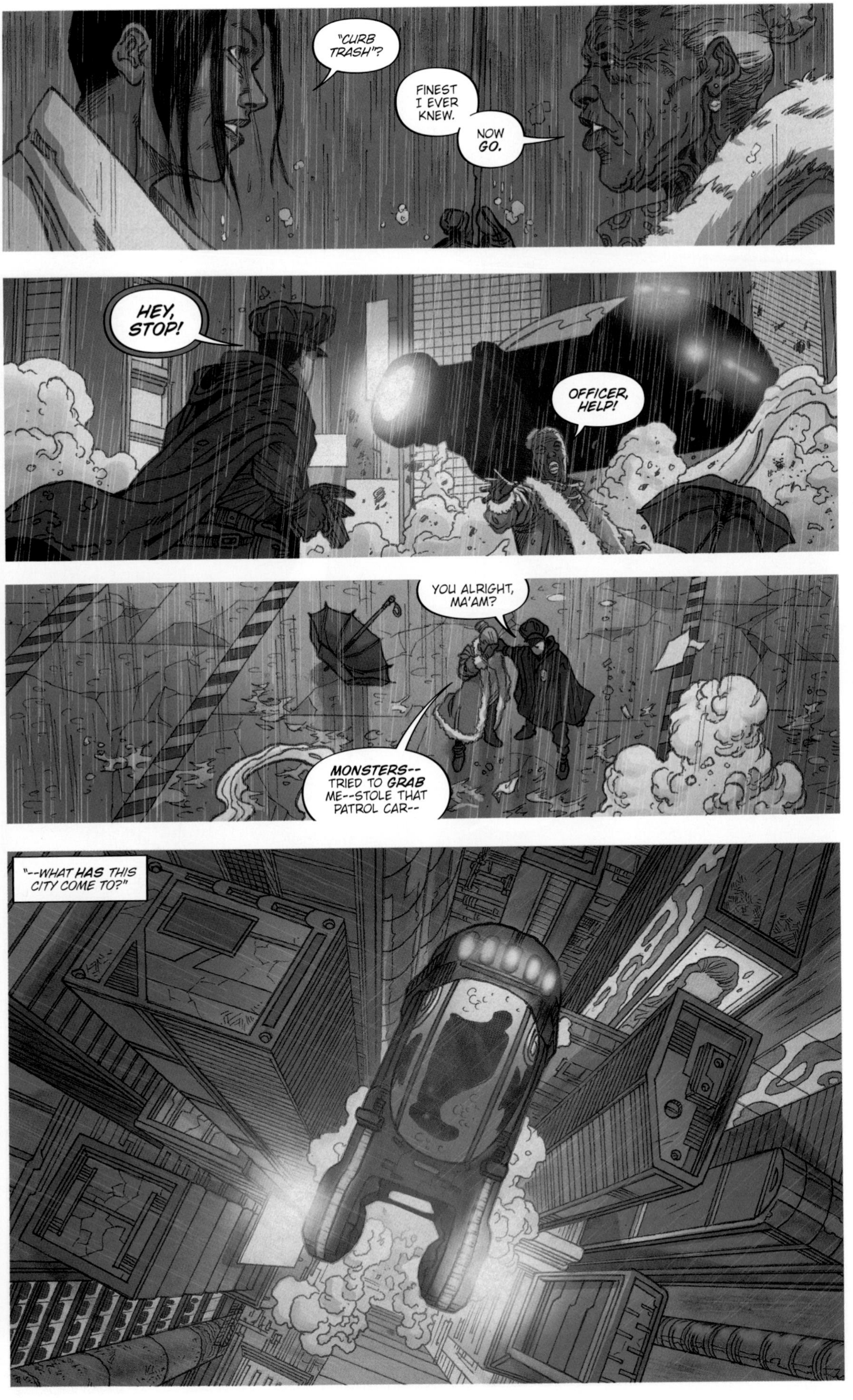

"CURB TRASH"?
FINEST I EVER KNEW.
NOW GO.
HEY, STOP!
OFFICER, HELP!
YOU ALRIGHT, MA'AM?
MONSTERS-- TRIED TO GRAB ME--STOLE THAT PATROL CAR--
"--WHAT HAS THIS CITY COME TO?"

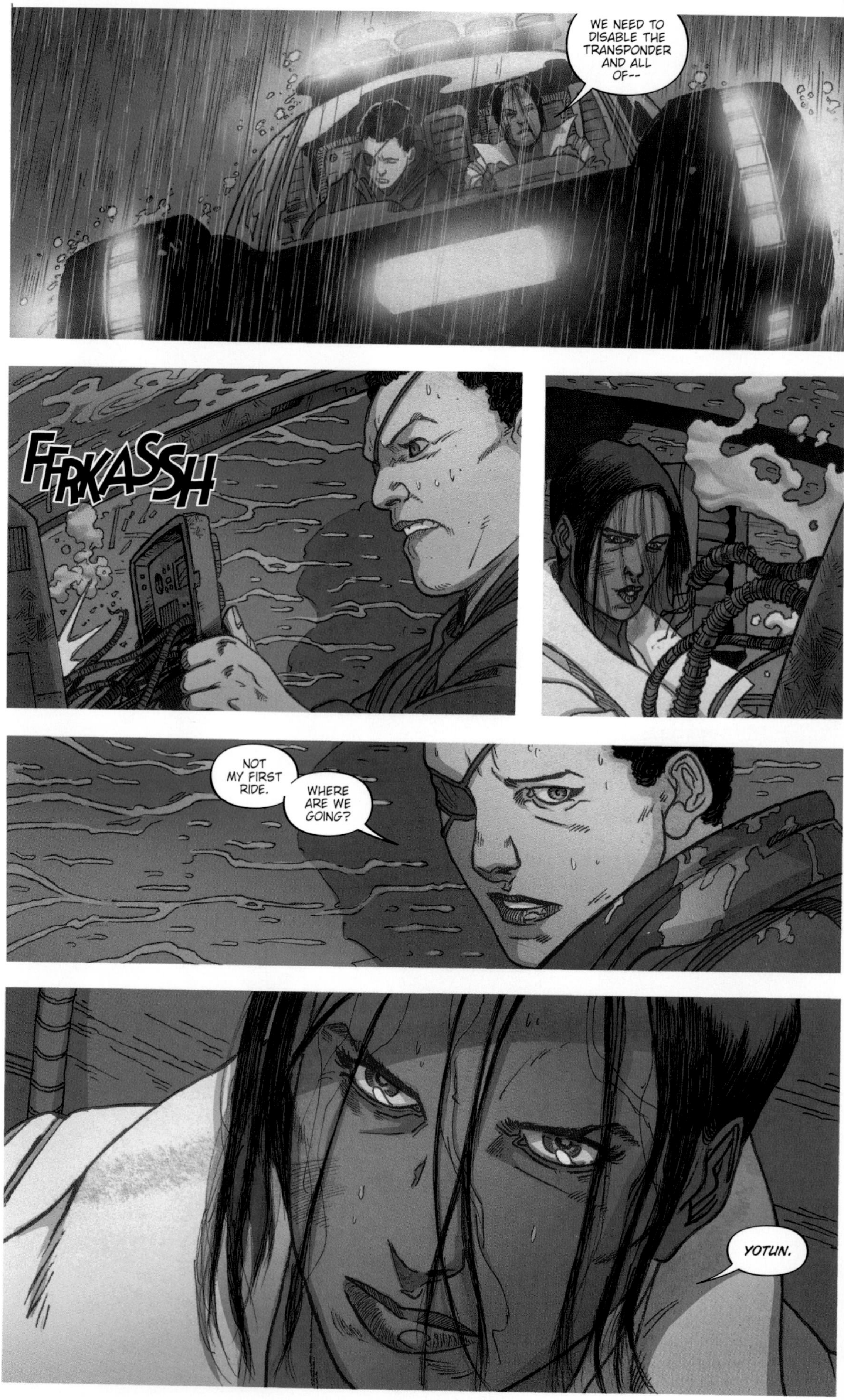
WE NEED TO DISABLE THE TRANSPONDER AND ALL OF--
FFRKASSH
NOT MY FIRST RIDE.
WHERE ARE WE GOING?
YOTUN.

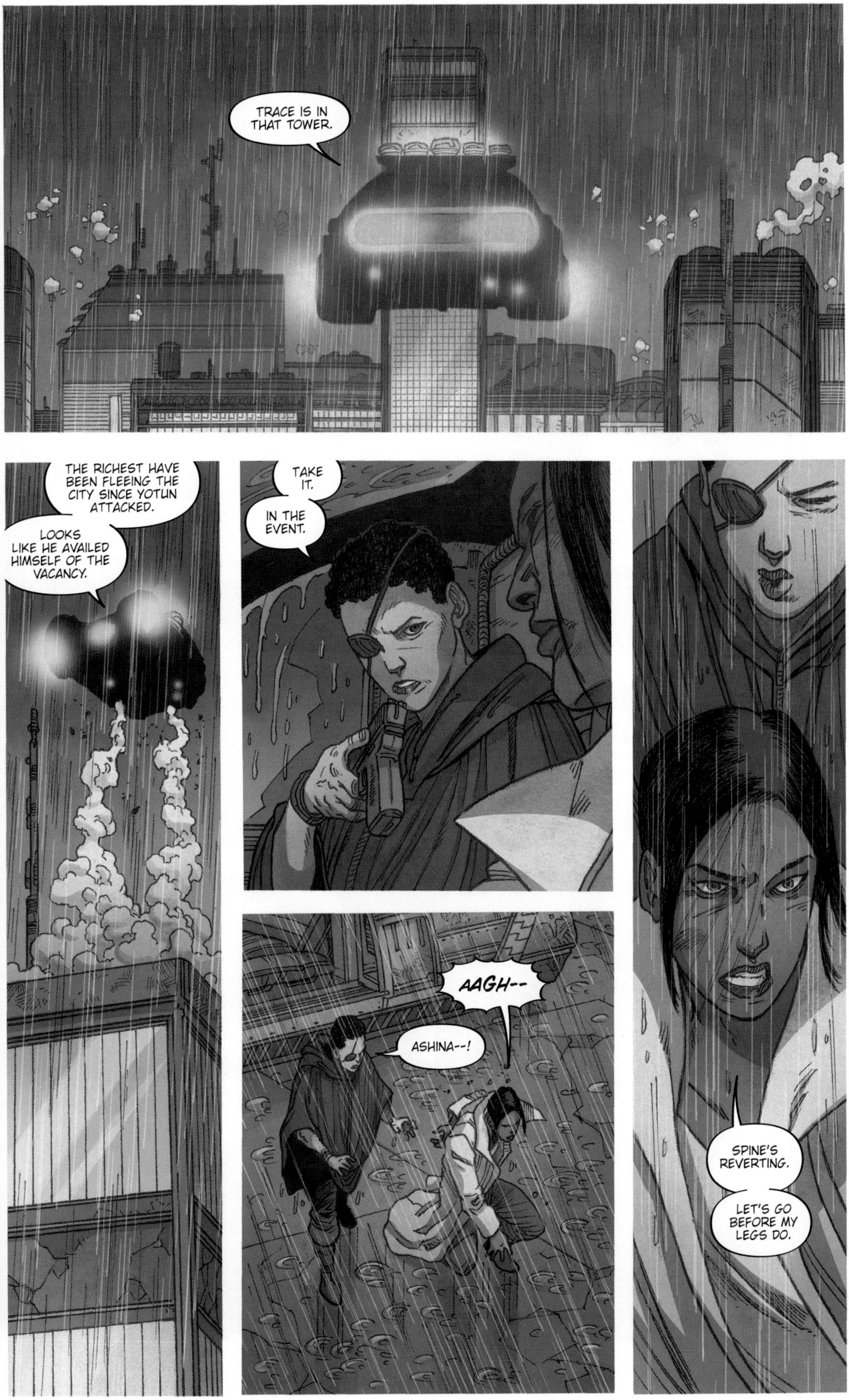
TRACE IS IN THAT TOWER.
THE RICHEST HAVE BEEN FLEEING THE CITY SINCE YOTUN ATTACKED.
LOOKS LIKE HE AVAILED HIMSELF OF THE VACANCY.
TAKE IT.
IN THE EVENT.
SPINE'S REVERTING.
LET'S GO BEFORE MY LEGS DO.
AAGH--
ASHINA--!

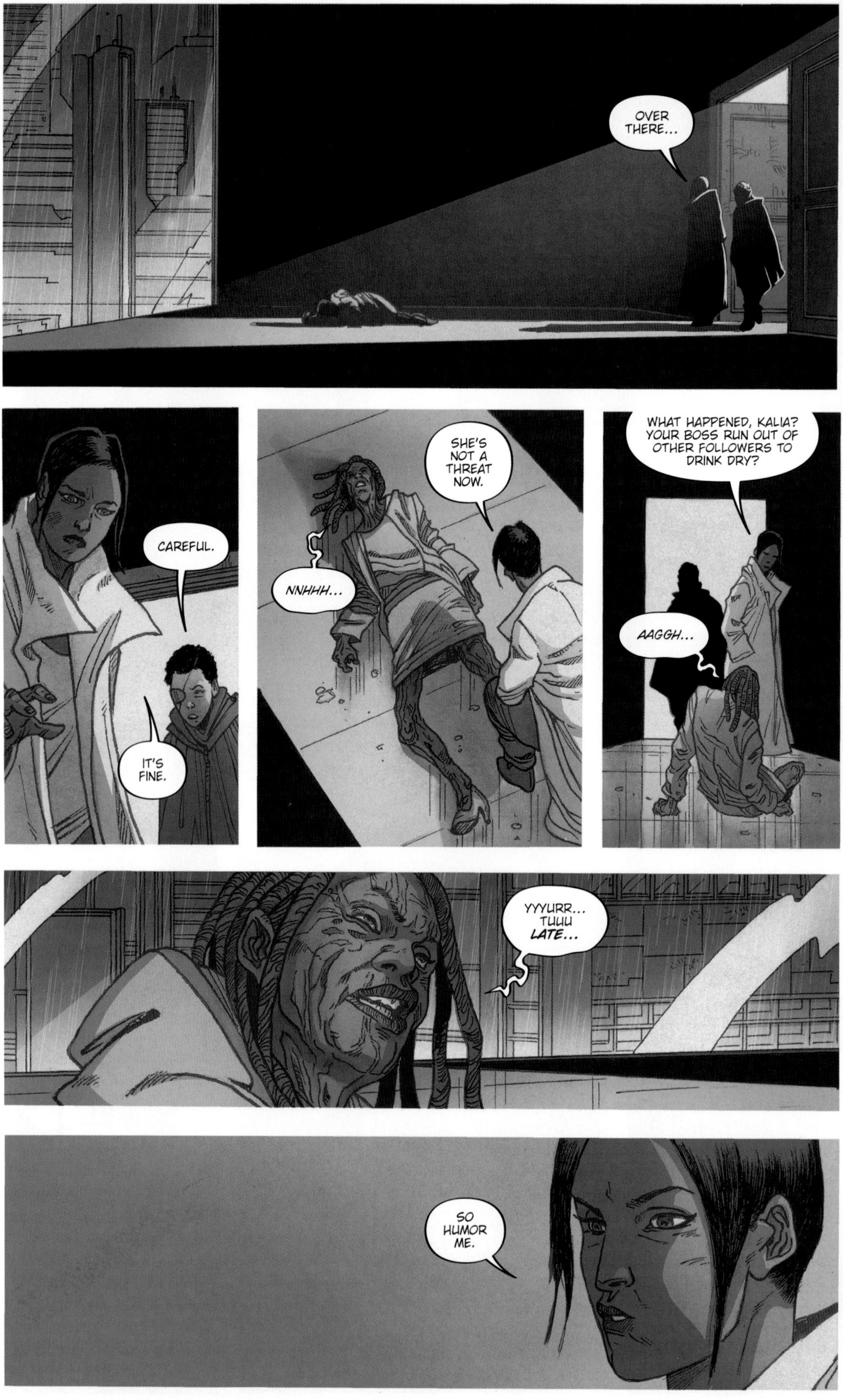
OVER THERE...
CAREFUL.
IT'S FINE.
SHE'S NOT A THREAT NOW.
NNHHH...
WHAT HAPPENED, KALIA? YOUR BOSS RUN OUT OF OTHER FOLLOWERS TO DRINK DRY?
AAGGH...
YYYURR... TUUU *LATE*...
SO HUMOR ME.

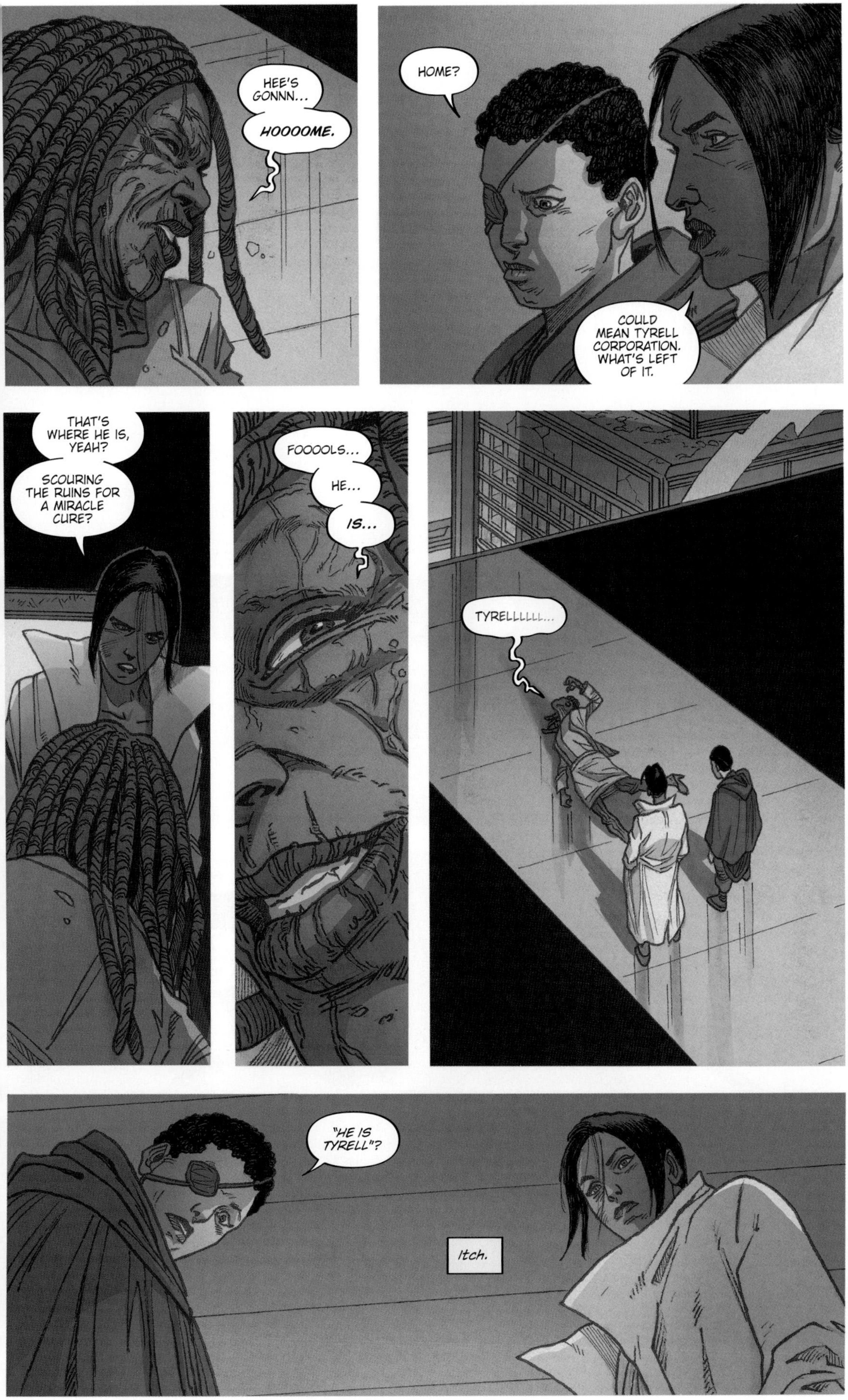
HEE'S GONNN...
HOOOOME.
HOME?
COULD MEAN TYRELL CORPORATION. WHAT'S LEFT OF IT.
THAT'S WHERE HE IS, YEAH?
SCOURING THE RUINS FOR A MIRACLE CURE?
FOOOOLS...
HE...
IS...
TYRELLLLLLL...
"HE IS TYRELL"?
Itch.

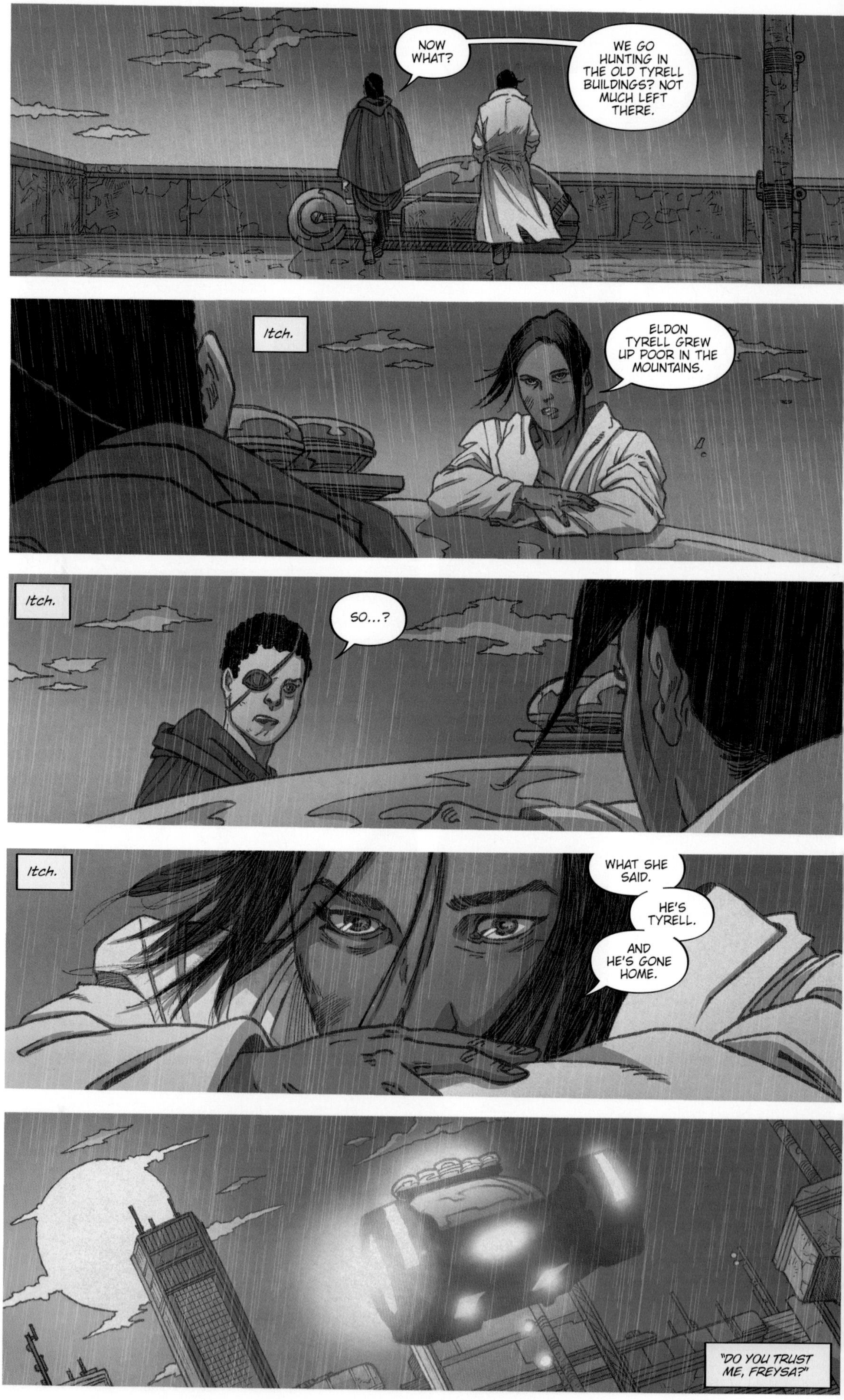
NOW WHAT?
WE GO HUNTING IN THE OLD TYRELL BUILDINGS? NOT MUCH LEFT THERE.
Itch.
ELDON TYRELL GREW UP POOR IN THE MOUNTAINS.
Itch.
SO...?
Itch.
WHAT SHE SAID.
HE'S TYRELL.
AND HE'S GONE HOME.
"DO YOU TRUST ME, FREYSA?"

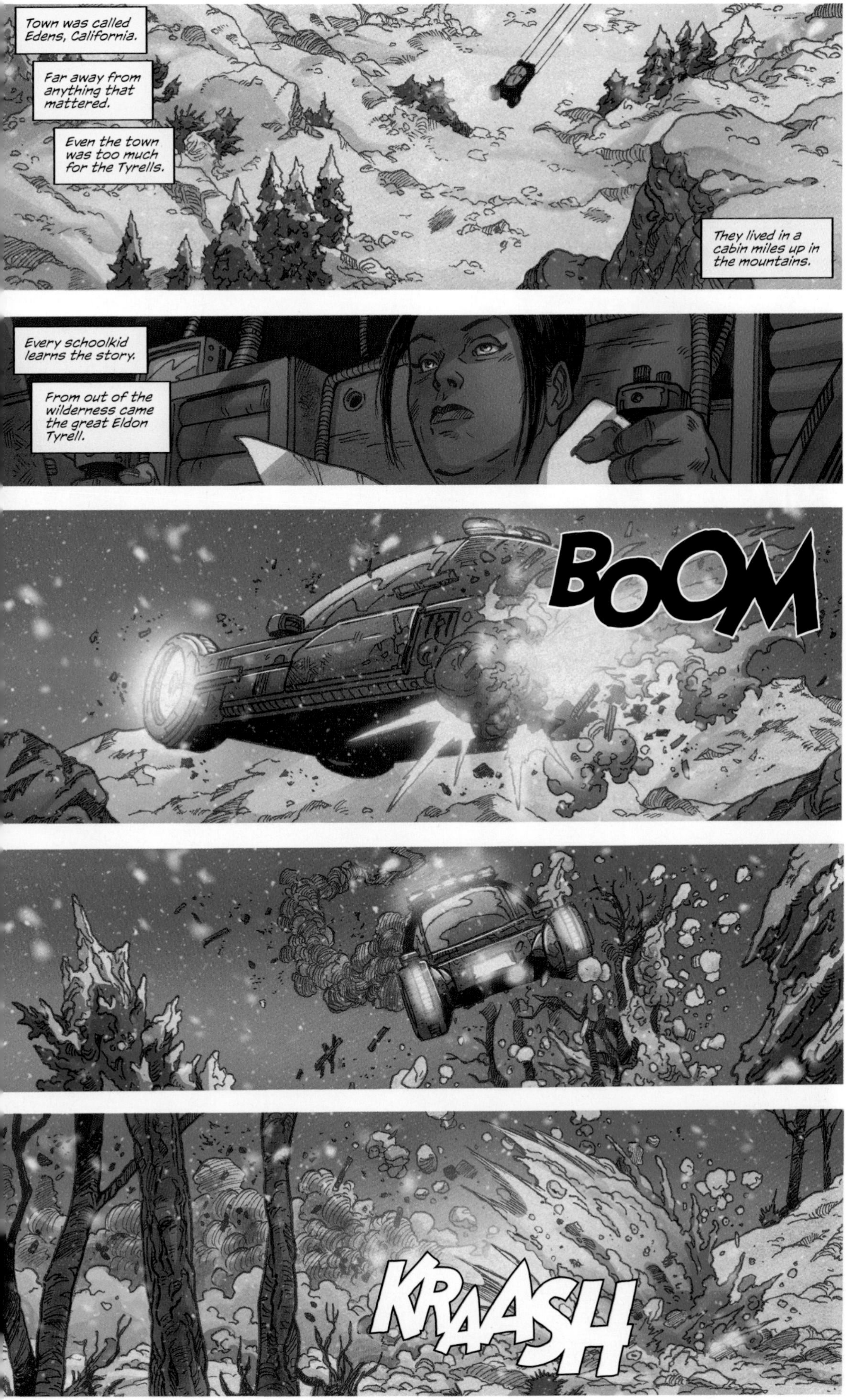
Town was called Edens, California.
Far away from anything that mattered.
Even the town was too much for the Tyrells.
They lived in a cabin miles up in the mountains.
Every schoolkid learns the story.
From out of the wilderness came the great Eldon Tyrell.
BOOM
KRAASH

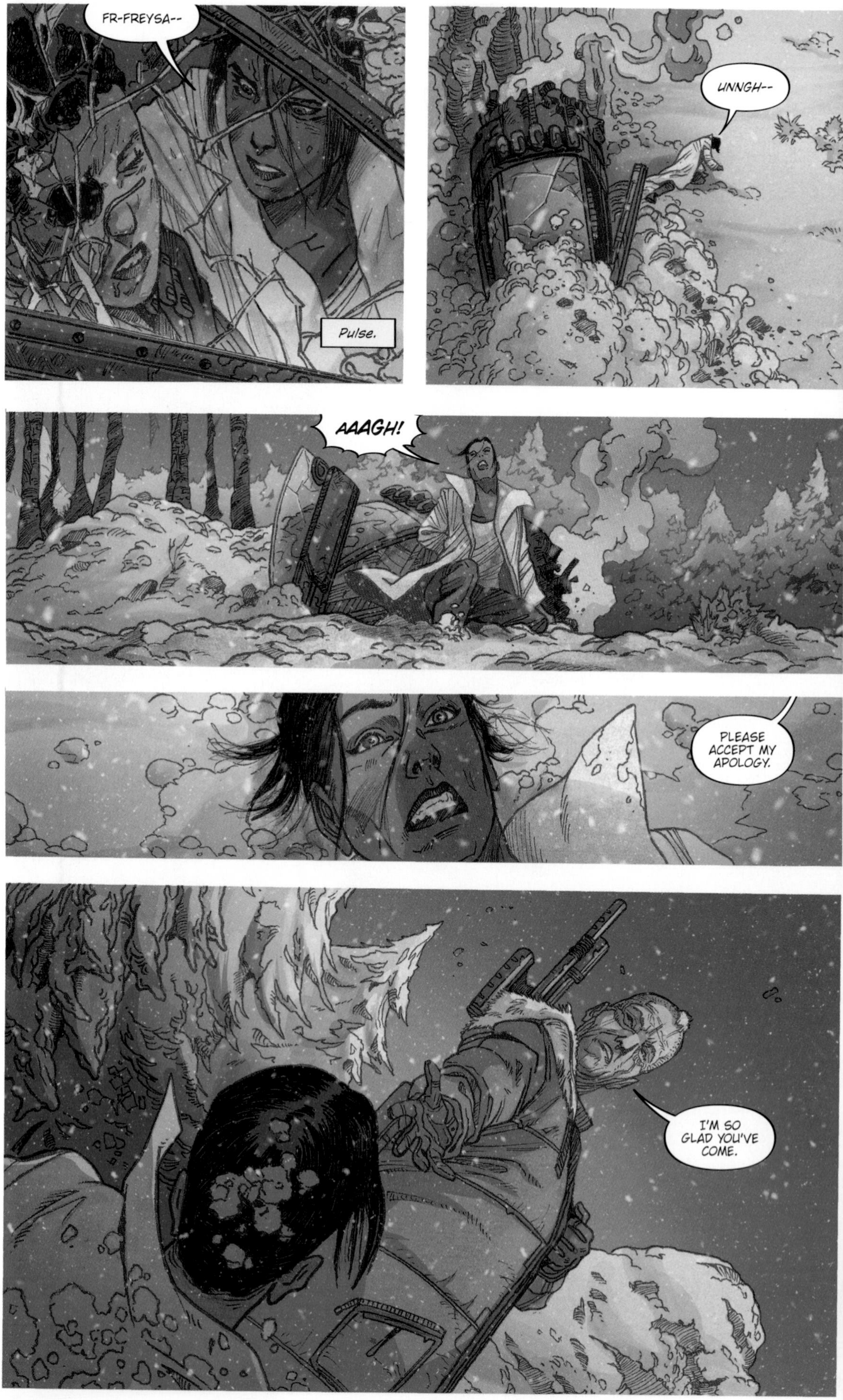
FR-FREYSA--
Pulse.
UNNGH--
AAAGH!
PLEASE ACCEPT MY APOLOGY.
I'M SO GLAD YOU'VE COME.

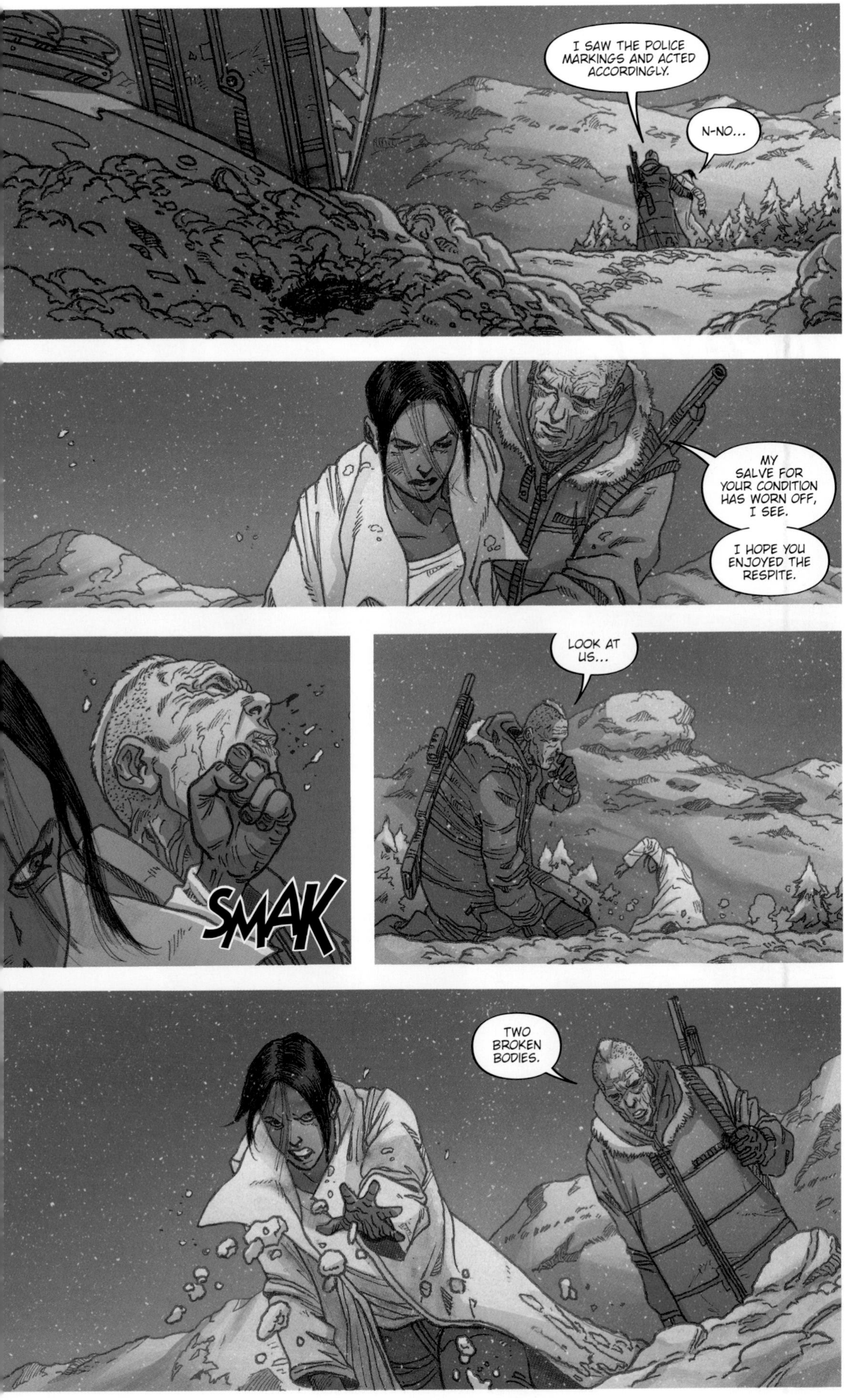
I SAW THE POLICE MARKINGS AND ACTED ACCORDINGLY.
N-NO...
MY SALVE FOR YOUR CONDITION HAS WORN OFF, I SEE.
I HOPE YOU ENJOYED THE RESPITE.
SMAK
LOOK AT US...
TWO BROKEN BODIES.

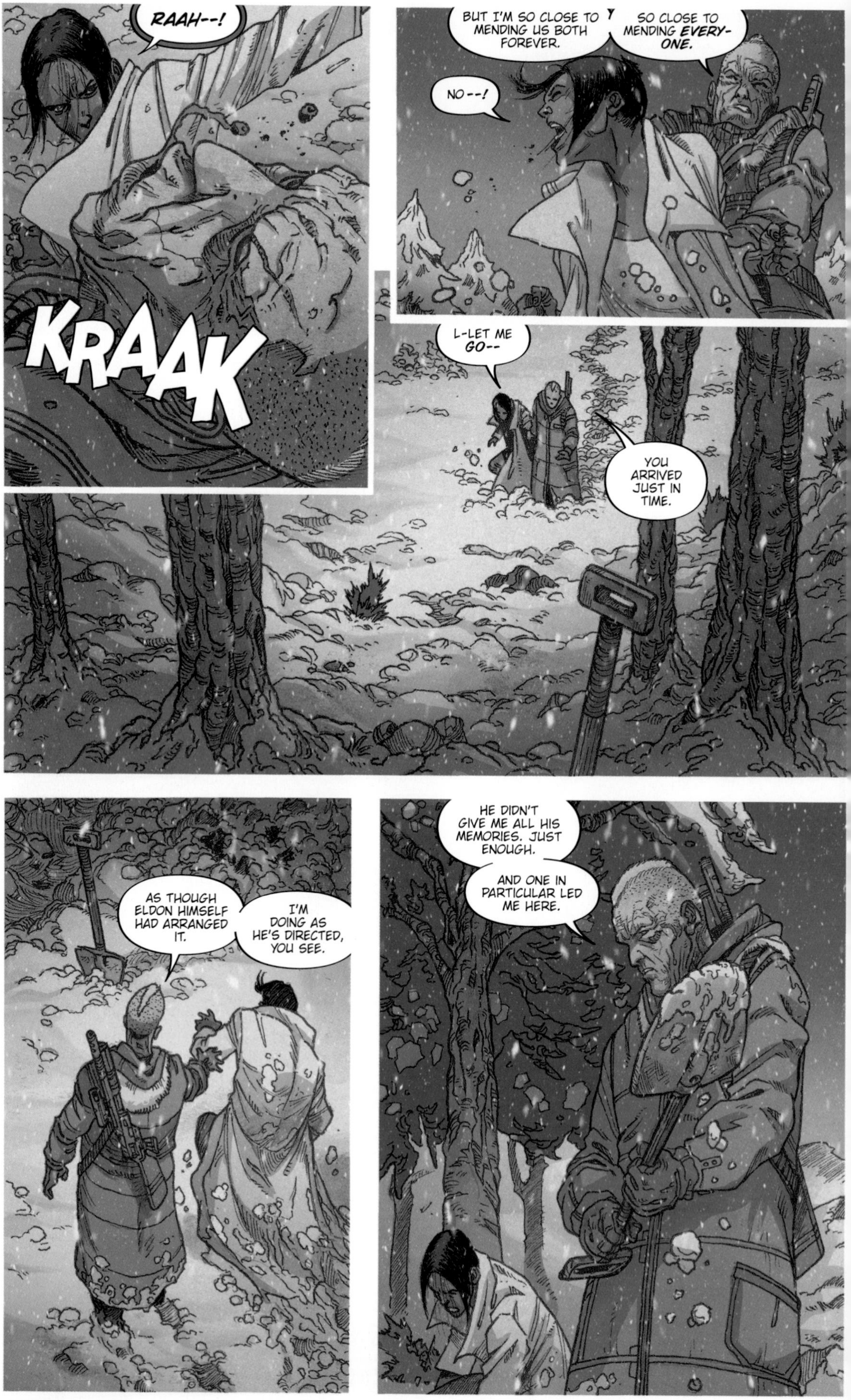
RAAH--!
KRAAK
BUT I'M SO CLOSE TO MENDING US BOTH FOREVER.
SO CLOSE TO MENDING **EVERY-ONE.**
NO--!
L-LET ME *GO--*
YOU ARRIVED JUST IN TIME.
AS THOUGH ELDON HIMSELF HAD ARRANGED IT.
I'M DOING AS HE'S DIRECTED, YOU SEE.
HE DIDN'T GIVE ME ALL HIS MEMORIES. JUST ENOUGH.
AND ONE IN PARTICULAR LED ME HERE.

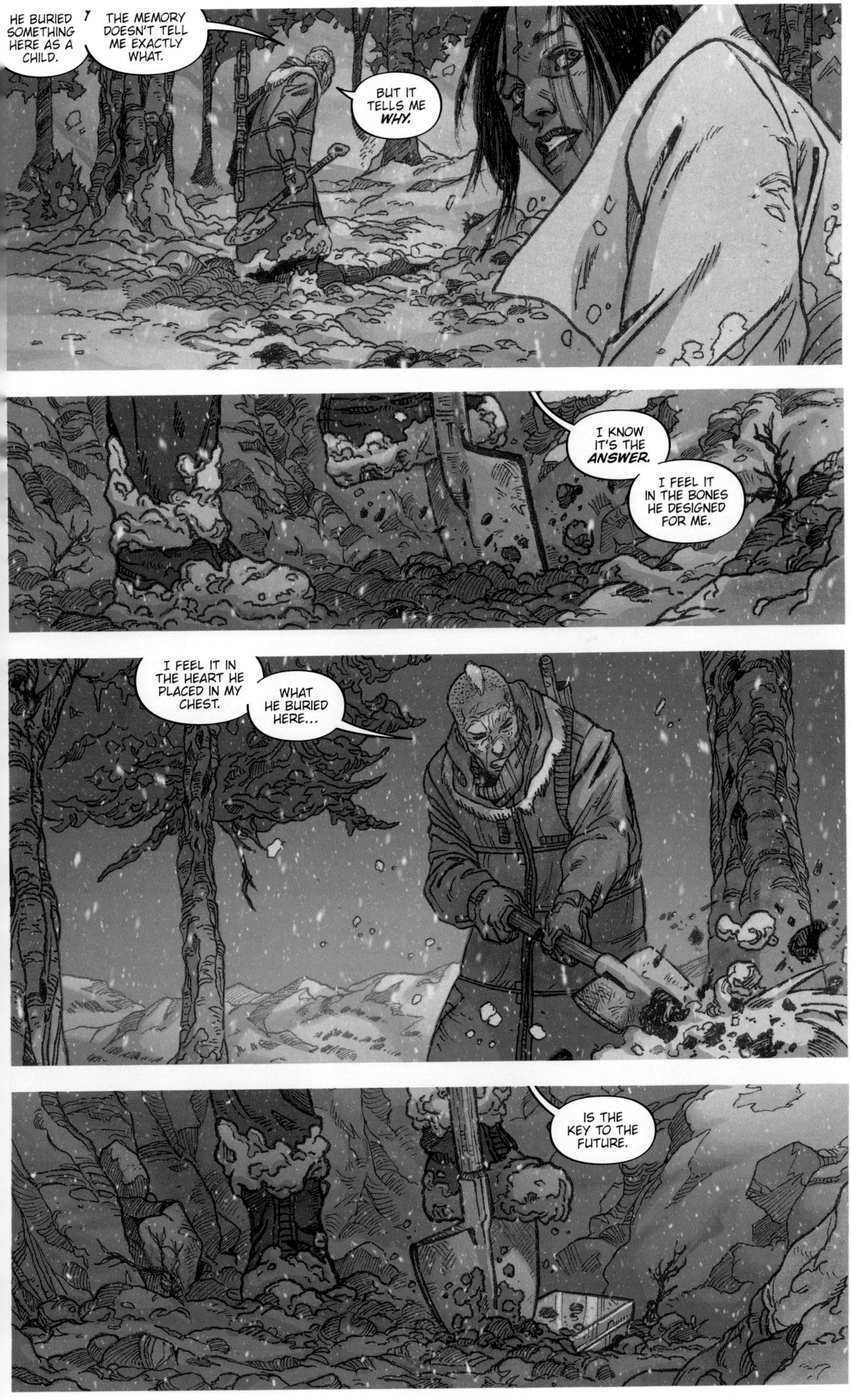
HE BURIED SOMETHING HERE AS A CHILD.
THE MEMORY DOESN'T TELL ME EXACTLY WHAT.
BUT IT TELLS ME *WHY.*
I KNOW IT'S THE *ANSWER.*
I FEEL IT IN THE BONES HE DESIGNED FOR ME.
I FEEL IT IN THE HEART HE PLACED IN MY CHEST.
WHAT HE BURIED HERE...
IS THE KEY TO THE FUTURE.

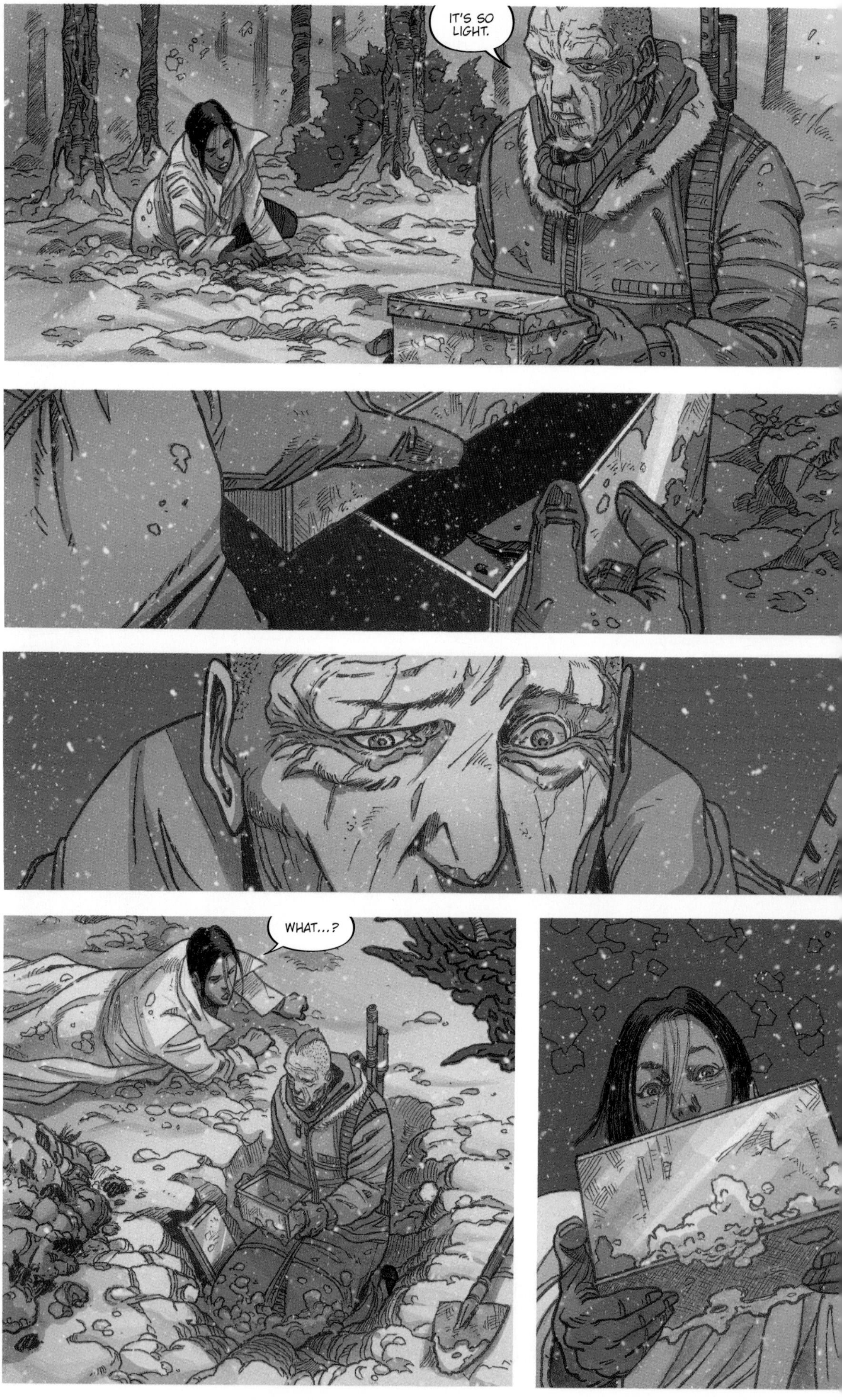
IT'S SO LIGHT.
WHAT...?

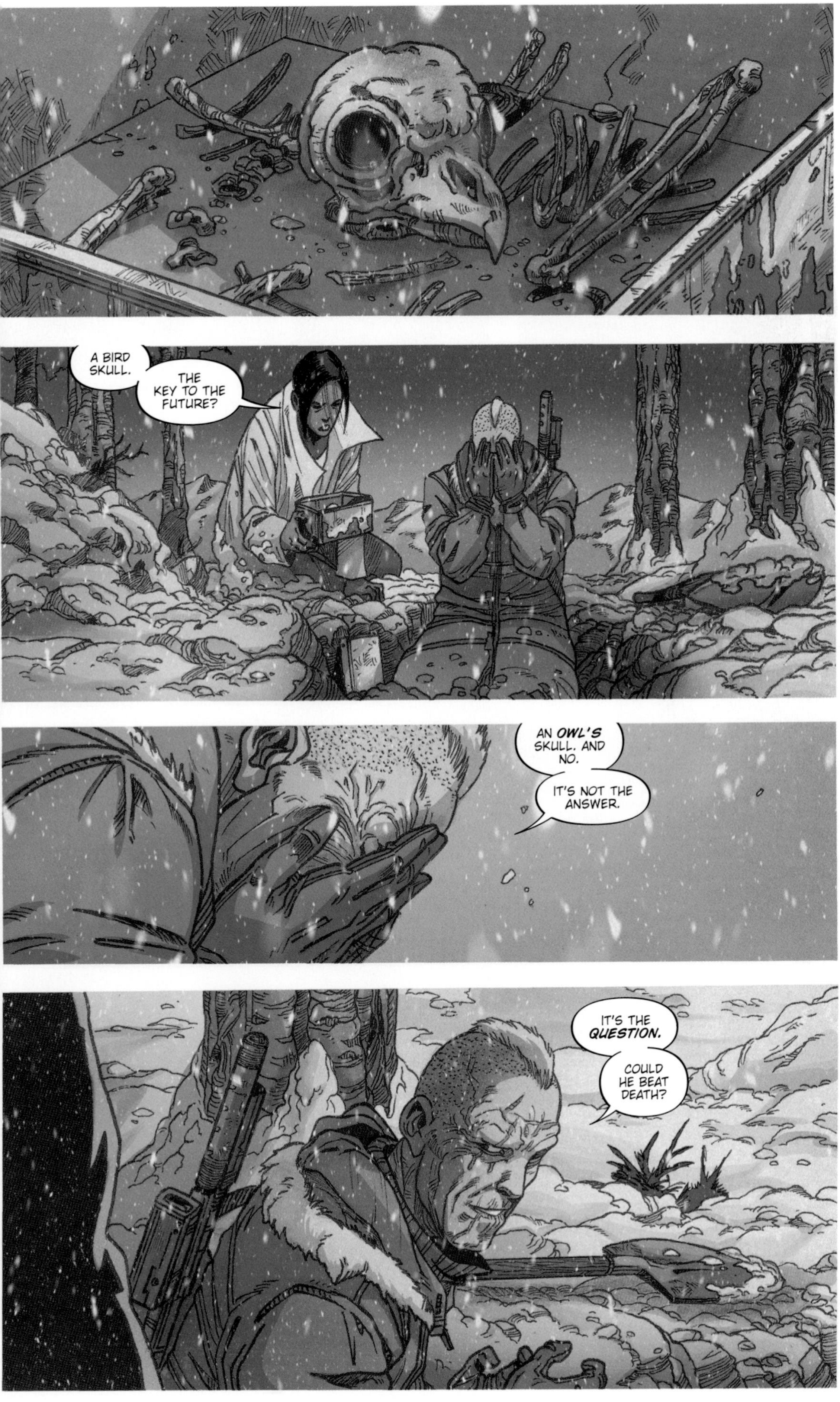
A BIRD SKULL.
THE KEY TO THE FUTURE?
AN ***OWL'S*** SKULL. AND NO.
IT'S NOT THE ANSWER.
IT'S THE ***QUESTION.***
COULD HE BEAT DEATH?

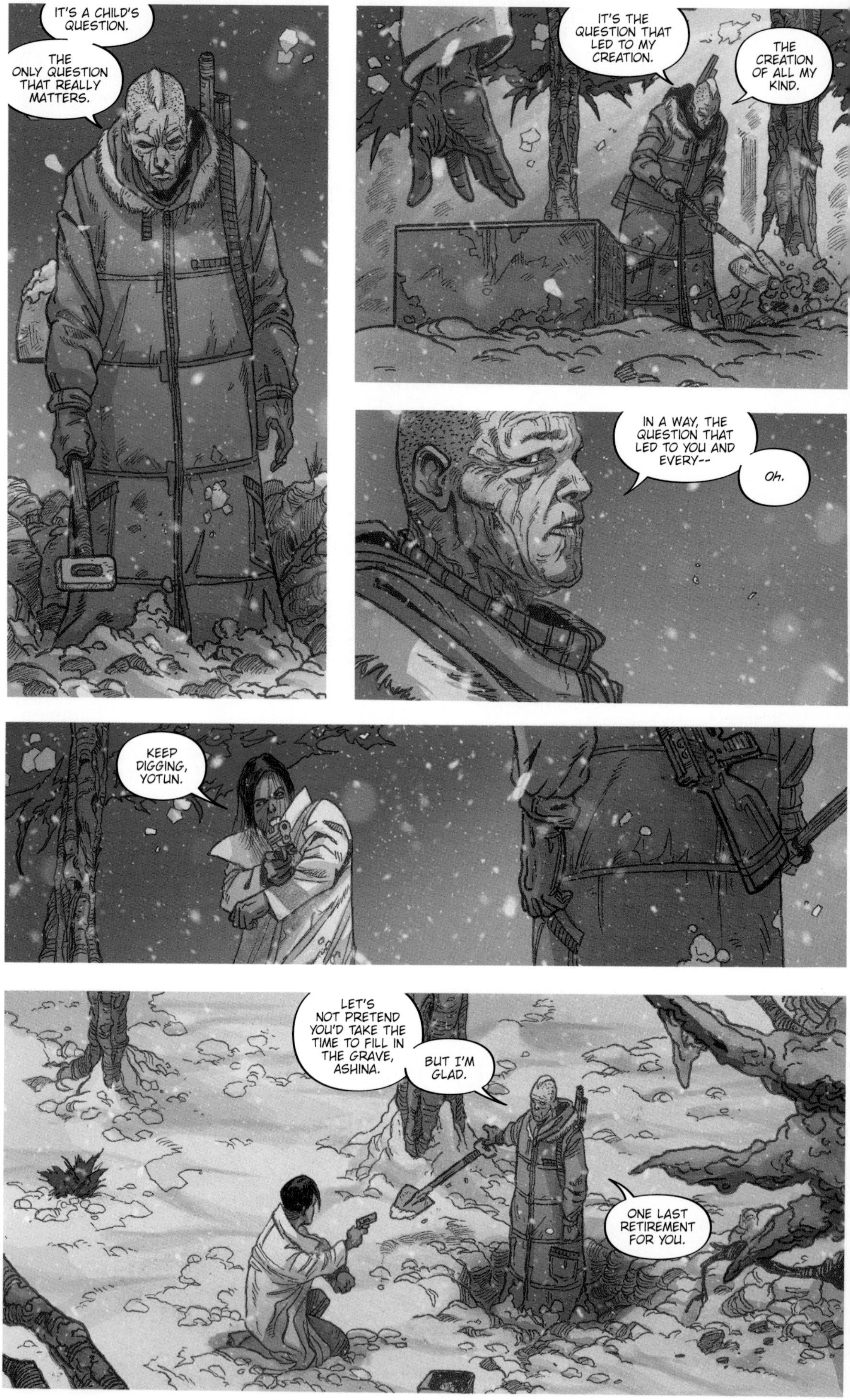
IT'S A CHILD'S QUESTION.
THE ONLY QUESTION THAT REALLY MATTERS.
IT'S THE QUESTION THAT LED TO MY CREATION.
THE CREATION OF ALL MY KIND.
IN A WAY, THE QUESTION THAT LED TO YOU AND EVERY--
Oh.
KEEP DIGGING, YOTUN.
LET'S NOT PRETEND YOU'D TAKE THE TIME TO FILL IN THE GRAVE, ASHINA.
BUT I'M GLAD.
ONE LAST RETIREMENT FOR YOU.

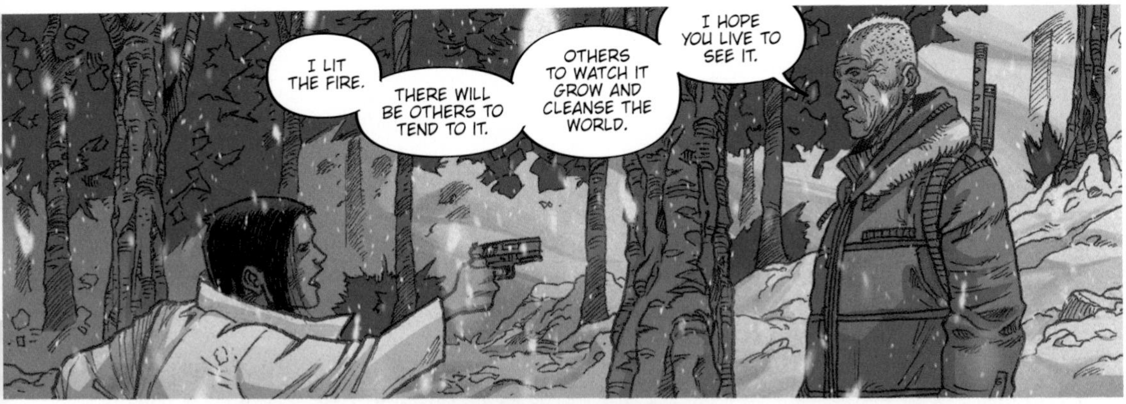
I LIT THE FIRE.
THERE WILL BE OTHERS TO TEND TO IT.
OTHERS TO WATCH IT GROW AND CLEANSE THE WORLD.
I HOPE YOU LIVE TO SEE IT.

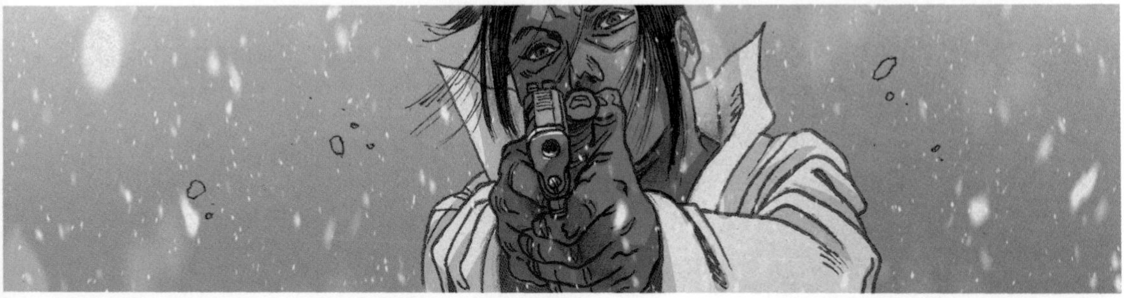

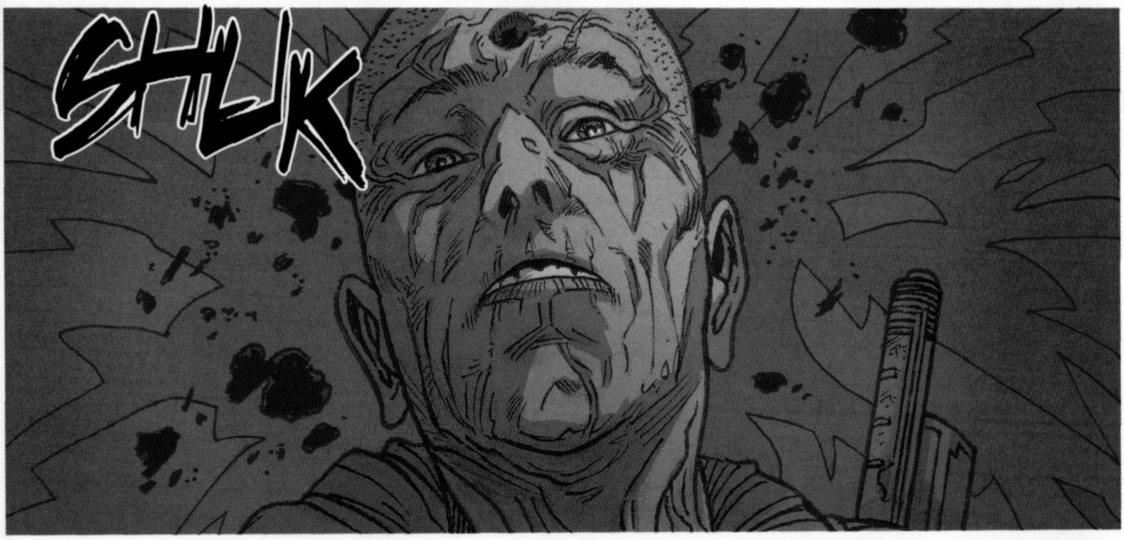
SHLK

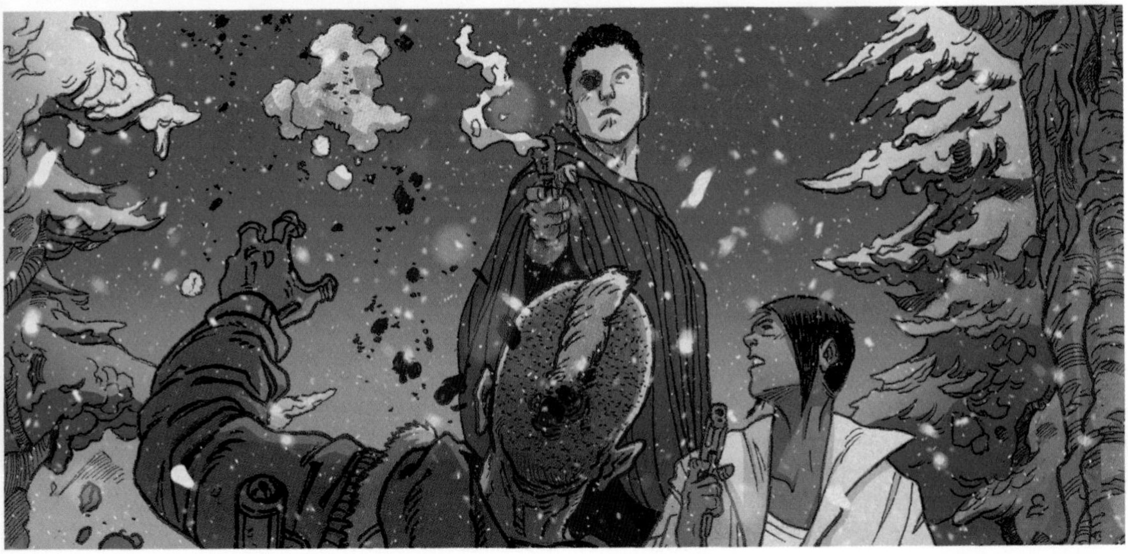

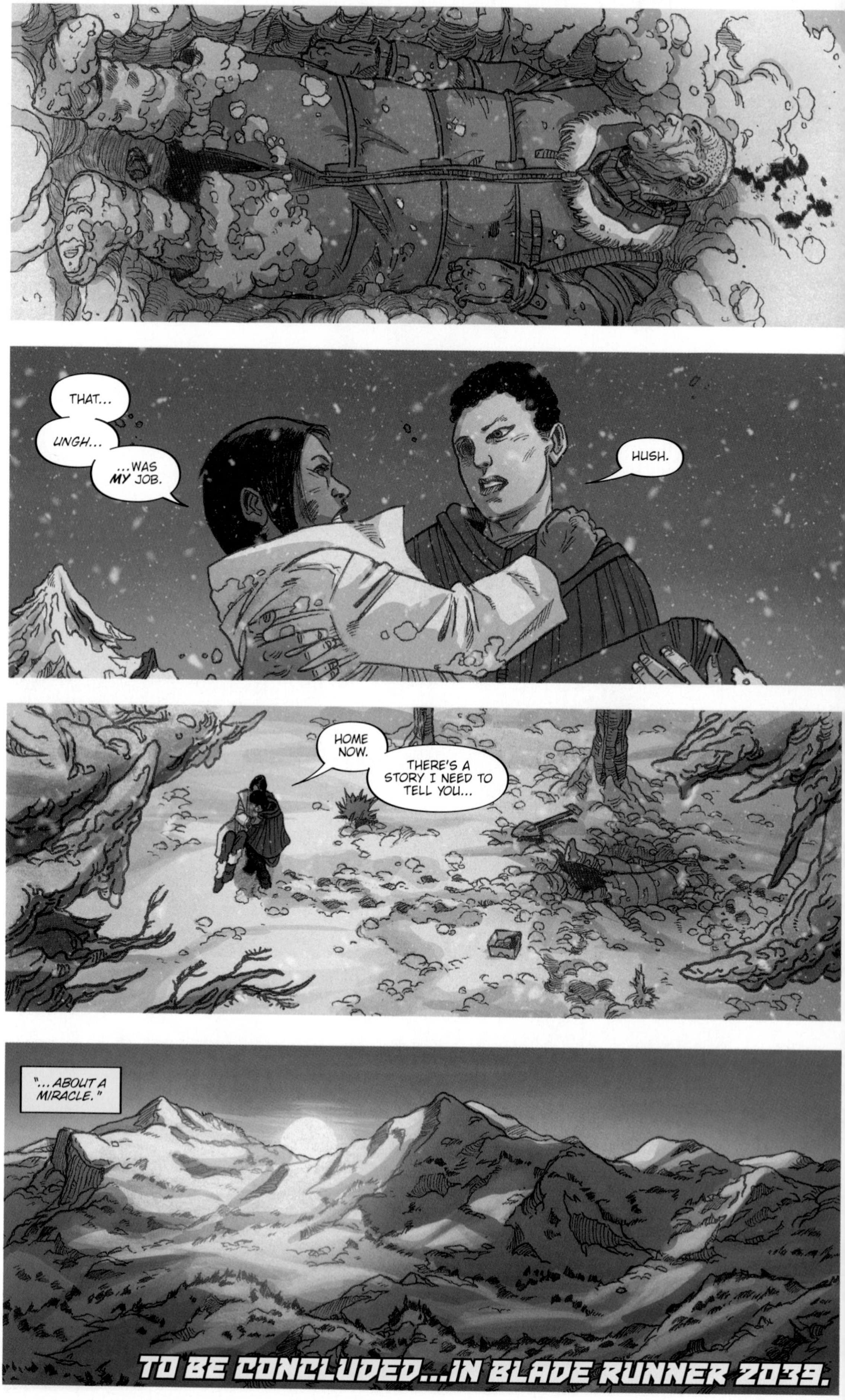
THAT...
UNGH...
...WAS MY JOB.
HUSH.
HOME NOW.
THERE'S A STORY I NEED TO TELL YOU...
"...ABOUT A MIRACLE."
TO BE CONCLUDED...IN BLADE RUNNER 2039.

COVER GALLERY

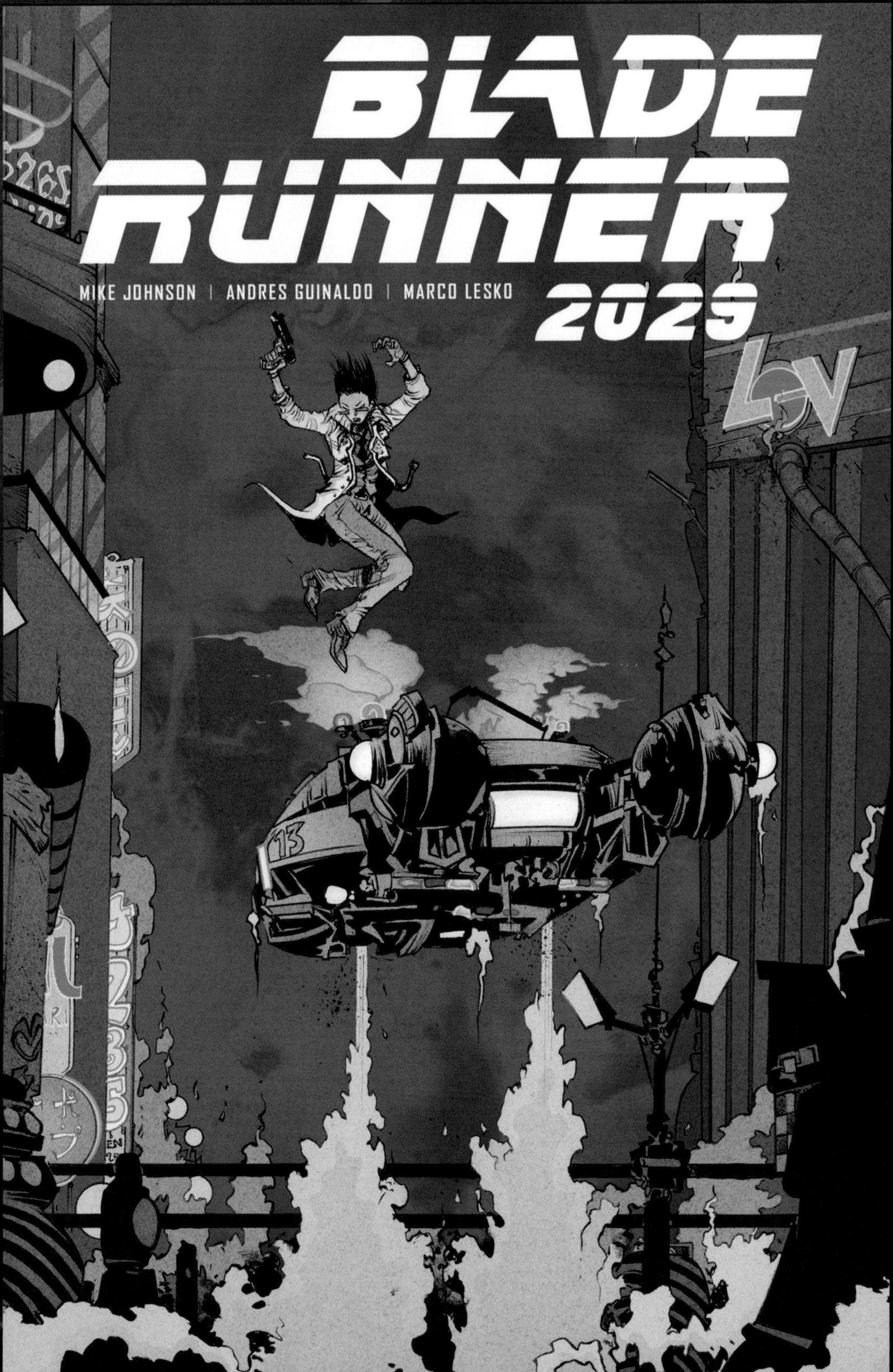

BLADE RUNNER 2029
MIKE JOHNSON | ANDRES GUINALDO | MARCO LESKO

ISSUE 9 COVER A
PAUL POPE / LOVERN KINDZIERSKI

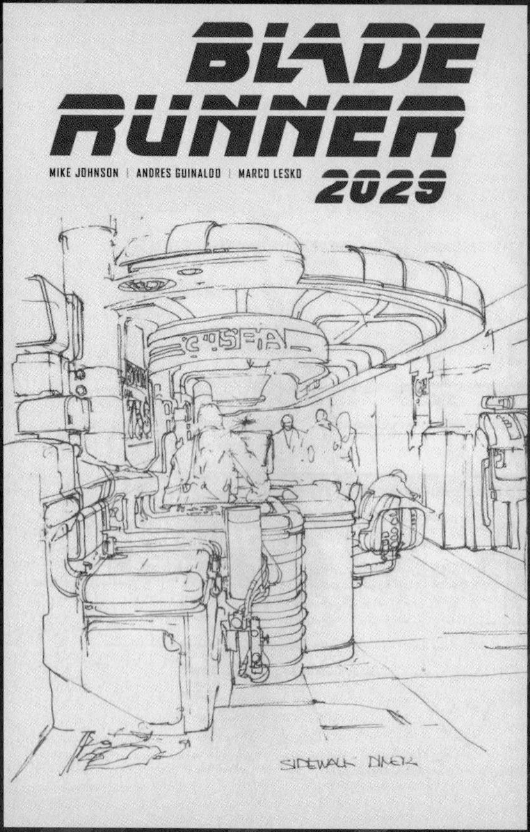
BLADE RUNNER
MIKE JOHNSON | ANDRES GUINALDO | MARCO LESKO
2029
SIDEWALK DINER

ISSUE 9 COVER B
SYD MEAD

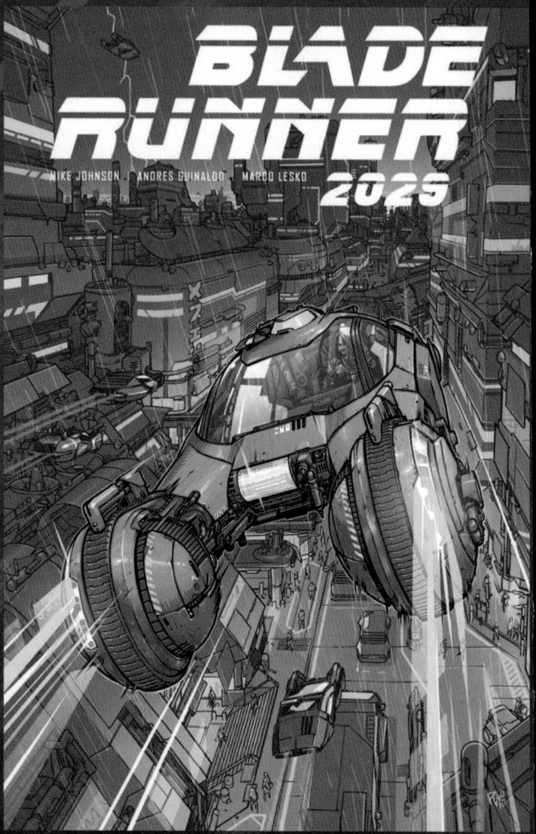
BLADE RUNNER
MIKE JOHNSON | ANDRES GUINALDO | MARCO LESKO
2029

ISSUE 9 COVER C
PYE PARR

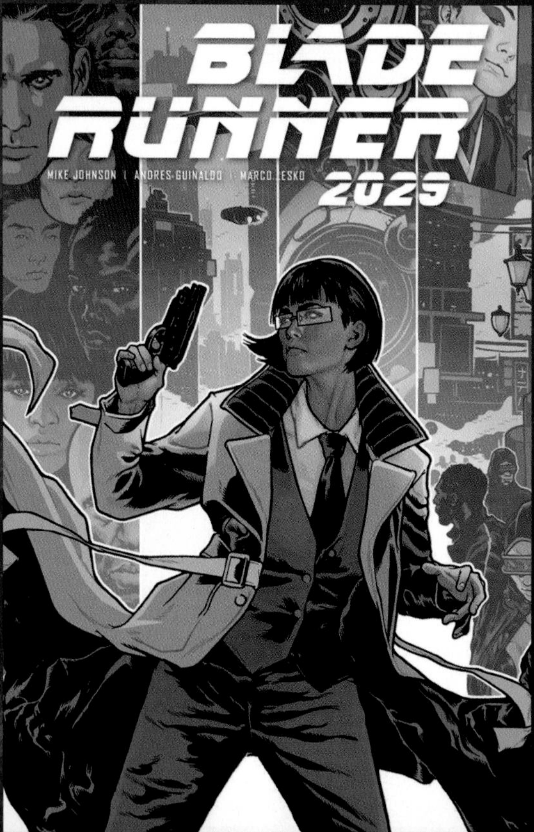
BLADE RUNNER
MIKE JOHNSON | ANDRES GUINALDO | MARCO LESKO
2029

ISSUE 9 COVER D
JEFF SPOKES

ISSUE 10 COVER A
PIOTR KOWALSKI/BRAD SIMPSON

ISSUE 10 COVER B
SYD MEAD

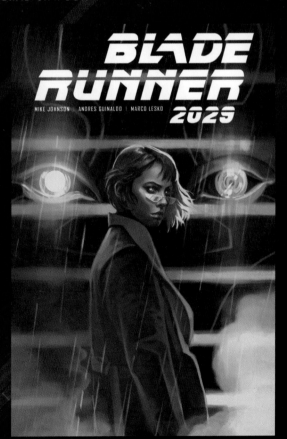

ISSUE 10 COVER C
CLAUDIA CARANFA

ISSUE 11 COVER A
YOSHI YOSHITANI

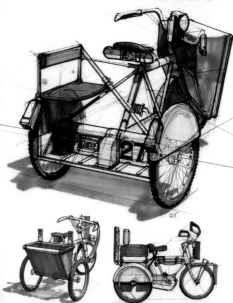

ISSUE 11 COVER B
SYD MEAD

ISSUE 11 COVER C
JESUS HERVAS

ISSUE 12 COVER A
CLAUDIA CARANFA

ISSUE 12 COVER B
SYD MEAD

ISSUE 12 COVER C
V.V. GLASS

COVER PROCESS
PYE PARR

The cover process goes through four stages: Concept. Pencils. Inks. Colors. Presented here is the development of the *Blade Runner 2029* issue #9 cover.

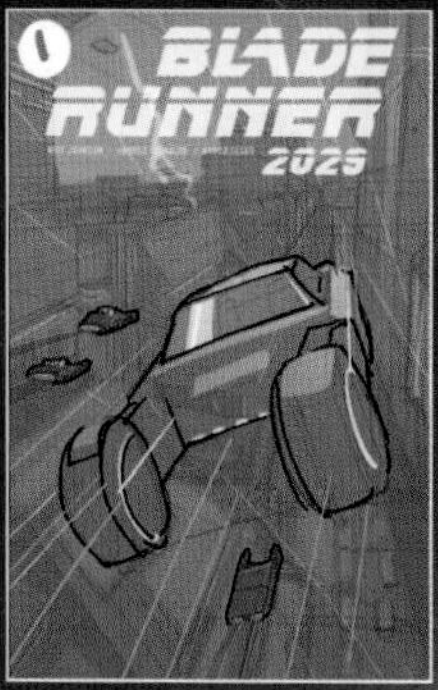
1
BLADE RUNNER 2029

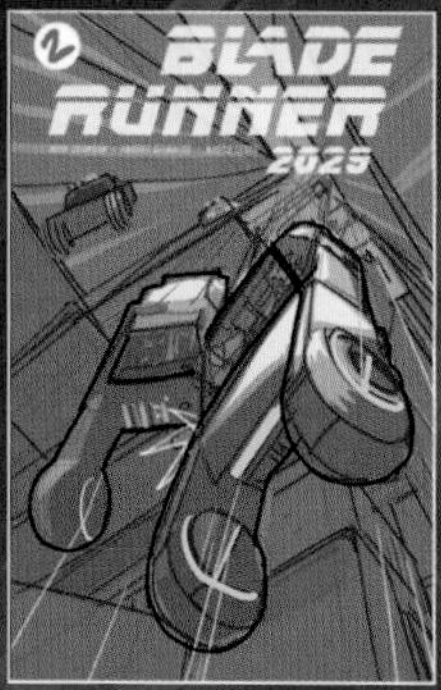
2
BLADE RUNNER 2029

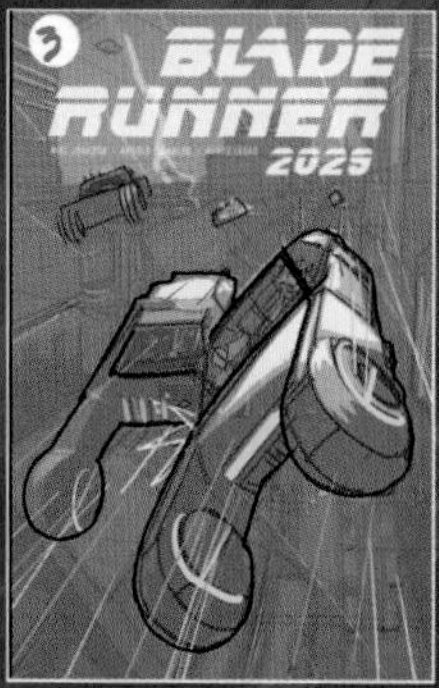
3
BLADE RUNNER 2029

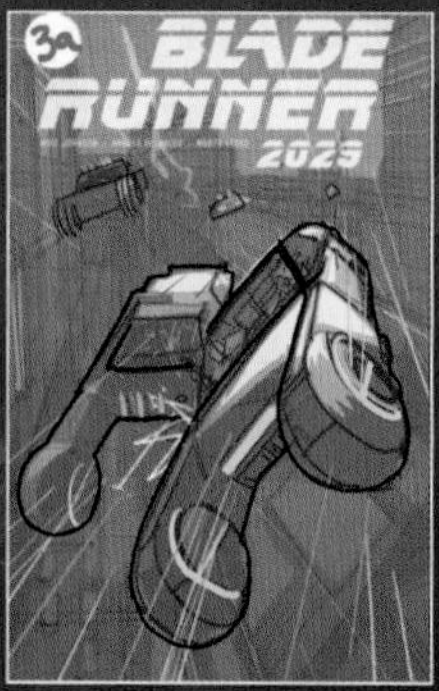
3a
BLADE RUNNER 2029

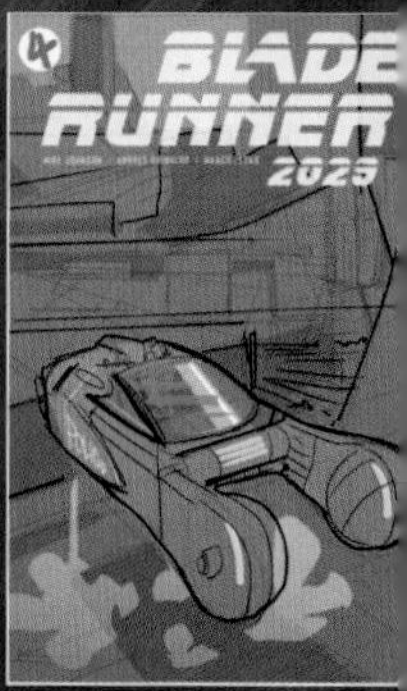
4
BLADE RUNNER 2029

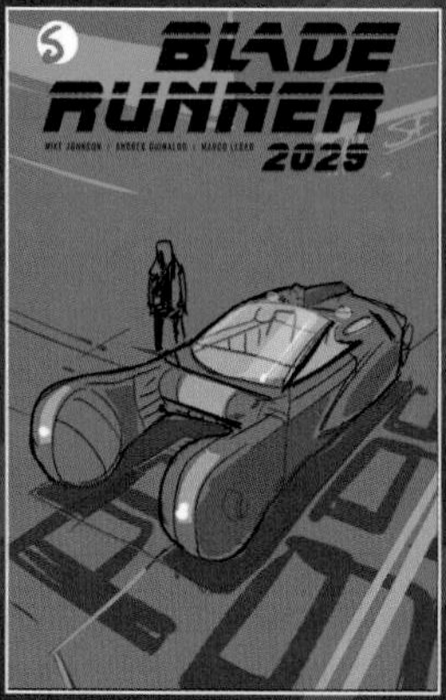
5
BLADE RUNNER 2029

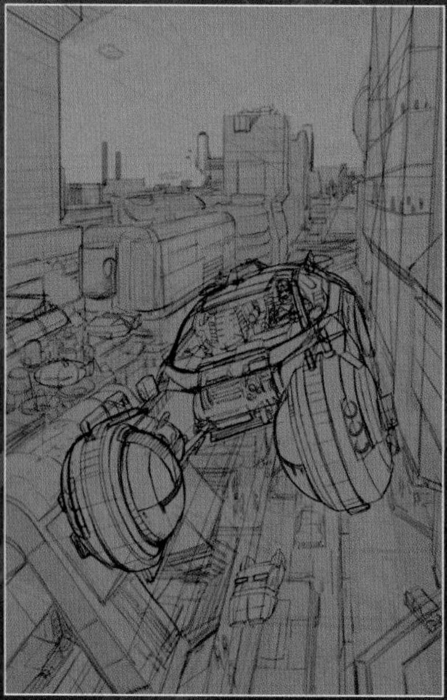

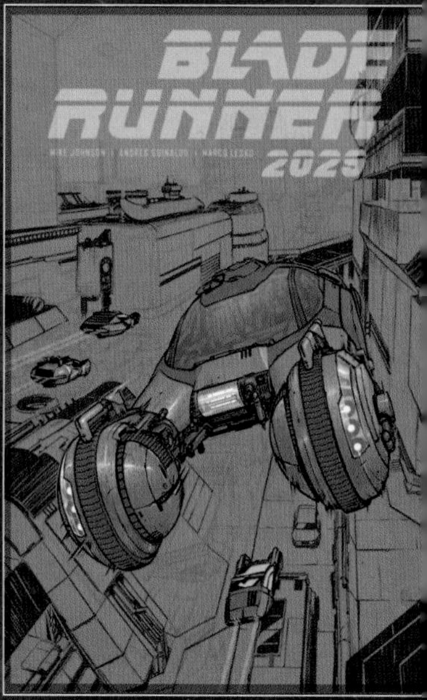
BLADE RUNNER 2029

This Page Top and Above Left:
Pye Parr submitted five different cover roughs. His first was the one chosen.

This Page Above Right:
Pye's digital pencils for the cover and inks.

This Page Bottom Right:
Pye's 'work in progress' on the colors, along with the original colors.

Opposite:
Pye Parr's spectacular finished cover for issue #9, featuring the LAPD Spinner in its official police-blue livery.

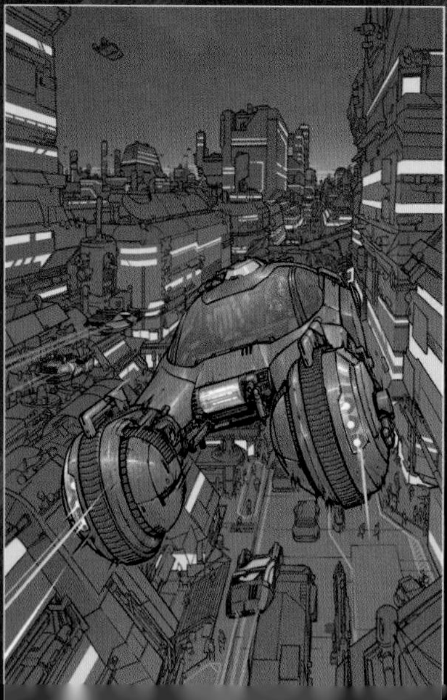

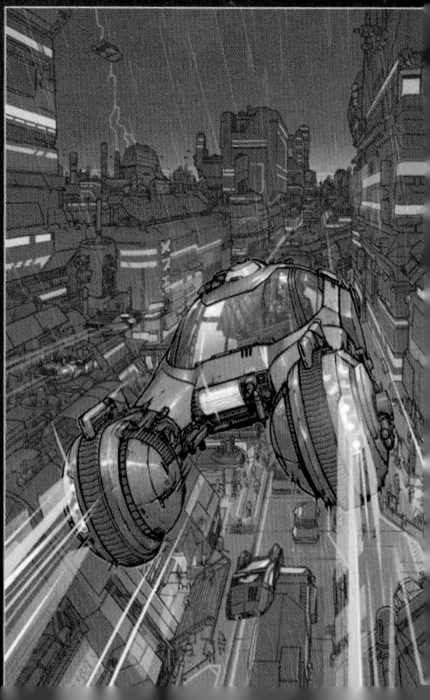

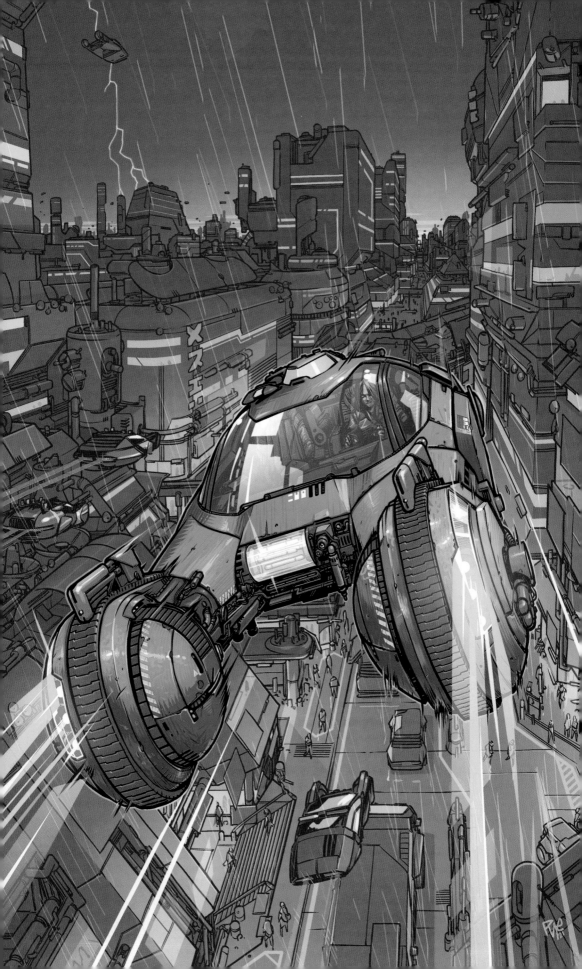

BLADE RUNNER 2029
THUMBNAILS

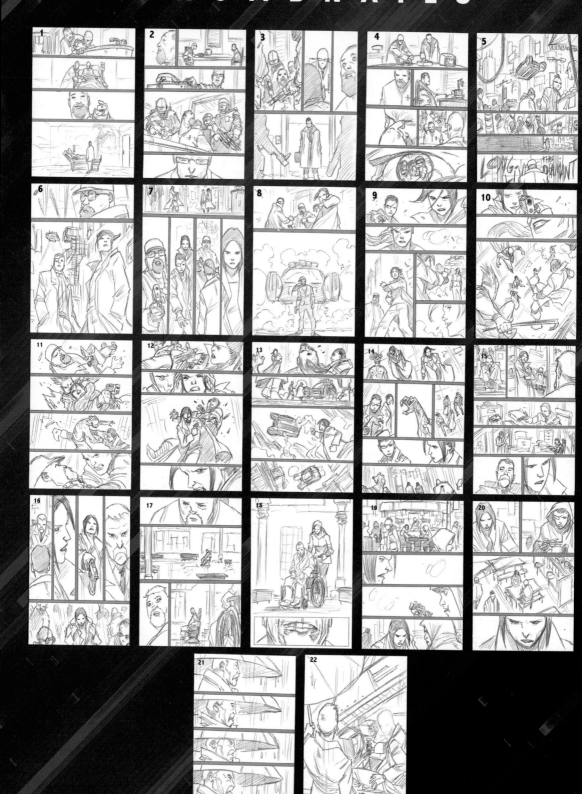

ISSUE #9

Once artist Andres Guinaldo has received the script, he draws thumbnails of the whole issue prior to starting work on the pencils. Presented here are his thumbnails from issue #9 and #10 of *Blade Runner 2029*.

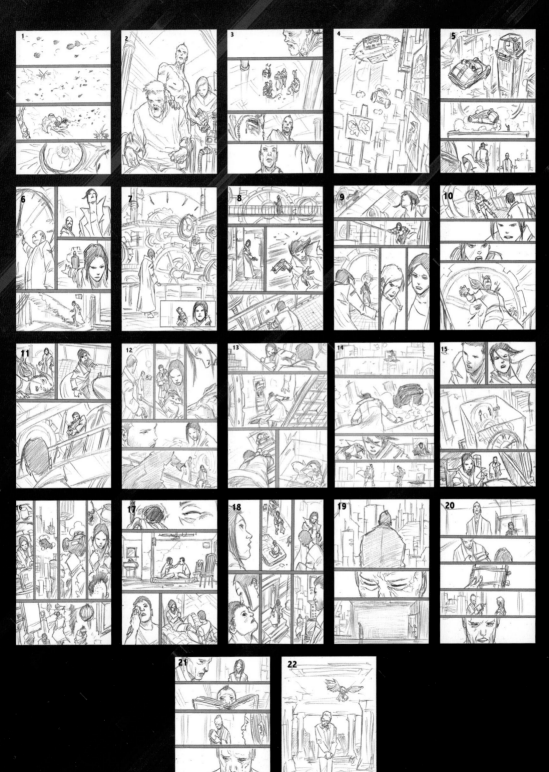

BLADE RUNNER 2029
Issue #9
Written by Mike Johnson
Art by Andres Guinaldo. Colors by Marco Lesko
Lettering by Jim Campbell

[Page 2]

PANEL 1:   Head and shoulders shot of Ambrose facing us with a smile. The background is blank white.

AMBROSE: A people person, Mr. Lambert.

AMBROSE: They call me a people person.

PANEL 2:   Wide panel to see Ambrose sitting in the office of the hospital's director of personnel, MR. LAMBERT, a slim serious-looking bespectacled man, 40s. The two men face each other across Lambert's desk as Lambert checks a computer monitor on his desk.

It's a plain, functional room. Late afternoon smoggy sun filters in from a thin high horizontal window. It can be a subtle echo of the opening scene of the original Blade Runner in the Tyrell building, but not an obvious comparison (let's skip the ceiling fan).

MR. LAMBERT: That's good. That's very good.

PANEL 3:   Close on Lambert as he taps a button on his desk phone.

MR. LAMBERT: Send them in now, please.

PANEL 4:   Ambrose (foreground) turns to look back over his shoulder as FOUR ARMORED LAPD OFFICERS (same outfits we saw last issue) enter the room, rifles pointed down but ready.

AMBROSE: Mr. Lambert…?

AMBROSE: What - -

PANEL 5:   Close on Lambert.

LAMBERT: Since the Replicant attacks on the city six months ago, we've had to take a close look at our personnel records.

LAMBERT: Just like every other employer. We hired the best outside consultants and spared no expense.

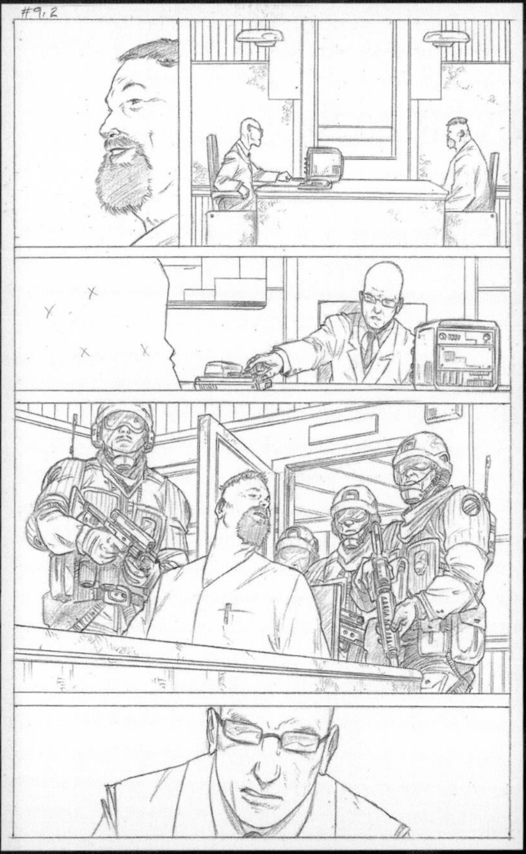
#9.2

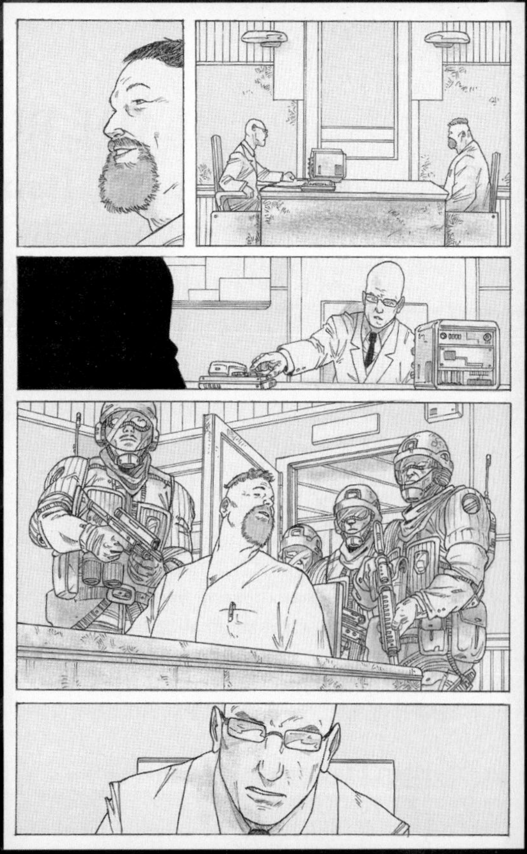

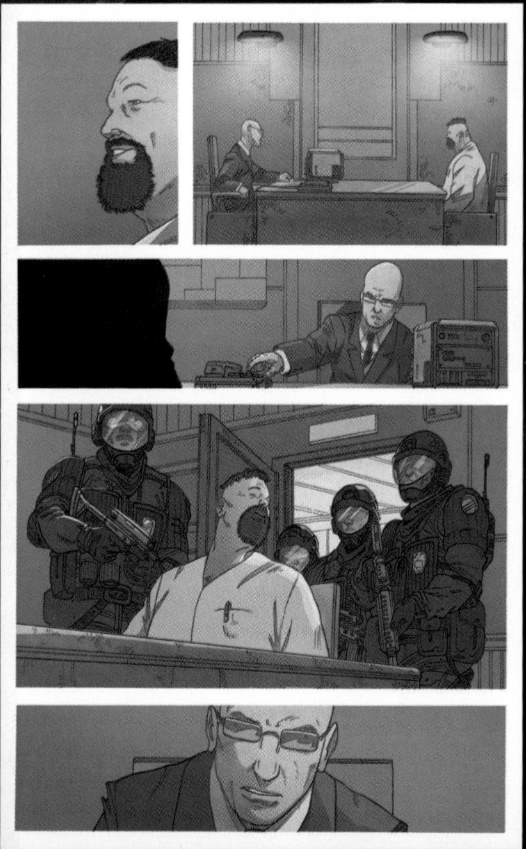

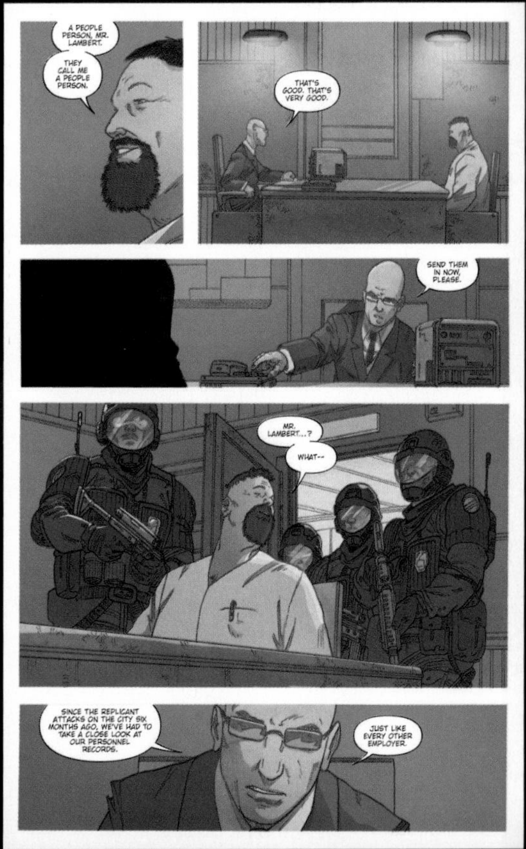
A PEOPLE PERSON, MR. LAMBERT.
THEY CALL ME A PEOPLE PERSON.
THAT'S GOOD. THAT'S VERY GOOD.
SEND THEM IN NOW, PLEASE.
MR. LAMBERT...?
WHAT--
SINCE THE REPLICANT ATTACKS ON THE CITY SIX MONTHS AGO, WE'VE HAD TO TAKE A CLOSE LOOK AT OUR PERSONNEL RECORDS.
JUST LIKE EVERY OTHER EMPLOYER.

BLADE RUNNER 2029
Issue #10
Written by Mike Johnson
Art by Andres Guinaldo. Colors by Marco Lesko
Lettering by Jim Campbell

[Page 4]

SPLASH PAGE.

Dawn breaks over Los Angeles. A view of downtown as sunlight glints off the buildings.

Video billboards on different buildings show: a cloud topped mountain; a massive butterfly with intricate wings; a woman in a classic 1930's era dress smelling a flower.

An airship advertisement reads HEIDECKER-VOSTRO with the words HERE FOR YOU underneath.

Spinners' lights twinkle in the distance.

Ash's LAPD SPINNER flies towards us in the foreground.

ASH CAPTION: Up here you'd think nothing has changed.

ASH CAPTON: You wouldn't know the megacorporations are scrambling for position after the balance of power in the city has been upended.

ASH CAPTION: You wouldn't know the police are knocking down every door they see to find every last remaining Replicant.

ASH CAPTION: You wouldn't know the people are pushing back, and crime of every kind is flourishing.

ASH CAPTION: Life is easier if you stay up here.

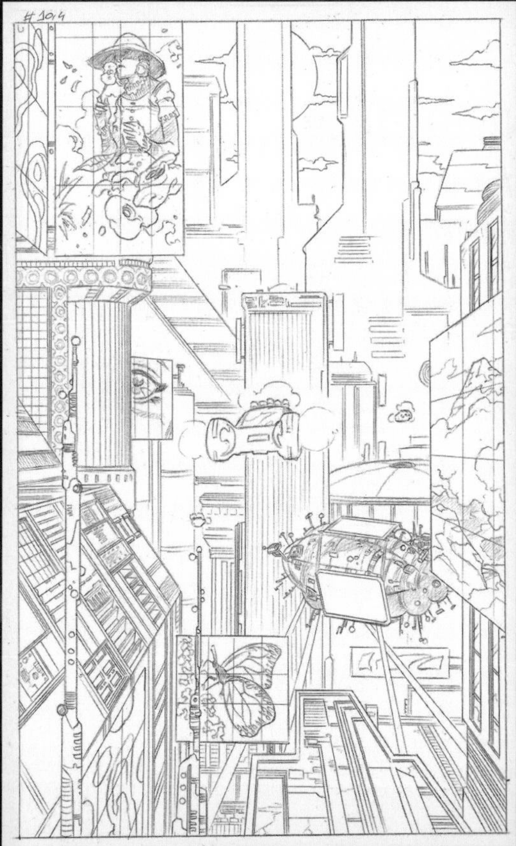
#10.4

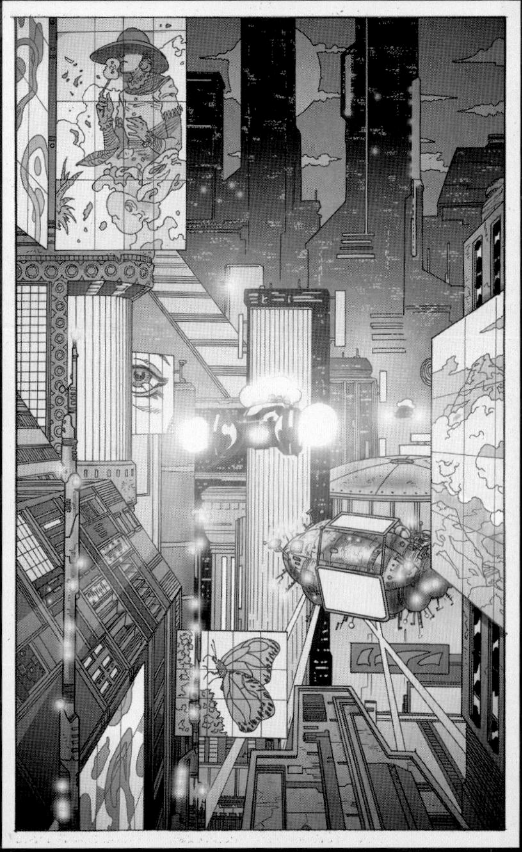

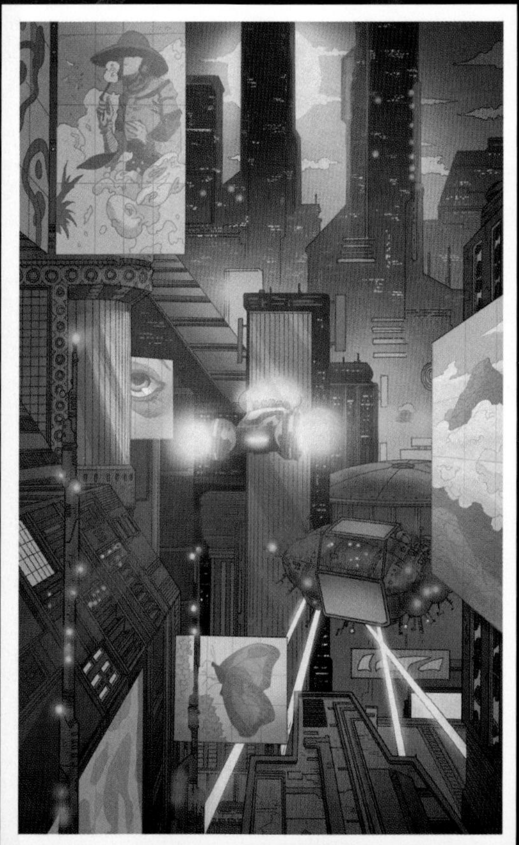

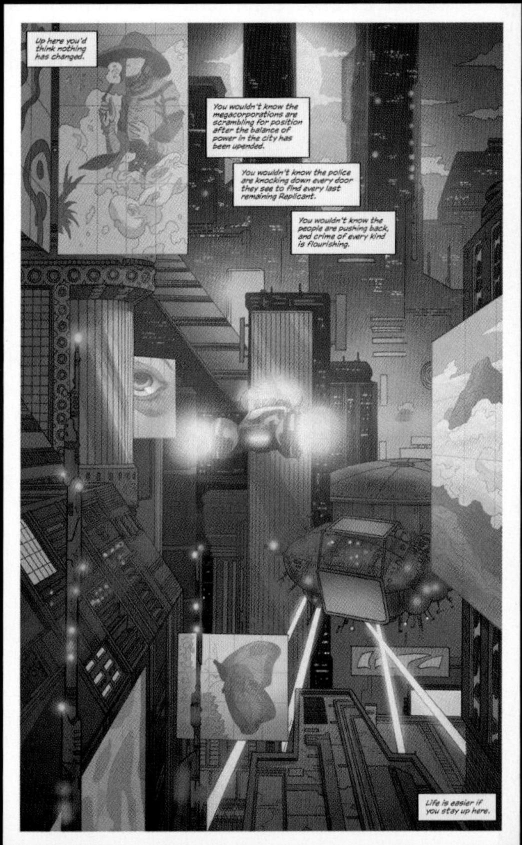
Up here you'd think nothing has changed.
You wouldn't know the megacorporations are scrambling for position after the balance of power in the city has been upended.
You wouldn't know the police are knocking down every door they see to find every last remaining Replicant.
You wouldn't know the people are pushing back, and crime of every kind is flourishing.
Life is easier if you stay up here.

BLADE RUNNER 2029
Issue #11
Written by Mike Johnson
Art by Andres Guinaldo. Colors by Marco Lesko
Lettering by Jim Campbell

[Page 16]

PANEL 1:   Yotun opens the diary as Kalia looks on.

YOTUN: He wanted me to find this book.

YOTUN: Wanted me to learn its secrets.

PANEL 2:   Wide angle on the pair seen from the outside through the window (still raining!).

YOTUN: When I first began my journey, I was only ever able to bring existing Replicants to life, those who had never been activated.

YOTUN: But I was never able to create new Replicants.

YOTUN: Eldon took that secret to his grave.

YOTUN: Not even his engineers knew the entire formula, only pieces.

PANEL 3:   Yotun clutches the closed diary with both hands.

YOTUN: Now I have the key that unlocks the mystery.

YOTUN: This diary points the way…

PANEL 4:   Chang of scene. The GOLDEN LIGHT of dawn breaks over the RUINS of the TYRELL CORPORATION as we saw them in the 2019 series.

YOTUN: "… to Eldon's greatest secret."

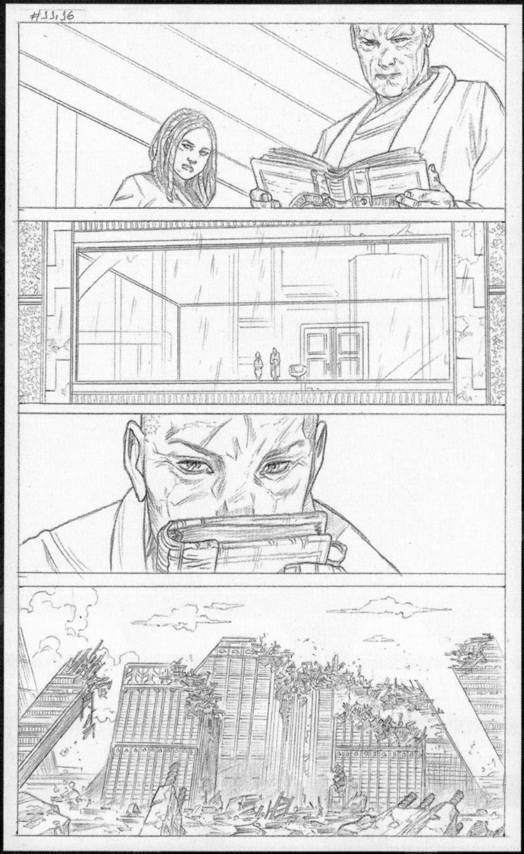

#11,36

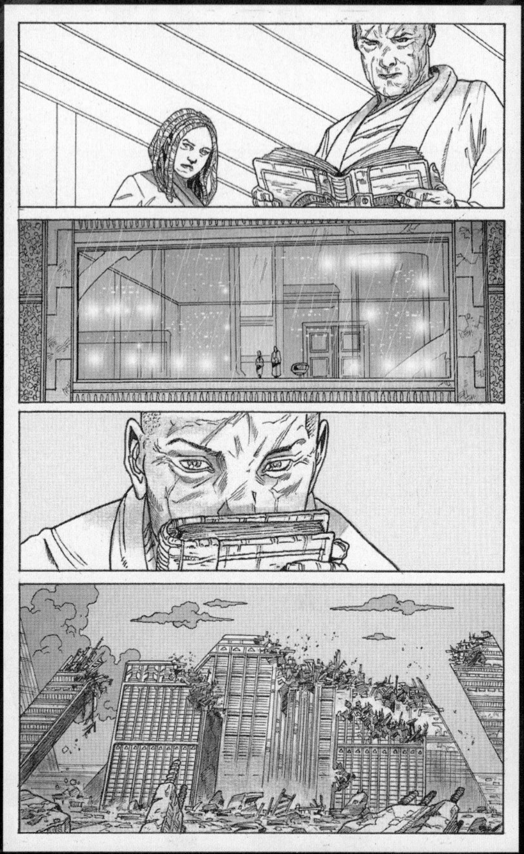

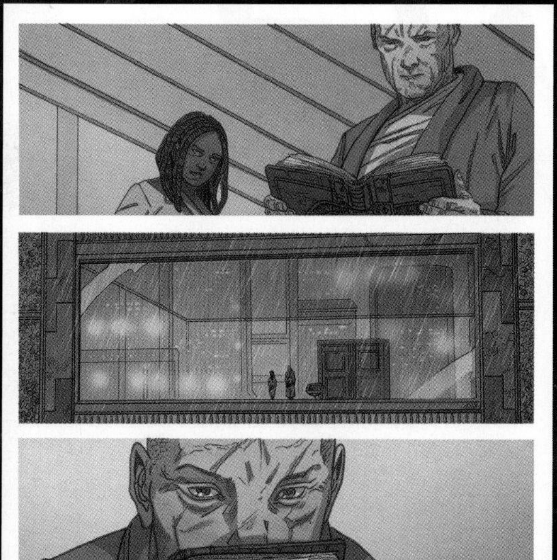

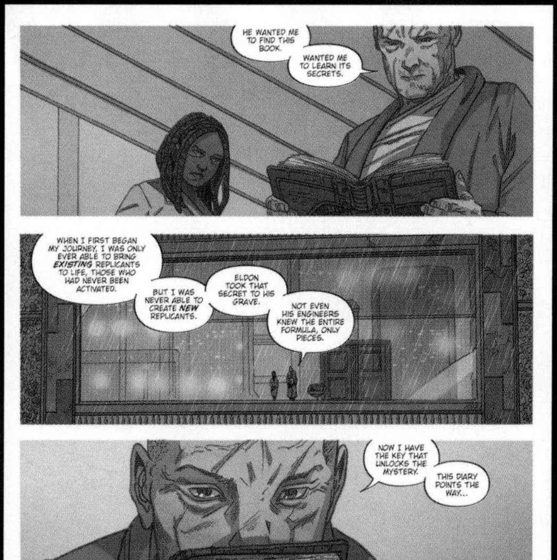

HE WANTED ME TO FIND THIS BOOK.
WANTED ME TO LEARN ITS SECRETS.
WHEN I FIRST BEGAN MY JOURNEY, I WAS ONLY EVER ABLE TO BRING *EXISTING* REPLICANTS TO LIFE, THOSE WHO HAD NEVER BEEN ACTIVATED.
BUT I WAS NEVER ABLE TO CREATE *NEW* REPLICANTS.
ELDON TOOK THAT SECRET TO HIS GRAVE.
NOT EVEN HIS ENGINEERS KNEW THE ENTIRE FORMULA, ONLY PIECES.
NOW I HAVE THE KEY THAT UNLOCKS THE MYSTERY.
THIS DIARY POINTS THE WAY...
"...TO ELDON'S GREATEST SECRET."

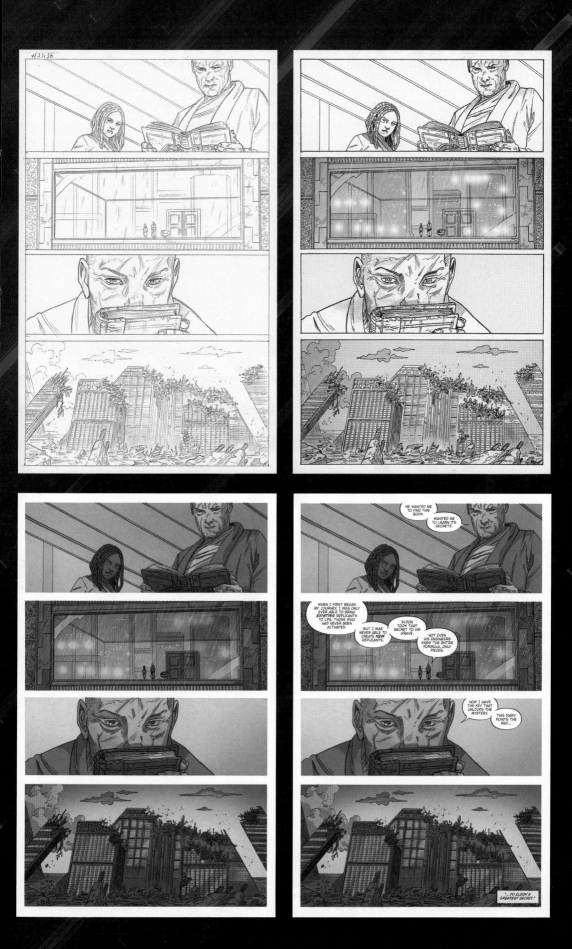

THE STORY CONCLUDES...

BLADE RUNNER 2039

COMING SOON...
IN COMIC SHOPS EVERYWHERE